Originally published in Padova by Franco Muzzio Editore as
La Cucina delle Murge

Classic Recipes and Traditions

Translated for the First Time

Oronzo Editions, LLC

New York

2008

Italy's Food Culture

Puglia

A Culinary Memoir

Maria Pignatelli Ferrante

ORONZO EDITIONS, LLC
11 West 30th Street
Suite 7R
New York, NY 10001
www.oronzoeditions.com

ISBN 978-0-9797369-1-9

Library of Congress control number: 2008904644

The launching of this series has been guided and nurtured by many generous people. We especially thank our intrepid translator and indefatigable consultant for the time and care they took with our first book.

—THE PUBLISHER

Originally published in Padova
by Franco Muzzio Editore as
La Cucina delle Murge
ISBN 88-7021-720-5

Italian Series Editor: Marco Guarnaschelli Gotti (d. 2003)

Translator: Natalie Danford, New York
Consultant: Maria Galetta, New York

Printed in China

contents indice

Foreword

PUGLIA: *A Culinary Memoir* by Maria Pignatelli Ferrante, launches Oronzo Editions' series of regional Italian cookbooks originally published by Franco Muzzio Editore and now translated into English. Each book contains hundreds of recipes culled from diverse sources—from treasured handwritten family notebooks to books from the libraries of nobility. These are traditional, regional, and sometimes extraordinary "rescued" recipes.

Italian journalist and gastronomist Marco Guarnaschelli Gotti and publisher Franco Muzzio joined together to document and publish Italy's unique regional histories and cuisines and their relationships to local culture. Gotti as series editor sought out local cultural experts who became "gastronomic anthropologists," researching centuries-old histories and traditions—some long forgotten, many still practiced. Honoring the legacy of Pellegrino Artusi, they emphasize the importance of traditional home cookery in the development of Italian cuisine. Italy's cultural and gastronomic nuances reflect complex micro-regional geographies and climates. These authors narrate and preserve traditions, all the while aware of Italy's fast-changing way of life.

In the tradition of Italian cookbook writing, Signora Ferrante's style is conversational, opinionated, and intimate. She weaves the story of Puglia's economic and cultural history throughout her comprehensive collection of traditional recipes. Her memories of life in Italy's southern agrarian society bring us the rich traditions of the *pugliesi* who developed a resilient, robust, and joyful local culture. Here is a story of Italy little-known to the outside world and even to many Italians.

—*Polly Franchini, Publisher*

Nota Bene

Most of these recipes come from a time before modern appliances and tools appeared in the Italian domestic kitchen. Ingredient amounts, times, and temperatures for food cooked in the family hearth or wood-burning oven were entirely up to the knowledgeable cook who, for the most part, passed along her wisdom verbally.

Although Signora Ferrante could well assume her Italian readers knew the basics of Italian cookery, those of us who were unfortunately not raised in Italy may need help. So we have added from time to time ingredient amounts and instructions to help our readers along, hoping to do this without intruding on her own very personal style.

Preface Premessa

THE LAST fifty years have witnessed many secular miracles, including the miracle of the cooking of Puglia. In this region, food was a matter of survival for centuries, as it was in other farming cultures of southern Italy. But today, Puglia's cuisine is enjoyable and substantial, all the while retaining its special character.

A good meal in Puglia now consists of numerous dishes, from appetizer to dessert, when just a few decades ago it would have featured a single dish. This is true throughout Puglia, including Capitanata (Foggia), and the Bari, Otranto, Salento, and Murgia areas. The latter is the extensive central plain that is the focus of Maria Pignatelli Ferrante's wonderful work on food and memory.

Cooks of all persuasions will be salivating while reading these simple and inventive recipes, which call on all the cultivated and wild produce that grows on this ancient land. Yet the cuisine presented here is rather modern, too, with its reliance on greens, legumes, pasta, a little fish, not much meat, extra-virgin olive oil, and simple cheeses. At the same time, Roman, Byzantine, medieval, and Arab influences can all be seen here. Just look at the recipe for "Sweet and Sour Shellfish" (*Cognotti*), which calls for oysters and mussels to be fried, then cooked in a mixture of honey and wine vinegar, with ground almonds and chestnuts, and bits of candied orange peel.

Emotions run deep in these pages, which recount the rhythms of life in a farming region—its social rhythms, the changing of the seasons, the harvesting methods and the way products are transformed; living spaces and buildings; architectural form; and the use of space in an agricultural system that has been profoundly changed by industry and tourism, but has not disappeared completely.

Maria Pignatelli Ferrante writes about all of this as an insider. Like a Renaissance diarist, she writes with emotion and spirit to create a

Left: a group of trulli

passionate personal narrative that brings it all to life. Here is what it is like to live among the *trulli* and farmhouses, to participate in the village social life that revolves around the simple task of peeling fava beans, to experience religious holidays and harvests. Here are the annual rituals of putting up products for the winter, and the relationship between the wealthy landowners and tenant farmers (represented splendidly by an anonymous letter from the author's own archives). The parts of that life that live on and the parts that have disappeared forever all contribute to this wonderful account.

—*Marco Guarnaschelli Gotti* (d.2003), *Italian series editor*

INTRODUCTION INTRODUZIONE

PUGLIA IS often referred to as "Italy's California," and while that may be an exaggeration, I can state fairly that this region often seems like an oasis of calm in the sea of contradictions that is southern Italy.

Puglia's history has far-reaching roots. "Diomedes' fields" in Gargano got their name from a Homeric hero, who, having survived the Trojan War, moved his horses there. Legend has it that Porto Badisco, a few miles south of Otranto, is where Aeneas docked. And, of course,

mythical Taras bounded across the Ionic Sea on the back of a dolphin in order to found the city of Taranto.

These are myths to be sure, but as usual these myths are based on a kernel of truth. The soil of Puglia has been dug up relentlessly over the years for its archeological treasures; the items found there adorn museums and houses in Europe and throughout the world.

Legend aside, the real-life people of Puglia have been subject to the rule of Carthaginians, Romans, Lombards, Byzantines, and Saracens. They have been ruled by Swabian kings, French princes, and Spanish viceroys. They have survived their conquerors' wars, invasions, revolutions, and restorations, all the while gritting their teeth and working hard to defend their own traditions, character, and identity.

This long and complex struggle is chronicled by stunning handiwork in the form of stone walls, temples, amphitheaters, Basilian crypts, Romanesque churches, castles, baroque palaces—all beautifully incorporated into urban and rural landscapes characterized by a strong, almost religious sense of order.

The culture of Puglia is made manifest in many ways, from true works of high art to more humble crafts, from the fairy tale fantasy of the region's *trulli* to its highly elaborate baroque architecture. However, there is one aspect of Puglia's culture that stands out above all others, and that is the cooking of its people.

This is the fruit of thousands of years of poverty—and the creativity and intelligence of a people struggling daily to keep their dignity while also struggling simply to survive. I have researched this culinary tradition in detail, and delved deeply into its origins and traditions.

—Maria Pignatelli Ferrante

Wheat and Wheat Products

Il grano e i suoi derivati

In Puglia, and indeed throughout the entire Mediterranean region, wheat has always been a major crop. Wheat is used to make various types of flour, although a distinction must be made between what we call in Italy "hard" wheat and "soft" wheat.

"Hard" wheat in Italy means durum wheat, *grano duro*. It has a crisp texture, so it splinters when it is ground. Hard wheat is the source of semolina flour, which is slightly yellow in color and is used almost solely for making pasta, and not for baked goods. [An exception is the world-famous "Bread of Altamura," made from "hard" wheat semolina flour in the Murgia area of Puglia. It is the only bread in Italy to have earned the European Union D.O.P.* quality stamp.]

"Hard" wheat yields less per acre than "soft" wheat, and sells at a higher price. Under the best of circumstances, the excellent *cappello* wheat variety had yielded 1,400 to 1,600 pounds per acre farmed. Today, in many areas, some varieties can yield more than 13,000 pounds per acre. This impressive growth in "hard" wheat yield has two sources: new varieties and improved irrigation methods.

"Soft" wheat, *grano tenero,* is milled to make grades of baking flour, sold in Italy as "00" (*doppio zero*—the highest grade and finest milled), "0," "1" "2," and *integrale* (the lowest grade and coarsest). The differences in these grades are due to how finely the wheat has been ground and how much of its fiber—wheat germ and bran—has been removed during the milling process. "Soft" white flour grades are processed with both hot and cold milling techniques.

*The EU D.O.P. (Protected Denomination of Origin) stamp identifies a unique and significant food produced in a specific region or town. Its geographical origin determines its quality or particular characteristics. Production of the product may only be carried out in its specified area.

White *Tipo* "00" has a talcum-powder texture and is most like American "cake" flour. White *Tipo* "0" is closest to American "all-purpose" flour. These are the two grades typically used in Italian baking.

MILLING

Hot milling refers to grinding with a millstone that in the past was either turned by hand or powered by horses, donkeys, or even water. The grinding mechanism itself consists of two large stone disks, each about four feet in diameter. The disks sit one on top of the other. The bottom disk remains immobile while the top disk turns in a circle. The lower stone is outfitted with small holes, so as the wheat is ground the smaller pieces of wheat fall through the holes and are collected below. Once the wheat has been ground to a powdery consistency, it is sifted and then sorted into grades of "soft" white flour, which are the main products, and coarse and fine bran, which are by-products used mainly in animal feed.

Only the higher grades of "soft" white flour are used to prepare bread. Adding even a small amount of *integrale*, which is produced from whole grains, would result in very heavy bread. [This grade is closest to American whole wheat flour.] Historically this was given to the mill operator, who sold it for the making of focaccia. In accordance with tradition, we will refer to *integrale*, with its brownish color, as *farina nera*, or "black flour."

Cold milling uses metal cylinders that roll parallel to each other to break the wheat. Each type of cylinder is indicated with a letter and number: b^1, b^2, b^3, b^4 and so on; each of these numbers corresponds to a certain type of product produced by the cylinders.

TRADITIONS

In addition to bread, high grades of "soft" white flour are used to make fresh or homemade pasta. Until World War II, high grades were used solely to prepare desserts and homemade pasta and were available only to the wealthy.

With very few exceptions, the poor and middle class, people who worked for a living with their minds or with their hands, used lower grades and "black flour," or *farina nera*. But even the wealthy often sacrificed a bit of their social status by adding a handful of "black flour" to traditional products such as bread, pasta, and focaccia, to make these tastier.

In the poorest ranks of society, the use of high grades of "soft" white flour was considered almost a wasteful luxury. I still have a very strong memory of a poor woman and child who came begging for a handful of *farina nera* or a fistful of dried figs, the latter being the only sweets available in those days.

Today, not only are eating habits more or less similar across social classes, but whole grain foods are sought after for their nutritional properties. Old social distinctions have fallen by the wayside, and it is generally accepted that mixing some of the lower grades and "black flour" with semolina flour results in more flavorful orecchiette and *fricieddi* (short pasta made using a round one-eighth inch diameter piece of metal known as a *fricieddu*).

Breads

In earlier days, women and children were responsible for making bread, and they sometimes worked during the night to do so, but in the late 1800s a law was introduced that forbade employing women and children for this type of work and at the same time enacted a prohibition against anyone working between the hours of ten p.m. and four a.m.

During the Italian Fascist period, working overnight was made legal again, with the caveat that there needed to be three teams working in shifts. Since then, working overnight has been banned once again. As a result, bread bakers have begun to use fast-rising yeasts in order to allow bread to be delivered in the early morning hours. At the same time, wood-burning ovens—which offer what is called "direct fire"—have gradually been replaced with ovens that supply "indirect fire." These employ a series of small tubes in which hot water circulates. While "direct fire" ovens effectively remove moisture from bread as it is baking, "indirect fire" ovens maintain a bread's humidity. Logically enough, then, bread made using the newer ovens becomes inedible twenty-four hours after it is baked, as it becomes too hard, or sometimes too gluey, to be eaten. A saying has it that in order to eat good bread, one must taste it twenty-four hours after it emerges from the oven!

In the days when the baking process removed moisture from bread, approximately two and one-half pounds of bread dough could be assumed to result in two and one-quarter pounds of baked bread, making it relatively easy to predict the amount of the finished product. Today's ovens with "indirect fire" risk turning out baked bread that can weigh more or less the same as the uncooked dough.

Pasta

Until the postwar period, dishes of pasta and sauce were reserved for our Catholic holidays, when the entire family, liberated from the demands of hard work, could gather together around the table. Today, the expression *invitare qualcuno a maccheroni e carne* ("to invite someone for macaroni and meat") is still used in southern Italy to mean someone is being invited for the most and the best that a household has to offer. And both the wealthy and the poor are in the habit of serving some raw vegetables known as *spingituro*

FIELDS near ALTAMURA

alongside pasta. *Spingituro* is the classic accompaniment to orecchiette. Usually this is celery, but chicory, fennel, and cucumbers may also be used. These are used to break up the strong taste of the region's sauces, encouraging diners to eat more.

ORECCHIETTE

Before giving you recipes for orecchiette (*see* First Courses/*Primi Piatti*) and discussing the methods for garnishing it, I will describe to you how this pasta is made, although I should warn you that if you were not born in Puglia and have never lived there, it will be difficult for you to get from the stage when the pasta dough is a simple roll to the point where the pieces of pasta have been shaped into those wrinkled disks that receive so much well-deserved admiration.

First, knead a mixture of flour and water until you have a smooth and fairly stiff dough. Then, cut off a small piece and roll it until it is one long cylinder of dough (as with dough for *taralli*) with a diameter of approximately one-half inch. Orecchiette ["little ears"] should be made on a rough wood surface, which is known as a *fizzatora* or a *tavuliere*, because a certain amount of imperfection is desired. A perfectly smooth surface would allow the pasta to slide around and would keep it from developing the wrinkled surface that orecchiette are meant to have. The women of Puglia move incredibly quickly as they take off a piece of the cylinder and hold it between the index fingers and thumbs of their left hands. They hold knives in their right hands and cut off thin slices of pasta, then stretch them in order to shape orecchiette that are properly [ear-shaped] concave and round. Some use their thumbs to make small cup shapes called *recchie* or *coppetedde.*

Fortunately, artisanal pasta makers produce packaged orecchiette. Otherwise, few people would ever have a chance to taste this food, which is the symbol of Puglia's traditions.

GARNISHING PASTA

Currently, the most popular way to serve orecchiette in Puglia is with fresh tomato sauce, basil, and generous amounts of grated *cacioricotta*. *Cacioricotta,* made throughout Puglia, is a soft, bright white cheese that varies slightly in taste from area to area. It can be made with cow's milk or sheep's milk. The cow's milk variety has a more delicate flavor, while the sheep's milk type is stronger.

In parts of southern Puglia, *cacioricotta* used to be made on farms in wheels about ten inches in diameter and thickness. The white mixture, which was soft and unsalted, was packed into *fesche*, small cylindrical containers made of braided reeds that allowed the whey to drip out. Once the *cacioricotta* was nice and firm, it was taken to the landowner's house or to stores, where it was cut into slices, sprinkled with sea salt, placed in a ceramic container called a *capasa*, and then topped with a weight. *Cacioricotta,* was a seasonal cheese, made only in summer. In the warm weather, milk used to be boiled for fear that it would go bad and could not be used for any other kind of cheese since the fat could no longer be separated from the casein. *Cacioricotta* was made by default. When it was stored in salt, it could be enjoyed all year long, though when it was removed from the salt it had to be rinsed with running water and then boiled for about fifteen minutes.

In many Murgia areas, local cheese makers are now producing excellent *cacioricotta* in circular forms with a diameter of approximately four inches and about one and one-half inches thick. *Cacioricotta* is lightly salted and aged for a short time, so that when grated it gives off large, soft flakes. *Cacioricotta* from the hills has a more delicate and less salty flavor than *cacioricotta* made on the plains. *Cacioricotta* from the plains is also delicious when eaten fresh.

Another classic topping for homemade pasta is pecorino, a raw whole sheep's milk cheese that is heated from 95° to 98° F. Three months of aging make it an excellent alternative to meat or fish. After six months it is the right consistency for grating. Pecorino can also be accompanied by *ragù*, a thick tomato sauce that includes meat—beef, pork, lamb, or veal, which would have been used as the second course—cooked with olive oil and onion.

In earlier times, *ragù* was made in an earthenware pot known as a *tiesto*, similar to a Neapolitan *tiano*, over a coal fire. Before going to bed, people doused the last pieces of burning wood with water, and then they carefully collected the coal from the fire and stored it in jute bags or in copper containers.

Perfect *ragù*—a dark tomato sauce that tends to be more dry than liquid—relied on tomatoes that had been puréed and then dried in the sun; another secret was to cook the sauce slowly for four to five hours. Modern life and the regular use of electricity and gas have made it much easier and faster to cook a delicious *ragù*.

These days, homemade pasta and specifically "fresh pasta" are experiencing a resurgence in popularity. By "fresh pasta" I mean the pasta made and sold at the small artisanal shops that have multiplied in our area. These stores create various kinds of pasta: tortellini, ravioli, *agnolotti*, cannelloni, crêpes, tagliatelle, and pastina for broth. Often multi-colored, these pastas can be seen as part of a blossoming local artisanal culture, although they have no place in Puglia's culinary traditions.

This reminds me of an anecdote that has been recited in my family for many years. Our table was always crowded at mealtime, because we lived in the same house with my grandmother and my uncle's family. Because we were very picky, our cook would serve several dishes in order to make everyone happy, while relying—as was common at the time—only on ingredients we received from our farms. My uncle was a brilliant, cultured, and personable man with many fine qualities, and he always boasted that he was an excellent cook, too. One day, he decided to prove himself in the kitchen and prepare a dish of pasta. So he sent someone to buy egg tagliatelle, seven ounces of butter, seven ounces of prosciutto, some mushrooms, and I don't know how much *Parmigiano-Reggiano*, a cheese that rarely appeared on our table. When the dish was ceremoniously presented, all the members of my family clapped and praised my uncle. Our cook, Addolorata, simply looked on, and then said (in dialect), "Sure, but anyone can cook that way."

Poor Addolorata made us orecchiette with several different sauces every day, even with *ricotta forte*, a soft spicy cheese kept in jars and served as a topping, spread on crostini, or added to tomato salad. It takes much effort to make *ricotta forte* and age it properly. From April to June, every week Addolorata added fresh ricotta to the wooden box where the cheese was aging until the correct volume and level of fermentation was achieved.

First courses

Primi Piatti

When it comes to the first course from Puglia, it's natural to start with orecchiette, the greatest symbol of the cuisine of Puglia.

But in order to pay even greater respect to tradition, we should start with *Recchietedd p'i pulupitt* or *Recchie cu li purpietti.* I could come up with various definitions for this dish, but the recipe would always be more or less the same in Puglia, whether prepared by someone from Martina Franca, Grottaglie, Lecce, or Francavilla.

This specialty of the region combines two items that are typically found in the Salento area: orecchiette and meatballs. Sunday calls for one to be served as the first course/*primo* and the other as the second course/*secondo*, but more typical tradition says that each dish of orecchiette tossed with sauce and cheese must also feature at least four or five meatballs taken from the second course to be eaten together with the pasta. In earlier days, especially on holidays, farmers placed a large ceramic dish full of orecchiette and meatballs in the center of the table. Diners, armed with their forks, all ate directly from the serving dish.

Above: orecchiette with broccoli rabe

ORECCHIETTE WITH MEATBALLS

Orecchiette con le polpette

Serves 4

Ingredients

1/3 cup extra-virgin olive oil
1 small onion, minced
1 cup white wine
2 cups fresh tomato purée
or 2 8-ounce cans
Basil leaves
1 pound orecchiette
Grated pecorino

Meatballs

2 slices day-old country bread, crusts removed
1/2 pound ground pork and veal, mixed
1 egg, lightly beaten
2 tablespoons grated pecorino
1 clove garlic, minced
Fresh flat-leaf parsley, chopped
Sea salt
Pepper

To make the meatballs, first immerse the bread in water, then squeeze it to rid excess water, and tear into small pieces. Combine the bread with the ground meat, egg, pecorino, a small amount of garlic, and parsley to taste in a large mixing bowl. Season with salt and pepper. Mix the ingredients with your hands until well combined.

Form the mixture into hazelnut-sized [about 3/4 inch diameter] meatballs. Heat the olive oil in a skillet large enough to hold the meatballs in a single layer. Fry the meatballs, turning them so that they brown on all sides. Add the onion to the skillet and cook until it is soft. Add the wine and cook until the wine has evaporated. At this point, add the tomato purée and basil and simmer until the sauce has thickened, about 30 minutes.

Fresh tomato purée: blanch and peel tomatoes, then purée them through a food mill.

Meanwhile, bring a large pot of salted water to a boil and cook the orecchiette until al dente. Drain the pasta and then mix it with the sauce and abundant grated pecorino. Transfer to individual plates, being sure to include 4 or 5 meatballs in each serving.*

*Traditionally, this dish is served with raw celery sticks, a *spingituro*. (See page 13.)

ORECCHIETTE WITH MEAT ROLLS

Orecchiette con le brasciole

Serves 4

*This recipe is made in the same way as the previous dish, except that stuffed rolls of meat—*brasciole *in the dialect of Puglia—are used in place of the meatballs.*

Ingredients

4 lean veal cutlets, preferably scaloppini, about 1 pound
Sea salt
Pepper
1 clove garlic, minced
Fresh flat-leaf parsley, chopped
1 teaspoon capers
Pecorino, shaved
1/3 cup extra-virgin olive oil
1 small onion, minced
1 cup white wine
2 cups fresh tomato purée or 2 8-ounce cans
Basil leaves
1 pound orecchiette
Grated pecorino

Sprinkle the cutlets with salt, pepper, garlic, and parsley to taste. Top each cutlet with a few capers, and then distribute shaved pecorino on top of the capers. Roll up one cutlet and tie it with kitchen twine or secure it with a toothpick. Repeat with remaining cutlets.

In a large skillet add the oil and fry the cutlets, turning them so that they brown on both sides. Add the onion and cook until it is soft. Add the wine and cook until the wine has evaporated. At this point, add the tomato purée and the basil and simmer the cutlets until the sauce has thickened, about 1 hour.

Fresh tomato purée: blanch and peel tomatoes, then purée them through a food mill.

Meanwhile, bring a large pot of salted water to a boil and cook the orecchiette until al dente. Remove the cutlets from the sauce. Drain the pasta and then mix it with the sauce and abundant pecorino. Transfer to individual plates, being sure to include a cutlet in each serving.

ORECCHIETTE WITH TOMATO SAUCE

Orecchiette con sugo di pomodoro

Serves 4

Ingredients

2 1/4 pounds fresh tomatoes
Extra-virgin olive oil
1 onion, diced
Basil leaves
1 pound orecchiette
Grated *cacioricotta**

Dice the tomatoes and fry them in a skillet in enough olive oil to cover the bottom, along with the onion. Season with a generous amount of basil. Bring a large pot of salted water to a boil and cook the orecchiette until al dente. Drain the pasta and transfer to a serving dish. Mix in a very generous amount of grated cheese, then toss it with the sauce.

*A local cheese (see page 16). A bright white farmer's "basket" cheese hard enough for grating is an alternative.

The cheese used here has a delicate flavor, so you need to use a lot of it. If you like, you can replace the diced tomato with fresh puréed tomatoes or canned peeled tomatoes.

ORECCHIETTE WITH RICOTTA

Orecchiette con la ricotta

Serves 4

*In Puglia, this dish is usually served as an appetizer/*antipasto*. While it is quite substantial, it is also delicately flavored. Some like it with a bit of tomato sauce mixed in as well. Usually orecchiette with* ragù *is served after this dish.*

Ingredients

Sea salt
3/4 pound orecchiette
1 cup ricotta

Bring a large pot of salted water to a boil and cook the orecchiette until al dente. While the pasta is cooking, whisk the ricotta in a large bowl with a pinch of salt and a few tablespoons of the pasta cooking water. Drain the pasta and add it to the ricotta, tossing to combine well.

ORECCHIETTE WITH BROCCOLI RABE

Orecchiette con le cime di rape

Serves 4

Ingredients

1 1/4 pounds broccoli rabe
Sea salt
1 pound orecchiette
1/2 cup extra-virgin olive oil
2 cloves garlic, any green shoots removed
Peperoncino, hot red chili pepper, sliced [or dried flakes]
4 anchovies, rinsed, boned, and coarsely chopped

Trim the broccoli rabe thoroughly and rinse it in several changes of cold water. Bring a large pot of salted water, at least 1 gallon, to a boil. Add the orecchiette and cook it for 5 minutes, then add the broccoli rabe and cook both over high heat until the pasta is al dente.

Meanwhile, in a large skillet heat enough oil to coat the bottom. Then add the garlic, chili, and anchovies. When the garlic has browned, remove the cloves from the pan and discard. Remove the skillet from the heat. Drain the pasta and broccoli rabe and transfer to a serving dish, with the chili and anchovies. Pour the remaining oil over the pasta, mix well to combine thoroughly, and serve immediately.

ORECCHIETTE WITH RAGÙ

Orecchiette col ragù

Serves 4

Ingredients

2/3 cup extra-virgin olive oil
1 onion, chopped
2 1/4 pounds meat, chopped (any combination of veal, beef, pork or lamb)*
1 cup dry red wine
2 cups tomato sauce
1 pound orecchiette
Grated pecorino

Heat the oil in a heavy-bottomed casserole and fry the onion and chopped meat. When the meat has browned, add the wine. When the wine has evaporated, add the tomato sauce.

It's best to use homemade tomato sauce though store-bought is OK as well. In place of pecorino, you can use *ricotta forte,* a spicy cheese that lends the pasta a markedly strong flavor.

Cook the sauce over low heat for 2 to 3 hours. When the sauce is finishing, bring a large pot of salted water to a boil and cook the orecchiette until al dente. Drain the pasta and transfer to a serving bowl. Top the cooked pasta with the sauce, then top the entire dish with abundant grated pecorino.

*Where I'm from, the meat mixture usually consists of lamb, veal, and pork, though you can make this with any combination you like.

BAKED ORECCHIETTE

Orecchiette stufate

Serves 4

Ingredients

2 cups fresh tomato purée or 2 8-ounce cans
1 onion, chopped
Extra-virgin olive oil
Basil leaves
Sea salt
Pepper
1 1/2 pounds orecchiette
7 ounces (2/3 cup) mozzarella, diced
3 1/2 ounces (1/3 cup) *provola*, diced
7 tablespoons grated *Parmigiano-Reggiano*
3 tablespoons grated pecorino

4 terracotta/ceramic individual baking dishes

Fresh tomato purée: blanch and peel tomatoes, then purée them through a food mill.

Using the tomato purée, onion, oil, and basil, prepare a light tomato sauce in a skillet and season to taste with salt and pepper. Bring a large pot of salted water to a boil and cook the orecchiette until al dente. Drain the pasta and transfer to a large bowl. Add the 4 cheeses and some of the tomato sauce. Stir to combine. Spread about 1/2 cup of tomato sauce in the bottom of each of the baking dishes. Divide the pasta among the 4 dishes, then top with additional sauce and additional basil leaves. Bake in a preheated 400° oven for about 15 minutes.

REHEATED ORECCHIETTE

Orecchiette riscaldate

This dish may be made from leftovers, but it's delicious. Take any orecchiette and sauce left over from lunch. Reheat them in a skillet with low sides so that a crunchy crust forms on the bottom. Stir frequently with a wooden spoon so that they brown on all sides. While tossing the orecchiette over the heat, add grated pecorino or Parmigiano-Reggiano *(but never* cacioricotta*).*

ORECCHIETTE WITH CAULIFLOWER

Orecchiette con i cavolfiori

Serves 4

Ingredients

1 pound purple "Sicilian" cauliflower [in Puglia, this is white with purple markings]
1/2 cup extra-virgin olive oil
2 cloves garlic, any green shoots removed
Spicy red chili pepper, sliced [or dried flakes]
4 salted anchovies, rinsed, boned, and chopped
1 pound orecchiette

Trim the cauliflower and cut it into florets. In a large pot of water, boil until al dente. In a wide skillet with low sides, heat the oil, then add the garlic, chili to taste, and anchovies. When the garlic has browned, remove it and discard it. Drain the cauliflower florets and add them to the skillet. Toss over the heat for a few minutes.

Meanwhile, bring a large pot of salted water to a boil and cook the orecchiette until al dente. Drain the pasta and add it to the skillet with the cauliflower. Toss over the heat for a few minutes and serve piping hot.

VERMICELLI WITH TUNA SAUCE

Virmicidd con sugo di tonno

Serves 4

This dish is usually served on the evening before a major Catholic holiday, when it is traditional to eat a meatless meal.

Ingredients

1 clove garlic, minced
1/4 cup extra-virgin olive oil
1 6-ounce can Italian tuna in olive oil, drained
10 ounces (1 1/4 cups) fresh tomato purée
2 3/4 cups flour
Sea salt
Pepper
Fresh flat-leaf parsley, chopped

In a skillet, fry the garlic in the oil, then add the tuna and tomato purée. Cook for about 20 minutes.

Meanwhile make the homemade pasta. Mound the flour on a smooth work surface. Add water in small amounts and knead until you have achieved a stiff dough. Then work by hand to make vermicelli ["little worms"]. Roll out long thin cylinders of dough, and then cut them into 3/4 inch long pieces.

Bring a large pot of salted water to a boil and cook the vermicelli for a few minutes until al dente. Drain the pasta, and transfer to a serving bowl. Toss the cooked pasta with the tuna sauce. Season with salt and pepper and sprinkle with parsley to taste.

Fresh tomato purée: blanch and peel tomatoes, then purée them through a food mill.

VERMICELLI WITH FISH SAUCE

Virmicidd con sughetto di pesce

This dish also is usually served on the eve of a major Catholic holiday.

Ingredients

2 3/4 cups flour
1 clove garlic, minced
1 onion, diced
Extra-virgin olive oil, enough to cover the bottom of the casserole
6 to 7 canned peeled tomatoes, chopped
1 whole scorpion fish, spines trimmed and cleaned*
1 eel, skinned, cleaned, and [if large] sliced*
Several oily fish (such as anchovies, mackerel, or sardines)
Pepper
Fresh flat-leaf parsley, chopped

Make the homemade pasta. Make a stiff dough with flour and water on a smooth work surface. Add water in small amounts until you have achieved the right consistency. Then work by hand to make vermicelli ["little worms"]. Roll out long very thin cylinders of dough, and then cut them into 3/4 inch long pieces.

In a large stockpot, fry garlic and onion in oil until golden, and then add 6 to 7 peeled tomatoes. When this mixture has thickened, thin it again with enough water to make the resulting sauce an amount that will cover all the fish to be added. Bring the liquid to a boil and add the fish, starting with the largest fish and going down in size so the smallest fish are added last. Cooking time should be about 30 minutes total.

When the sauce is finishing, bring a large pot of salted water to a boil and cook the vermicelli for a few minutes until al dente. Drain the pasta and transfer to a large serving bowl.

Remove a few of the smaller fish and carefully remove their bones, then flake the fish flesh and mix it with the cooked pasta. Top the pasta with the remaining sauce and all the fish. Season with a generous amount of pepper and parsley to taste and serve.

You will need to remove the skin and bones of the scorpion fish after presenting the dish.

*A good fishmonger will do this for you.

COUNTRY-STYLE TAGLIATELLE WITH MUTTON RAGÙ

Tagliatelle rustiche con ragù di castrato

Serves 6

Ingredients

Pasta

2 1/2 cups finely ground semolina flour
1 1/2 cups semolina flour
1 1/2 cups whole wheat flour

Grated pecorino
Grated *Parmigiano-Reggiano*

Sauce

1 onion, minced
3/4 cup extra-virgin olive oil
1 1/4 pounds mutton leg, chopped
1 cup red wine
10 ounces (1 1/4 cups) tomato paste, diluted
Sea salt
Pepper
Basil leaves

For the homemade pasta, combine the 3 types of flour on a smooth surface adding enough lukewarm water and kneading to create a fairly stiff dough. Using a pasta machine, make tagliatelle that are slightly thicker than normal, about 1/8 inch. Put the noodles on a lightly floured tea towel and set them aside to rest for at least 2 hours.

Meanwhile, to make the sauce, fry the onion in the oil in a heavy-bottomed casserole. Add the chopped mutton and brown on all sides. Add the red wine, and cook until the wine has evaporated. Add the diluted tomato paste about 1 tablespoon at a time, stirring to combine with each addition. Season with salt and pepper. Simmer over low heat (a "flame tamer" is useful for this) for at least 3 hours. When the sauce *(ragù)* is cooked, stir in the basil leaves.

When the *ragù* is almost finished, cook the tagliatelle in a large pot of boiling salted water for a few minutes, and drain well. Combine the pasta with the *ragù* in a serving bowl, then sprinkle on the grated cheeses to taste.

Before stirring the sauce into the pasta, remove the pieces of meat and serve them as a second course with a good side dish/ *contorno.*

COUNTRY-STYLE TAGLIATELLE WITH BOAR RAGÙ

Tagliatelle rustiche con ragù di cinghiale

The preceeding recipe can be made using boar meat as well. Boar meat can be a little difficult to track down, but if you're lucky enough to get some, it results in a delicious sauce that marries perfectly with country-style tagliatelle, orecchiette, or even large-size dried semolina pasta.

MACCHERONI TIMBALE

Timballo di maccheroni

Serves 4

Ingredients

1 onion, chopped
1/2 cup extra-virgin olive oil
1 1/4 pounds mixed chopped meat, veal and pork
1 cup wine
10 ounces (1 1/4 cups) tomato sauce
Sea salt
Pepper
Basil leaves
3/4 pound egg lasagna noodles
8 ounces (1 cup) mozzarella, diced
2 hard-boiled eggs, diced
4 ounces (1/2 cup) mortadella and *prosciutto cotto*, diced
4 tablespoons grated *Parmigiano-Reggiano*
4 tablespoons grated pecorino

Meatballs

6 ounces ground meat (any combination of veal, beef, pork or lamb)
1 slice day-old country bread (remove crust, soak in water, squeeze dry, and tear into small pieces)
2 tablespoons grated pecorino
1 egg yolk
Sea salt
Pepper
Extra-virgin olive oil

In a skillet, cook the onion in the oil, then add the chopped meat. Add the wine and allow it to evaporate completely. Add the tomato sauce, salt, pepper, and basil, and simmer for at least 2 hours.

For this *timballo*, you can either make homemade egg noodles or use packaged lasagna noodles. For homemade noodles, make a dough with 5 cups of "0" Italian flour [or unbleached all-purpose] and 6 whole eggs. On a smooth work surface, mound the dough and make a well in the middle. Add eggs one at a time, incorporating them into the flour. Then knead the dough. It should be fairly stiff. Use a pasta machine to create sheets of dough. Cut the dough into large pieces, about 3 1/4 by 6 inches and about 1/16 inch thick.

Bring a large pot of salted water with 1 tablespoon of oil added to a boil. Whether using packaged or homemade noodles, boil them a few at a time. When the noodles are al dente, remove them using a strainer and place them on damp tea towels that have been wet and then wrung out. Meanwhile, prepare meatballs using the ingredients listed, except the olive oil. Make the meatballs about the size of hazelnuts and brown in a skillet on all sides in the oil. In a baking dish, spread about 1/2 cup of tomato sauce on the bottom, then cover with a layer of noodles. Put some of the diced mozzarella, eggs, cold cuts, and meatballs on top, sprinkle with some of the grated cheeses, then top with another layer of sauce.

Top the sauce with a layer of noodles. Repeat layers in the same order until you have used all the ingredients, ending with a layer of noodles topped with cheese and covered with a generous amount of sauce. Bake in a preheated 400° oven for about 30 minutes. Allow to rest 10 minutes before serving.

RICOTTA LASAGNA

Sagna con la ricotta

Serves 4

Ingredients

- 1/4 cup extra-virgin olive oil
- 1 onion, cut into large pieces
- 2 cups fresh tomato purée or 2 8-ounce cans
- Sea salt
- Pepper
- Basil leaves, torn
- 3/4 pound egg lasagna noodles
- 3/4 pound ricotta
- 7 tablespoons grated *Parmigiano-Reggiano*
- 6 ounces (3/4 cup) *provola*, thinly sliced

In a skillet, heat the oil, then fry the onion pieces. Remove and discard the onion pieces and add the tomato purée. Add salt, pepper, and basil leaves to taste. Simmer the sauce for 20 minutes.

Fresh tomato purée: blanch and peel tomatoes, then purée them through a food mill.

Bring a large pot of salted water to a boil, with 1 tablespoon of oil added, and boil noodles a few at a time. When the noodles are al dente, remove them using a strainer and place them on damp tea towels that have been wet and then wrung out.

Meanwhile, in a mixing bowl, wisk the ricotta and *Parmigiano-Reggiano* together with a fork until smooth. (Reserve about 1 tablespoon *Parmigiano-Reggiano.*) Add a few tablespoons of the tomato sauce, 1 tablespoon at a time, to the ricotta mixture and whisk until until you produce a thick creamy mixture. Spread 1/2 cup of the remaining tomato sauce on the bottom of a baking dish. Top with a layer of cooked noodles and spread a layer of the ricotta mixture evenly over the noodles. Add a layer of *provola* slices and a little tomato sauce. Continue to layer noodles, then the ricotta mixture, then *provola,* ending with a layer of noodles topped with sauce and sprinkled with the reserved *Parmigiano-Reggiano*. Bake in a preheated 400° oven for approximately 30 minutes. Allow to rest 10 minutes before serving.

If you wish, you can also add layers of hazelnut-sized meatballs made from: 6 ounces ground meat, 1 tablespoon grated *Parmigiano-Reggiano*, 1 egg yolk, and 1 slice day-old country bread (remove crusts, sprinkle with water, and then squeeze dry, and tear into small pieces). In a skillet, brown the meatballs in olive oil, then add them to the tomato sauce and let them cook in the sauce for a few minutes.

BAKED PASTA

Pasta al forno

Serves 4

Ingredients

1 onion, chopped
1/2 cup extra-virgin olive oil
1 1/4 pounds mixed chopped meat, veal and pork
1 cup red wine
1 1/4 cups tomato purée
Sea salt
Pepper
Basil
1 pound rigatoni, penne, *ziti spezzati*, or *reginette*
8 ounces mozzarella, diced
2 hard-boiled eggs, diced
4 ounces (1/2 cup) mortadella and *prosciutto cotto*, diced
4 tablespoons grated *Parmigiano-Reggiano*
4 tablespoons grated pecorino

Meatballs

6 ounces ground meat, any combination of veal, beef, pork or lamb
1 slice day-old country bread (remove crust, soak in water, squeeze dry, and tear into small pieces)
2 tablespoons grated pecorino
1 egg yolk
Sea salt
Pepper
Extra-virgin olive oil as needed

In a skillet, cook the onion in the oil, then add the chopped meat. Add the wine and allow it to evaporate completely. Add the tomato purée, salt, pepper, and basil, and simmer the sauce for at least 2 hours.

Fresh tomato purée: blanch and peel tomatoes, then purée them through a food mill.

Meanwhile, prepare meatballs using the ingredients listed except for the oil. Make the meatballs about the size of hazelnuts and brown in a skillet on all sides in the oil.

Bring a large pot of salted water to a boil and cook the pasta until al dente. Drain the pasta. Transfer to a bowl together with some sauce and cheese. Toss to combine.

Spread about 1/2 cup of the tomato sauce in the bottom of a baking dish and top with half of the pasta and sauce. Layer on the other ingredients, then top with another layer of pasta. Sprinkle with a generous amount of *Parmigiano-Reggiano* and top with sauce. Bake in a preheated 400° oven for about 30 minutes.

CURLY LASAGNA WITH BREAD CRUMBS

Sagna riccia con la serratizza

Serves 4

Serratizza *is dialect for the Italian word* segatura, *which means sawdust. In a culinary context, it means "bread crumbs." This dish used to be eaten during Lent, when meat and dairy products are forbidden.*

In my grandmother's time it was traditional for the cook to pass the grater through a lit flame before using it to grate the bread crumbs in order to eliminate any small amounts of cheese that might have gotten stuck between the teeth of the grater and would have caused diners to break Lent unwittingly.

Ingredients

- Extra-virgin olive oil
- 1 clove garlic, any green shoot removed
- 6 salted anchovies, rinsed, boned, and chopped
- Heaping espresso cup bread crumbs
- 3/4 pound thin curly lasagna noodles (also called *reginette*)
- Sea salt
- Pepper

Cover the bottom of a large skillet with olive oil, heat and then add the garlic. When the garlic turns golden, remove and discard it and add the anchovies. Briefly stir with a wooden spoon over the heat and then set aside.

Add 1 tablespoon of olive oil to a small non-stick skillet. Heat the oil and then add the bread crumbs. Stir continuously so that the bread doesn't burn. The bread crumbs should be browned. They do burn easily, so keep an eye on them.

Bring a large pot of salted water to a boil, add 1 tablespoon of oil, and boil the noodles a few at a time. When the noodles are al dente, remove them using a strainer and place them on damp tea towels that have been wet and then wrung out. Transfer them to a serving dish when they are all cooked.

Reheat the olive oil with the anchovies and pour this over the pasta, then sprinkle on the bread crumbs as if they were cheese. Combine thoroughly and season with salt and a generous amount of pepper.

CURLY LASAGNA WITH BREAD CRUMBS AND SAUCE

Sagna riccia con la serratizza al sugo

This recipe is the same as the preceding one with one small variation. When you cook the garlic and then the anchovies in olive oil, add 1 peperoncino, *sliced [or dried chili flakes] to taste, and 6 ounces (about 3/4 cup) tomato purée. The recipes are similar, but the results taste completely different.*

TURKEY LASAGNA

Lasagne stampate

Serves 6 to 8

This dish is usually served during the Christmas holidays.

Ingredients

7 eggs
Finely ground semolina flour

Broth

1 small turkey
1/2 onion
2 stalks celery
1 bunch fresh flat-leaf parsley
2 carrots
2 to 3 tomatoes
6 ounces (3/4 cup) fresh tomato purée
1 pound mozzarella, diced
6 tablespoons grated pecorino
Pepper

Meatballs

3/4 pound ground beef
2 slices day-old country bread (remove crusts, soak in water, squeeze dry, and tear into small pieces)
2 tablespoons grated pecorino
1 clove garlic, minced
Fresh flat-leaf parsley, chopped

Lightly beat the 7 eggs and combine with as much semolina flour as you need to create a dough. Using a pasta machine, roll the dough into sheets about 1/16 inch thick and cut them into squares that are roughly 4 inches by 4 inches.

Bring a large pot of salted water to a boil. Cook 10 of these pasta squares at a time. As soon as each square rises to the surface, remove it with a strainer and transfer to a bowl of ice water. Drain the pasta squares well and arrange them in a single layer on wool cloths. Let them rest overnight on the cloths, and then cut them into smaller squares.

Fresh tomato purée: blanch and peel tomatoes, then purée them through a food mill.

Meanwhile, make a broth with the turkey, onion, celery, parsley, carrots, and tomatoes. Put the ingredients in a stockpot with water to cover, bring to a boil, then simmer until vegetables are soft and turkey is cooked, about 45 minutes. Remove vegetables and turkey from the broth. Set aside the broth. Reserve the turkey meat.

In a mixing bowl, combine the ground beef with the moistened bread, egg yolk, pecorino, garlic, and parsley to taste. Combine thoroughly, then shape into meatballs the size of hazelnuts and brown them in a skillet in olive oil. Put the cooked meatballs and the tomato purée in a pot and simmer briefly over low heat until the purée has thickened somewhat and the meatballs have absorbed its flavor.

In a heavy-bottomed casserole, arrange a layer of the pasta squares. Top with a few of the cooked meatballs in sauce, some diced mozzarella, some grated pecorino, then a layer of turkey meat pieces. Repeat the layers in the same order until you have used up all the ingredients. Pour the broth over the pasta, then place over low heat and simmer for about 10 minutes before serving.

Spaghetti with Yellow Squash

Spaghetti con la zucca gialla

Serves 4

Ingredients

1 pound yellow squash (2 to 3 medium), thinly sliced
1 pound onions, thinly sliced
1/2 cup extra-virgin olive oil
Sea salt
Pepper
1 cup white wine
3/4 pound spaghetti
4 tablespoons grated *Parmigiano-Reggiano*
4 tablespoons grated pecorino

In a large skillet, fry the squash and onions in the olive oil. When they have given up all of their liquid, season with salt and pepper and add the white wine. Cook until the wine has evaporated. The mixture should be very dense and pulpy. If it has not reached that stage, add a little water and cook until it has. Bring a large pot of salted water to a boil and cook the spaghetti until al dente. Drain and transfer to a serving bowl. Add the cooked squash and grated cheeses to the pasta. Toss to combine thoroughly and serve.

SPAGHETTI WITH CRABS

Spaghetti con i cauri (granchi)

Serves 4

Ingredients

1/2 cup extra-virgin olive oil
1 clove garlic, chopped
12 small crabs, scrubbed and rinsed
2 cups fresh tomato purée or 2 8-ounce cans
3/4 pound spaghetti
Sea salt
Pepper

Fresh tomato purée: blanch and peel tomatoes, then purée them through a food mill.

In a large skillet, heat the olive oil with the garlic, then add the crabs, covering the skillet immediately as you do to keep from splattering. After a few minutes turn the crabs and add the tomato purée. Cook over low heat for about 30 minutes.

Bring a large pot of salted water to a boil and cook the spaghetti until al dente. Drain and add the spaghetti to the skillet with the sauce and crabs. Season with salt and a generous amount of pepper. Divide the spaghetti and crabs onto individual plates and allow diners to crack crabs and extract the meat themselves.

SPAGHETTI WITH MUSHROOMS

Spaghetti con i funghi

Serves 4

Ingredients

1/2 cup extra-virgin olive oil
1 clove garlic, chopped
10 ounces (1 1/4 cups) mushrooms, preferably the *pezza* variety, trimmed and diced
1 pound tomatoes, chopped
Sea salt
Pepper
3/4 pound thick spaghetti
Fresh flat-leaf parsley, chopped

In a large skillet, heat the olive oil and cook the garlic in it until it begins to turn golden, then add the mushrooms. When the mushrooms have given up all their liquid, add the tomatoes. Season with salt and pepper and cook until the sauce thickens.

Bring a large pot of salted water to a boil and cook the spaghetti until al dente. Drain well, and transfer to a serving bowl. Pour on the mushroom sauce and toss to combine. Sprinkle with minced parsley to taste.

SPAGHETTI WITH LEEKS

Spaghetti con gli spunzali

Serves 4

Ingredients

1/2 cup extra-virgin olive oil
5 leeks, trimmed, rinsed of all grit, cut into long strips (including some of the green part)
5 tomatoes, blanched, peeled, and chopped
Sea salt
Peperoncino, hot red chili pepper, sliced [or dried flakes] to taste
3/4 pound spaghetti
3 tablespoons grated pecorino

In a skillet, heat the olive oil and add the leeks. Cook, stirring frequently, until they are very soft, but do not allow them to brown. If necessary, add a little water to keep them from browning. When the leeks have melted into a pulp, add the tomatoes, salt, and chili.

Bring a large pot of salted water to a boil and cook the spaghetti until al dente. Drain the pasta and transfer to a serving dish, then top with the leek sauce and the grated pecorino. Toss to combine and serve.

SPAGHETTI WITH STRING BEANS

Spaghetti con i fagiolini

Serves 4

Ingredients

1 1/2 pounds plum tomatoes
1/4 cup extra-virgin olive oil
1 clove garlic, minced
Sea salt
3 1/2 pounds thin string beans, trimmed
10 ounces spaghetti
7 tablespoons grated *cacioricotta**
6 basil leaves

Blanch and peel the tomatoes and then purée them through a food mill. Put the olive oil and garlic in a small pot, add the tomato purée, and cook for 20 minutes. Season to taste.

In a large pot, bring 5 quarts of salted water to a boil. Add the green beans and when the water returns to a boil add the spaghetti. When the spaghetti is al dente, drain both the spaghetti and the green beans and transfer to a serving dish. Add the tomato sauce, *cacioricotta,* and basil leaves. Stir to combine and serve immediately.

*A local cheese (see page 16). A bright white farmer's "basket" cheese hard enough for grating is an alternative.

SPAGHETTI WITH WHITE CLAM SAUCE

Spaghetti con le vongole in bianco

Serves 4

Ingredients

1/2 cup extra-virgin olive oil
1 clove garlic
1 1/2 pounds baby clams in their shells, scrubbed and rinsed
3/4 pound spaghetti
Pepper
1/4 cup fresh flat-leaf parsley, minced

In a sauté pan, heat the olive oil, then add the garlic. Allow the garlic to turn just golden, then remove and discard. Add the clams, cover, and cook over high heat to open their shells. (Discard any that resist opening.)

Bring a pot of salted water to a boil and cook the spaghetti until al dente. Drain the pasta and transfer to a large serving dish. Transfer the clams to the serving dish with the pasta, along with any liquid from the skillet. Sprinkle with pepper and parsley to taste.

IN PUGLIA, the clams are always served in their shells in this dish, but if you'd rather serve the clams without their shells, clean the clams thoroughly, then place them in a large skillet over high heat until they begin to open. (Discard any that resist opening.)

Remove the clams from the heat, remove the clam meat from the shells, and strain the resulting liquid. Then heat the olive oil and garlic in a skillet, remove the garlic once it's brown, and add the clams and their juices and cook for 2 to 3 minutes only. Continue with the recipe above.

SPAGHETTI WITH RED CLAM SAUCE

Spaghetti con le vongole al pomodoro

Serves 4

Ingredients

1/2 cup extra-virgin olive oil
1 clove garlic
3 1/2 pounds salad tomatoes, not too ripe, diced
1 1/2 pounds baby clams in their shells, scrubbed and rinsed
3/4 pound spaghetti
1/4 cup fresh flat-leaf parsley, minced
Pepper

In a large pot with a tight-fitting lid, heat the olive oil and brown the garlic. Remove and discard garlic, then add the tomatoes. Cook, stirring continuously, until the tomatoes are very dense and all their liquid has evaporated. Add the clams. Cover the pot and cook for no more than 5 minutes. (Discard any that resist opening.)

Meanwhile, bring a pot of salted water to a boil and cook the spaghetti until al dente. Drain the pasta and transfer to a large serving dish. Add the clams and sauce, a generous amount of pepper and parsley, and serve immediately.

SPAGHETTI WITH MUSSELS

Spaghetti alle cozze

Serves 4

Ingredients

2 1/4 pounds mussels, scrubbed and rinsed
1/2 cup extra-virgin olive oil
1 clove garlic
10 ounces salad tomatoes, diced
3/4 pound spaghetti
Sea salt
Fresh flat-leaf parsley, chopped
Pepper

Open the mussels by hand, collecting their juices in a small bowl, keeping the mussels in their shells. Strain the liquid to remove any grit and set aside. In a skillet, heat the olive oil and garlic. As soon as the garlic begins to brown, remove and discard it. Add the diced tomato and cook until the sauce is quite thick. Add the mussels and some of their liquid. Bring to a boil, then remove from the heat.

Bring a pot of salted water to a boil and cook the spaghetti until al dente. Drain the pasta and transfer to a serving dish. Top with the mussels and sauce. Sprinkle with parsley and a generous amount of pepper to taste, and serve immediately.

To vary the recipe, transfer the cooked spaghetti to a skillet with low sides, the type you would use to make a frittata. Add the sauce and a little fresh oregano. Shake the skillet to keep the pasta in motion and cook until lightly browned.

MUSSEL SOUP WITH TUBETTINI

Tubettini in brodetto di cozze

Serves 4

Ingredients

2 1/4 pounds mussels, scrubbed and rinsed
1/2 cup extra-virgin olive oil
1 clove garlic
6 ounce salad tomato, diced
3/4 pound *tubettini*
Fresh flat-leaf parsley, chopped
Pepper

Open the mussels by hand, collecting their juices in a small bowl, keeping the mussels in their shells. Strain the liquid to remove any grit and set aside.

In a heavy-bottomed casserole, heat the olive oil and garlic. As soon as the garlic begins to brown, remove and discard it. Add the diced tomato and cook until the sauce is quite thick. Add the liquid from the mussels and cook for a few minutes. Add the mussels, cover the pot, and cook 2 to 3 minutes. Do not add salt. The sauce should be fairly thin.

Bring a pot of salted water to a boil and cook the *tubettini* until al dente, drain, and then add them to the mussels and their liquid. Transfer to a serving dish and sprinkle with parsley to taste and a generous amount of pepper. Serve immediately.

LINGUINE WITH SHELLFISH

Linguine ai frutti di mare

Serves 4

Ingredients

- 3/4 cup extra-virgin olive oil
- 3 cloves garlic, any green shoots removed
- 1/2 pound mussels in their shells, scrubbed and rinsed
- 1/2 pound date mussels* in their shells, scrubbed and rinsed
- 1/2 pound clams in their shells, scrubbed and rinsed
- 1/2 pound cockles in their shells, scrubbed and rinsed
- A few shrimp, shelled
- 3/4 pound linguine
- Fresh flat-leaf parsley, chopped
- Pepper

Heat the olive oil in a large pot with a lid. Add the garlic cloves and cook until they just begin to brown, then remove and discard. Add the shellfish and cook, covered, for 3 to 4 minutes. (Discard any that resist opening.) Bring a large pot of salted water to a boil and cook the linguine until al dente. Drain and place on a large serving dish. Pour the shellfish and their juices over the pasta. Garnish with parsley, season to taste with pepper, and serve immediately.

*Although date mussels are a traditional ingredient in this recipe, they are now an endangered, protected shellfish and are no longer available.

If you prefer to serve the shellfish out of their shells, open them by hand and add them to the hot olive oil without their shells. In any case, leaving the shells attached to at least some of the shellfish is recommended, as it makes the final presentation prettier.

DITALONI WITH POTATOES

Pasta e patate

Serves 4

Ingredients

1/4 cup extra-virgin olive oil
1 clove garlic
1 pound potatoes, peeled and diced
1 celery heart, trimmed and sliced into rounds
2 canned peeled tomatoes
Sea salt
Pepper
3/4 cup *ditaloni*

In a heavy-bottomed casserole, heat the olive oil until almost smoking. Add the garlic and when it browns, remove it and discard it. Add the potatoes and celery, fry briefly, then add the tomatoes and season with salt and pepper. Stir a few times, then add water to cover and bring to a boil. Cook until the potatoes begin to break apart.

Bring a pot of salted water to a boil and cook the *ditaloni* until they are about half cooked. Then drain them, reserving a few cups of the pasta water. Add the pasta and water to the potatoes. Cook for a short while longer. The dish should not be overly dense. Serve immediately.

RIGATONI WITH UNCOOKED TOMATO SAUCE

Rigatoni alla crudaiola

Serves 4

I've given a recipe with rigatoni here, but this quick and appetizing summer dish is just as good when made with penne, orecchiette, or even spaghetti.

Ingredients

10 ounces salad tomatoes
Extra-virgin olive oil
Sea salt
Pepper
Fresh oregano
Basil leaves
3/4 pound rigatoni
7 ounces (about 2/3 cup) grated *cacioricotta*

Chop the tomatoes and combine them with the olive oil, salt, pepper, oregano, and a generous amount of basil in a large serving bowl. Bring a large pot of salted water to a boil and cook the rigatoni until al dente. Drain the pasta. Add it to the serving bowl. Stir well and top with the grated *cacioricotta,* then toss again to combine and serve.

Penne with Eggplant

Pasta con le melanzane

Serves 4

In this dish, eggplant serves as the spingituro, *a role usually played by celery.*

Fresh tomato purée: blanch and peel tomatoes, then purée them through a food mill.

Ingredients

2 medium eggplants
Extra-virgin olive oil
1 onion, chopped
10 ounces (1 1/4 cups) fresh tomato purée
Sea salt
Basil leaves
3/4 pound penne
4 tablespoons grated pecorino

Wash the eggplant, slice them thinly, salt them, and let them release their bitter juices. In a large skillet, fry the eggplant slices in olive oil, enough to cover the bottom of the skillet, then place them on a plate and set aside. Prepare a tomato sauce by frying the onion in a small amount of oil, then adding the tomato purée, salt, and a generous amount of basil.

Bring a large pot of salted water to a boil and cook the penne until al dente. Drain the pasta. Toss it with the tomato sauce, additional basil leaves, and the grated pecorino. Divide among individual dishes and top each portion of pasta with 3 to 4 slices of eggplant.

BUCATINI WITH TOMATO AND MOZZARELLA

Bucatini alla pizzaiola

Serves 4

This dish is equally delicious when served cold and makes a nice choice for a buffet.

Ingredients

Extra-virgin olive oil
1 small onion, diced
2 cups fresh tomato purée or 2 8-ounce cans
Sea salt
Basil leaves
Fresh oregano
1 pound *bucatini*
3 tablespoons grated *Parmigiano-Reggiano*
1/2 pound mozzarella, sliced
2 ripe tomatoes, sliced
Pepper
Bread crumbs

Heat some olive oil in a skillet, enough to cover the bottom, with the onion and add the tomato purée and a pinch of salt. Cook the purée, then tear some basil leaves and add them, along with some oregano.

Bring a large pot of salted water to a boil and add the *bucatini*. Cook for 2 to 3 minutes, just until the pasta can be folded without breaking. It should still be fairly raw. Drain the *bucatini* and transfer them to a large bowl. Toss the *bucatini* with some of the tomato sauce (reserve at least 1/2 cup) and the *Parmigiano-Reggiano*.

Fresh tomato purée: blanch and peel tomatoes, then purée them through a food mill.

Spread 1/2 cup of the tomato sauce on the bottom of a baking dish. Spread 1/3 of the *bucatini* over it. Cover with half the mozzarella and a little more oregano. Top with another 1/3 bucatini and the rest of the mozzarella and finish with a third layer of *bucatini*. Top the *bucatini* with a layer of sliced tomatoes, then sprinkle on additional basil and oregano, season with salt and pepper, sprinkle on bread crumbs, and drizzle on some olive oil. Bake for about 20 minutes in a 400° preheated oven. Allow to rest for 30 minutes before serving.

CAVATELLI WITH ARUGULA

Cavatelli con la rucola

Serves 4

Ingredients

1 3/4 cups flour (or 10 ounces dry *cavatelli*)
6 ounces (3/4 cup) wild arugula, rinsed and trimmed, stems removed and discarded
1/2 cup extra-virgin olive oil
1 clove garlic
5 small tomatoes, chopped
Peperoncino, hot red chili pepper, sliced [or dried flakes] to taste
2 tablespoons grated *Parmigiano-Reggiano*
2 tablespoons grated pecorino

To make homemade *cavatelli,* mound the flour on a smooth work surface and create a small well in the middle. Pour in a small amount of water. Combine the flour and enough water to create a soft dough. Knead until the dough it is no longer sticky. Working with small amounts of dough at a time, roll out long, roughly shaped cylinders about 1/2 inch thick. Cut each cylinder into 1 inch pieces, and then make grooves around each piece with the tines of a fork. In a large pot of boiling salted water, cook the *cavatelli* for a few minutes, then toss in about 3/4 of the arugula. Cook until the *cavatelli* are cooked through.

Meanwhile, heat the olive oil in a skillet and cook the garlic until it begins to turn golden. Remove and discard garlic. Add the tomatoes and the chili. Cook 10 minutes. Drain the *cavatelli* and the arugula and transfer to a serving dish. Add the cooked tomatoes and the uncooked arugula to the dish with the *cavatelli* and toss to combine. Sprinkle with *Parmigiano-Reggiano* and pecorino and serve.

You can make *cavatelli* or purchase them for ease of preparation. If you do purchase them, make sure you buy them from an artisanal pasta shop and that they are freshly made in-house.

MUSHROOM RISOTTO

Risotto con i funghi

Serves 4

Ingredients

10 ounces (1 1/4 cups) mushrooms, trimmed and diced
3/4 cup extra-virgin olive oil
1 clove garlic, chopped
3 1/2 tablespoons butter
1 onion, minced
1 pound yellow rice
1 cup white wine
2 quarts broth (broth made with a bouillon cube is fine)
Sea salt
Pepper
Fresh flat-leaf parsley, chopped
Grated *Parmigiano-Reggiano* (optional)

Fry the mushrooms in 1/4 cup olive oil with the garlic in a skillet. Remove from the heat and set aside.

In a pan, melt the butter with the remaining olive oil and fry the onion until golden. Add the rice and stir for a minute or so, then pour in the wine. Stir until the wine has evaporated completely, then add the cooked mushrooms and garlic. Add broth to the pan 1/2 cup at a time, stirring until the liquid has been absorbed with each addition. Add broth until the rice is cooked. Season to taste with salt and pepper, garnish with parsley, and serve with *Parmigiano-Reggiano*, if desired.

RICE TIMBALE

Sartù di riso

Serves 4

Ingredients

- Extra-virgin olive oil
- 1 onion, quartered
- 2 cups fresh tomato purée or 2 8-ounce cans
- Basil leaves
- 2 3/4 cups rice
- 10 ounces (1 1/4 cups) mozzarella, diced
- 2 hard-boiled eggs, diced
- 3 1/2 ounces (1/3 cup) mortadella, diced
- 5 tablespoons grated *Parmigiano-Reggiano*
- 3 tablespoons grated pecorino

Meatballs

- 6 ounces ground meat, any combination of veal, beef, pork or lamb
- 1 egg yolk
- 1 slice day-old country bread (remove crust, soak in water, squeeze dry, and tear into small pieces)
- 2 tablespoons grated *Parmigiano-Reggiano*
- 1 tablespoon grated pecorino
- Sea salt
- Pepper

Using your hands, in a medium bowl combine the ground meat, egg yolk, bread, *Parmigiano-Reggiano*, pecorino, salt, and pepper. Shape the mixture into meatballs the size of hazelnuts. In a large skillet, brown the meatballs in olive oil and then set aside.

In another skillet, fry the onion in a little olive oil, then remove and discard it and add the tomato purée and basil leaves. Season with salt and pepper. The sauce should be fairly thin.

Cook the rice in 1 quart of boiling water until al dente. Drain the rice and season it with a little *Parmigiano-Reggiano*, a little pecorino, and about 1 cup of the tomato sauce. Toss to combine.

Spread about 1/3 of the remaining sauce on the bottom of a baking dish, then pour half the rice over it. Smooth the top of the rice and sprinkle the mozzarella, hard-boiled eggs, and mortadella on top. Arrange the cooked meatballs on top, then sprinkle on the remaining *Parmigiano-Reggiano* and pecorino. Add half the remaining sauce and then cover with the remaining rice. Smooth the top of the rice and drizzle the remaining sauce over it. Bake in a preheated 400° oven for 30 minutes.

Fresh tomato purée: blanch and peel tomatoes, then purée them through a food mill.

WHEAT BERRIES WITH RAGÙ

Grano pesato

Serves 4

This is an ancient dish from the Salento area, traditionally served during Carnevale, *just before Lent.*

Ingredients

10 ounces (1 1/4 cups) wheat berries [unprocessed whole wheat kernels]
1 pinch salt
1 tablespoon *ricotta forte*
4 tablespoons grated pecorino
Peperoncino, hot red chili pepper, sliced [or dried flakes] to taste
Ragù made with pork, lamb, and veal (see *Orecchiette col Ragù* on page 22)

To hull the wheat berries, put them in a stone mortar, moisten them with a little bit of water, and grind them with a wooden pestle using a circular motion until the outer skin has flaked off. As you do this, try to keep from breaking or squashing the grains, but at the same time you want to be sure to remove the skin from each piece. Rinse the wheat berries and discard their skins.

If you don't have the right equipment, you can purchase hulled wheat berries in specialty stores.

Put them in a pot with cold water to cover and a pinch of salt. Bring the water to a boil, then reduce the heat to a low simmer. Do not stir. When the liquid has been absorbed by the wheat berries but they are not so dry that they risk sticking together, remove the pot from the heat. Transfer the cooked wheat berries to a large bowl and stir in the *ricotta forte*, and chili. Ladle the wheat berries into individual serving bowls, then sprinkle with grated pecorino and top with generous amounts of *ragù.*

"SPONGE CAKE" IN BROTH

Pan di Spagna in brodo

Serves 4

This dish is served during the Christmas holidays.

Ingredients

5 eggs, separated
7 tablespoons grated *Parmigiano-Reggiano*
4 tablespoons grated pecorino

4 tablespoons bread crumbs
Sea salt
Pepper
1 pinch grated nutmeg
1 cup beef broth

Beat the egg yolks with the *Parmigiano-Reggiano*, pecorino, and bread crumbs. Season with salt, pepper, and nutmeg. Whip the egg whites to a soft peak and fold them into the yolk mixture. Transfer the mixture to a baking dish and pour 1/2 cup broth over it.

Bake in a preheated 350° moderate oven until the broth has been absorbed completely and the dish looks like sponge cake. Cool, then cut into 8 large pieces. Put 2 slices in individual serving bowls and pour additional hot broth over them.

If you like, you can cut the finished cake into small squares rather than large slices.

RICOTTA SOUP

Sciusciello con ricotta

Serves 4

This, too, is a dish that is served only during the Christmas holidays.

Ingredients

4 eggs
4 tablespoons *Parmigiano-Reggiano*
4 tablespoons grated pecorino
6 ounces (3/4 cup) ricotta
Sea salt
Pepper
1 pinch grated nutmeg
4 cups beef broth

In a bowl, beat the eggs with the *Parmigiano-Reggiano* and pecorino, then add the ricotta. Season with salt, pepper, and nutmeg. Beat vigorously until the mixture is very creamy. Bring broth for 4 portions to a boil then pour in the mixture. Stir very quickly and continuously in order to keep the mixture from stiffening. Serve piping hot.

Focaccia LE FOCACCE

FLOUR serves as the basis for many baked goods in Puglia, including focaccia. Our focaccia dough is made by adding water alone to flour, or by adding water plus olive oil, or by incorporating olive oil and lukewarm wine—or even by incorporating boiled potatoes that have been passed through a ricer.

Each type of dough results in a different kind of focaccia. The most common type is topped with fresh tomatoes. This type of focaccia makes an excellent substitute for bread and was once made weekly in almost every home.

Puglia was quite a poor part of Italy before World War II, so focaccia was a luxury then, not only because it was garnished, but because making focaccia meant there was less flour for making bread. Once a wood-burning oven was lit, its fire had to be exploited as much as possible. Bread was baked when the oven was at its hottest, and once it was cooked—and the oven was less hot—there was time to cook focaccia and *friselle.*

Friselle are shaped like large *taralli* [or bagels], about 4 or 5 inches in diameter, made with bread dough. Halfway through their baking time, they are cut in half horizontally, and then returned to the oven so that the cut surfaces turn brown and crispy. *Friselle* are used very frequently in Puglia. They can be stored for long periods of time and are very useful to have on hand when throwing together a meal at the last minute. *Friselle* are moistened a little with water and then arranged on a serving platter and topped with fresh tomatoes, basil, oregano, salt, pepper, olive oil, and, if desired, a little minced garlic.

After focaccia and *friselle* had been baked, the oven and its dying fire was used to bake potatoes. These were washed, dried, and then buried in hot ash, where they cooked slowly. When the potatoes were cooked, they were wiped clean of ash with a kitchen towel, split in two, and then seasoned with olive oil, salt, and pepper. (See page 92.) Today, they are sometimes topped with a little butter.

Focaccia with Fresh Tomato

Focaccia con pomodoro fresco

Serves 4

Ingredients

2 3/4 cups flour
1 cake yeast [or 1 package active dry yeast], dissolved in 3/4 cup lukewarm water
1 tablespoon salt
Extra-virgin olive oil
6 tomatoes
Sea salt
Fresh oregano leaves

On a smooth work surface, mound the flour and form a well. Add the dissolved yeast and salt, incorporating them into the flour, and adding additional lukewarm water as necessary. Knead the dough until it is tender but not too sticky. Put the dough in a lightly oiled bowl, turn to coat all sides, cover, then let the dough rise for at least 1 hour. Stretch the risen dough and press into an oiled shallow rectangular baking pan. Break up the tomatoes with your hands (do not slice them) and scatter over the top. Sprinkle on a generous amount of sea salt and oregano and drizzle on a little oil. Bake in a preheated 450° oven for about 30 minutes.

If you like, you can use room temperature milk rather than water to make the dough.

WHITE FOCACCIA

Focaccia bianca

Serves 4

Ingredients

2 3/4 cups flour
1 cake yeast [or 1 package active dry yeast], dissolved in 3/4 cup lukewarm water
1 tablespoon salt
1/2 cup extra-virgin olive oil
Sea salt
Pepper

On a smooth work surface, mound the flour and form a well. Add the dissolved yeast and salt, incorporating them into the flour, and adding additional lukewarm water as necessary. Knead the dough until it is tender but not too sticky. Put the dough in a lightly oiled bowl, turn to coat all sides, cover, then let the dough rise for at least 1 hour.

Using a rolling pin, roll out the dough to about 1/2 inch thickness. Transfer the dough to an oiled shallow baking pan and brush the top with a generous amount of olive oil, then add sea salt and pepper. Bake in a preheated 450° oven for 20 minutes.

FOCACCIA WITH RICOTTA

Focaccia con la ricotta

Serves 4

Ingredients

2 3/4 cups flour
1 cake yeast [or 1 package active dry yeast], dissolved in 3/4 cup lukewarm water
1 tablespoon salt
10 ounces (1 1/4 cups) ricotta
2 eggs
2 ounces spicy salami *or* mortadella, diced
8 to 12 ounce fresh mozzarella, diced
Grated *Parmigiano-Reggiano*
Scant grated nutmeg
Pepper
Extra-virgin olive oil

On a smooth work surface, mound the flour and form a well. Add the dissolved yeast and salt, incorporating them into the flour, and adding additional lukewarm water as necessary.

Knead the dough until it is tender but not too sticky. Put the dough in a lightly oiled bowl, turn to coat all sides, cover, then let the dough rise for at least 1 hour.

Meanwhile, in a mixing bowl, whisk the ricotta with the eggs until very smooth. Stir in the salami *or* mortadella, mozzarella, *Parmigiano-Reggiano*, and nutmeg. Season with salt and pepper and set aside. Cut the dough into 2 pieces, one slightly larger than the other. Roll out the larger piece, shaping it into a circle just slightly larger than a [12 inch] round baking pan.

Oil the pan and press the dough into it. Using your fingers, pinch the dough up around and above the rim of the pan. Pour in the ricotta mixture and smooth it. Roll out the second piece of dough into a circle and place it on top of the filling. Fold the bottom dough edge over the top dough edge, then seal all around with the tines of a fork. Brush the top of the pie with a generous amount of olive oil and bake in a preheated 450° oven for 30 minutes.

Focaccia with Cracklings

Focaccia con i frizzoli

Ingredients

- Pork belly, cut into strips [enough to produce 6 ounces of cooked skins]
- 2 3/4 cups flour
- 1/2 cup extra-virgin olive oil
- 1 cake yeast [or 1 package active dry yeast], dissolved in 3/4 cup lukewarm water
- 1 tablespoon salt
- Pepper

Cook the pork belly over low heat in a skillet. Drain off the fat (lard) into a jar. Once the lard produced has solidified, you can use it for cooking and even for baking certain desserts. Thoroughly cook the skin left in the skillet.

On a smooth work surface, mound the flour and form a well.Incorporate 1/2 cup olive oil, dissolved yeast, salt, lukewarm water, a generous amount of pepper, and about 6 ounces (3/4 cup) of the crumbled skins.

Oil a shallow rectangular baking pan. Roll out the dough to about 1 inch thick and press it into the pan. Allow the dough to rise for at least 1 hour, then bake in a preheated 450° oven for 25 minutes.

SAVORY PIE

Pizztidd o pizzutello

Serves 4

Ingredients

2 3/4 cups flour
1 1/4 cups extra-virgin olive oil
1 cake yeast [or 1 package active dry yeast], dissolved in 3/4 cup lukewarm water
1 tablespoon salt
2 1/4 pounds leeks, cleaned and cut into strips
4 heads escarole
5 salted anchovies, rinsed, boned, and chopped
3 peeled tomatoes, fresh or canned, crushed
Handful of capers
3/4 cup water-cured black olives, pitted and chopped
Sea salt
Pepper

On a smooth work surface, mound the flour and form a well. Pour 1/2 cup of olive oil into the middle of the well. Rub the flour and olive oil together to make a crumbly mixture. Reshape the well and pour the dissolved yeast into the center. Add 1 tablespoon salt. Gently pull in flour from the sides of the well and incorporate into the liquid. Then when the liquid has mostly been absorbed, collapse the remaining flour over the moist part. Knead until thoroughly combined into a smooth dough. Put the dough in a lightly oiled bowl, turn to coat all sides, cover, then let the dough rise for about 2 hours.

In many parts of Puglia this dish is made without escarole, but I think the greens add a delicate yet strong flavor.

In a large skillet, heat 1/2 cup of olive oil and add the leeks. Tear the escarole leaves into pieces and add to the skillet. When the greens have begun to cook down, add the anchovies, tomatoes, capers, and olives. Season with salt and pepper and continue cooking until the greens are cooked through. If necessary, add a little water to keep the greens from burning.

Divide the dough into two equal pieces. Press one piece into the bottom of an oiled [12 inch] round baking pan. Spread the cooked leek and escarole mixture over the dough. Roll out the second piece of dough and place it on top of the filling. Seal the edges together and then press their edges together with a fork. Brush the top of the pie generously with olive oil and poke some holes in the top with a fork. Bake in a preheated 450° oven for about 30 minutes.

Fritters and Turnovers

Frittelle e Panzerotti

Puglia boasts a wide variety of deep-fried foods due to the large amount of olive oil that has been produced in the region since ancient times.

The women of Puglia have always enjoyed free rein and expressed great creativity in inventing fried foods. Many of these dishes are nothing short of true gastronomic masterpieces. They range from simple fritters that, once cooked, are topped with tomato sauce and grated pecorino to turnovers with more elaborate fillings. Indeed, these fritters and turnovers are the closest the people of Puglia come to consuming "fast food." They often serve as dinner. Everyone likes turnovers; I've never seen anyone fail to eat heartily when they are served. Currently, it's fashionable for restaurants to serve them as appetizers, together with a few pieces of focaccia and some other snacks, but if they are to be eaten as a second course, they should be larger in size, and you will need more of them.

The dough for fritters can be varied according to taste and, of course, the preference of the person making them. There are many options when it comes to preparing and filling them. Some people add milk to the dough, others olive oil, still others extra-virgin olive oil and wine. Some people prefer to make the dough with water alone, or with water and a cooked potato passed through a ricer (potato makes the dough softer, but a little harder to digest). In any case, the results are always a hit.

Fritters and Sauce

Frittelle vuote

Serves 4

Ingredients

3 cups flour
1 teaspoon salt
1 potato, boiled and passed through a ricer (optional)
1 cake yeast [or 1 package active dry yeast], dissolved in 3/4 cup lukewarm water

Topping

1/4 cup extra-virgin olive oil
1 clove garlic
8 ounces (1 cup) canned peeled tomatoes
Handful of capers

Extra-virgin olive oil
Grated pecorino

To make the dough, combine the flour and salt in a large bowl, and the potato if using. Add the dissolved yeast. Stir until the ingredients form a dough. Transfer to a smooth work surface and knead until the dough is smooth and compact. Transfer to a lightly oiled bowl, turn to coat all sides of the dough, then cover with a wool cloth and set aside to rise for 1 to 2 hours.

Meanwhile, to make the topping, heat the olive oil in a skillet and fry the garlic until it turns golden. Remove and discard garlic. Add the tomatoes and the capers and cook the sauce until it is very thick, with no liquid left at all.

In a heavy-bottomed pot, bring a generous amount of olive oil to a boil. Cut off small pieces of the dough, flatten them with your hand, and fry them a few at a time in boiling oil. Use a strainer to remove and arrange them on a serving dish as they are cooked. Top each fritter with a spoonful of sauce and a sprinkling of pecorino.

Fritters

Pettole

Serves 4

Ingredients

1 cake yeast [or 1 package active dry yeast], dissolved in 3/4 cup lukewarm water
1 tablespoon salt
6 cups flour
Extra-virgin olive oil

Pour the dissolved yeast into a large bowl and stir in the salt. Add the flour about 1/4 cup at a time, mixing with your hands between additions. Use your hands like a whisk to beat the mixture. Continue to mix with your hands in this way until you have a smooth, somewhat liquid dough. If the dough seems too dense, add a little more water. Set aside in a warm place to rise for 2 to 3 hours.

In a heavy-bottomed pot, bring a generous amount of olive oil to a boil. Set the bowl with the dough and a small bowl of lukewarm water near the stove. Dip your left hand into the dough and make a fist. Use your thumb and index finger to form a small ball of the dough. Wet your right hand with some lukewarm water and then with a quick motion use your right hand to remove the ball of dough from your left and allow it to drop into the olive oil. Be sure your right hand is moist, but not dripping, as any drops of water that drip into oil will splatter. Continue until the olive oil is full of fritters. The fritters should float in the oil and should not touch the bottom of the pot.

Cook the fritters until they are golden. Remove them with a strainer and transfer to a wire strainer or colander to drain.

The traditional method for forming the pieces of dough sounds complicated, but once you've done a few you should get the hang of it. If you feel uncomfortable using your hands, you can drop small amounts of the dough into the boiling oil from a spoon. They will taste just as good, but they won't have the characteristic look of *pettole*.

ANCHOVY FRITTERS

Pettole con le acciughe

Serves 4

Ingredients

6 cups flour
Scant salt
1 cake yeast [or 1 package active dry yeast], dissolved in 3/4 cup lukewarm water
6 anchovies in salt, rinsed, boned, and minced
Extra-virgin olive oil

To make the dough, combine the flour and salt in a large bowl (keep in mind that the anchovies are salty). Add the dissolved yeast. Stir until the ingredients form a somewhat liquid dough. Add more water if necessary.

Cover and set aside to rise for about 1 hour. Stir in the anchovies and set aside to rise for 1 additional hour.

In a heavy-bottomed pot, bring a generous amount of olive oil to a boil. Fry spoonfuls of the dough in the boiling oil. Remove them with a strainer and drain.

country-style fritters

Pettole rustiche

Ingredients

1 tablespoon salt
6 cups flour
1 cake yeast [or 1 package active dry yeast], dissolved in 3/4 cup lukewarm water

Filling

1 small head escarole
3 salted anchovies, rinsed, boned, and minced
2 peeled canned tomatoes
1 tablespoon capers
1/4 cup black olives, pitted and chopped
Sea salt
Pepper

Extra-virgin olive oil

Prepare the dough. Combine the flour and salt in a large bowl (keep in mind that the anchovies are salty). Add the dissolved yeast. Stir until the ingredients to form a somewhat liquid dough. Add more water if necessary. Cover and set aside to rise for about 1 hour.

For the filling, cook the escarole, anchovies, tomatoes, capers, and olives together in a skillet. Season to taste with salt and pepper. The filling should be very dense. If necessary, add a little water when cooking to stop from burning. When the dough has risen, take about 1 tablespoon of the dough and fill it with about 1 teaspoon of the filling by pressing the filling into the center of the dough and closing the dough up around it.

In a heavy-bottomed pot, bring a generous amount of olive oil to a boil. Fry spoonfuls of the dough in the boiling oil. Remove them with a strainer and drain.

EGG AND CHEESE TURNOVERS

Panzerottini ripieni di uova e formaggio

Serves 4

Ingredients

3 cups flour
Salt
1 cup olive oil
1 cake yeast [or 1 package active dry yeast], dissolved in 3/4 cup lukewarm water

Filling

3 eggs
7 tablespoons grated *Parmigiano-Reggiano*
7 tablespoons grated pecorino
Fresh flat-leaf parsley, chopped
Sea salt
Pepper

Extra-virgin olive oil

To make the dough, combine the flour and salt in a large bowl. Add the dissolved yeast and 1 cup of oil. Stir until the ingredients form a dough. Transfer to a smooth work surface and knead until the dough is smooth and compact. Transfer to a lightly oiled bowl, turn to coat all sides of the dough, then cover and set aside to rise for 1 hour.

Meanwhile, combine the ingredients for the filling. Season with salt and pepper. The filling should be very dense and not liquid. If it seems too liquid, add additional grated cheese.

Roll out the dough very thin and, using a cookie cutter or drinking glass, cut out circles about 4 inches in diameter. Put 1 tablespoon of the filling on each piece of dough, then fold the dough over to make half-moons. Seal the edges with a fork.

In a heavy-bottomed pot, bring a generous amount of olive oil to a boil. Fry the turnovers until they are golden, and remove them with a strainer. Serve as an appetizer.

RICOTTA FORTE TURNOVERS

Panzerottini con la ricotta forte

These are made like the egg and cheese turnovers, but the cheese in the filling is ricotta forte.

MOZZARELLA AND TOMATO TURNOVERS

Panzerotti mozzarella e pomodoro

Serves 4

These are excellent as either a second course or as a one-dish meal.

Ingredients

- 4 1/2 cups flour
- Salt
- 1 cake yeast [or 1 package active dry yeast], dissolved in 3/4 cup lukewarm water
- 1 large potato, boiled and passed through a ricer (optional)
- Extra-virgin olive oil

Filling

- 1 16-ounce can peeled tomatoes, drained
- 10 ounces (1 1/4 cups) mozzarella, diced
- Sea salt
- Pepper

To make the dough, combine the flour and salt in a large bowl. Add the dissolved yeast and the potato if using. Stir until the ingredients form a dough. Transfer to a smooth work surface and knead until the dough is smooth and compact. Transfer to a lightly oiled bowl, turn to coat all sides of the dough, then cover and set aside to rise for 2 hours.

Meanwhile, crush the tomatoes through your fingers and set them in a colander to drain. When the tomatoes have drained, combine the diced mozzarella and the tomatoes in a small bowl and season to taste with salt and pepper. Shape pieces of dough into disks about 8 inches in diameter and 1/8 inch thick. Top each disk with a heaping tablespoon of the tomato and mozzarella mixture, then fold the dough over to form half-moons. Seal the edges with a pastry wheel.

In a heavy-bottomed pot, bring a generous amount of olive oil to a boil. Fry the turnovers, taking care to turn them frequently so they don't brown too much on one side. Remove them with a strainer and drain.

Fava Beans  Le Fave

Many areas of Puglia, especially the Salento, have long been known for a variety of crops. Since in the past produce was only available in season—a situation that no longer exists today—the harvests Puglia offered had to be preserved for as long as possible.

This meant the housewives of Puglia were kept busy preparing a wide variety of items through the summer and fall so that when the cold, barren winter arrived, they would have something to eat.

Fava Beans, which have fed the poor for centuries, were grown on every plot of land. The beans harvested in April and May were tender and green, and were most commonly served with bread, in place of tomatoes. When paired with chunks of pecorino or pancetta, fava beans were transformed into a true delicacy.

Another cheese that matches perfectly with young fava beans and with chicory is *ricotta marzotica*, or March ricotta, a local cheese which is produced in that month after the lambs have been weaned. It's made with sheep's milk and is generously salted, then covered with young herbs so it doesn't dry out too much and is aged in cool, well-ventilated areas for a maximum of two weeks. This cheese has a slightly acidic and very refined taste. It's not used very frequently anymore, at least not nearly as much as it used to be. It is, however, still made by local cheese makers and sometimes served in grated form. Sad to say today's *ricotta marzotica* just doesn't provide the same fresh, pure flavor of the old kind that was brought to the table covered in herbs.

Above: fava bean pods

In late June, any pods left until the plants have dried up are then harvested and thrashed. The beans are then separated from the pieces of dry pod by sieving them through big sifters (large circular containers with holes in the bottom that allow the dried pieces of pod to fall out). The fava beans are then kept in the sun for a few days until they dry completely. They are then transferred to containers, where boiling water is poured over them and then they are covered with cloths. This is done to ensure that the fava beans are kept safe from the parasites that are drawn to them (known as *favaruli*). Once they are completely dry, the beans are transferred to copper or earthenware containers where they can be stored for two or three years without losing their flavor.

Fava Rituals

I can still picture how, when I was a girl, people would gather together to shell fava beans. There is much to say about the social aspect of this daily ritual, which was performed all summer long. In the afternoon, when the sun had fallen a little lower on the horizon, the oldest woman in the family sat by the door to the house on a low chair (known as a *siggitedda*). Next to her she had another, higher chair that held a large polished stone plate. In her hand she held a smaller stone that looked like a Neolithic almond-shaped ax, and she struck each fava bean with it to break its shell. Once their shells were broken, the beans were placed in a basket, and the other members of the family, who gathered around the old woman, took a handful at a time and used a knife with a short, blunt tip (similar to a cheese knife) called a *puntarulo* to split the beans in half, keeping them inside their skins.

I've called this activity a "ritual" because it truly was one. Once the day's work was finished, the whole family got together in the *nchiostre** and in the streets as if the outdoors were a big living room. They talked to their neighbors and passersby. They told each other about the events of that day, or their plans for the next day. They chatted about what they'd eat for dinner, speculated about possible marriages, and compared notes on their illnesses. Everyone had a chance to speak her piece, though priority was given according to age and wisdom. Breaking news, gossip, and slander made the rounds, and through this unique method of communication, the inhabitants of the street or the whole neighborhood learned the news of the day. Girls would scoop up some of the fava beans cracked by their grandmothers in their aprons, and then they'd go off and form groups separate from the adults. One day they'd be in front of one girl's house, the next in front of another's. In these groups, the young people talked about love, who was courting whom, and the color and style of their dresses for the holidays. Boyfriends and admirers made discreet

*This word derives from the medieval Latin *enclostrum* and the classical Latin *enclaustrum* and indicates the small courtyard inside the landowner's house.

View of Ostuni street

appearances, walking down the street in front of the girls with great nonchalance in order to parade before the girls without raising their mothers' suspicions.

As it grew dark, the woman of the house would step out to meet her husband as he returned from the fields, and after a very frugal dinner she would return to sit at the door of the house and chat and enjoy the cool evening air, but this time with the head of the family at her side.

cucina povera

As I've already noted, fava beans were a part of the food of the poor in southern Italy for centuries—and a kind of inverse status symbol, an emblem of social and economic conditions that teetered on the edge of survival. Anyone who, when asked what he or she had eaten the previous day, had to confess that it had been fava beans did so with a resigned and almost embarrassed expression.

Cooking fava beans consisted of nothing more than seeing that the earthenware pot where they had been placed in the morning sat over a fire for a couple of hours. The only flavoring was a little olive oil that was added once the beans were cooked as they were being beaten with a *cucchiara,* a long heavy wooden spoon, to turn them into purée. When and where possible, fava beans were served with greens, peppers, tomatoes, olives, and other vegetables. Leftover fava beans made another appearance in the evening. A little onion was fried in olive oil, and then the beans were softened and reheated (these were called *fave scarfate*) and a few small pieces of stale bread or rice were added to the mix. It's not an exaggeration to say that eating *fave scarfate* was humiliating and even depressing. This dish was recognized as a food one would eat only if there was nothing else.

Today's "Peasant" Food

As "peasant" food has become all the rage, fava beans have become fashionable. The restaurants that serve fava beans present them with the pride that comes with offering their customers a "typical" dish with an absolutely unique flavor. They are often accompanied by chicory or *sevoni,* wild greens with a pleasantly bitter edge.

Fava beans are at their tastiest when beaten with a large amount of olive oil and served with a variety of vegetables—fried eggplant and peppers, pickles, water-cured olives, artichokes, and anything else that whets the appetite.

Fava Bean Purée

Puré di fave

Serves 4

As noted, the purée may be served with boiled field greens (chicory or other bitter greens), fried vegetables, tomato salad, pickled vegetables, or anything else you like.

Ingredients

10 ounces (1 1/4 cups) dried white fava beans, sorted and rinsed
2 large potatoes, peeled and diced
Sea salt
1 1/4 cups extra-virgin olive oil

Put the beans in an earthenware pot together with the potatoes. Add water to cover and bring to a boil over low heat. Boil, covered, for about 20 minutes. Do not stir the beans. Drain the beans and potatoes, add fresh water to cover and season with salt. Bring to a boil again and cook for an additional 30 minutes. At this point, the true fava bean purist will hold the pot between her legs and vigorously beat the beans with a wooden spoon while slowly drizzling in the olive oil. Not everyone is capable of this, however, so—with some trepidation—I recommend putting the fava bean mixture through a food mill, then returning the purée to the earthenware pot and vigorously mixing with a wooden spoon while you add the olive oil.

Leftover Fava Beans

Fave scarfate

Ingredients

1 small onion, diced
1/2 cup extra-virgin olive oil
Fava bean purée leftover from the morning meal, or set aside to rest for 3 to 4 hours
3/4 cup stale semolina/country bread, torn into pieces
1/4 cup boiled chicory (optional)

In a skillet, fry the onion in the olive oil, then add the fava beans. Thin the purée with 1/2 cup water. Stir vigorously, and stir in the bread. Stir in the chicory if using.

Fava Beans and Rice

Fave e riso

This is a variation on leftover fava beans.

Ingredients

1 small onion, diced
1/2 cup extra-virgin olive oil
Fava bean purée leftover from the morning meal, or set aside to rest for 3 to 4 hours
1/2 cup rice

In a skillet, fry the onion in olive oil, then add the fava beans. Thin the purée with 3 cups water. Bring to a boil and stir in the rice. Cook, stirring continuously (as if you were cooking a risotto), until the rice is cooked through.

Fava Beans and "Wild Onion" Bulbs

*Fave e lampasciuni**

Serves 4

Ingredients

10 ounces (1 1/4 cups) dried white fava beans, sorted and rinsed
2 large potatoes, diced
Sea salt
1 1/4 cups extra-virgin olive oil
1 pound "wild onions" [bulbs]
Toasted bread crumbs

Prepare the fava bean purée recipe. Clean and blanch the "wild onions" and mix them in with the fava beans. Drizzle on additional olive oil and sprinkle with bread crumbs.

* *Lampasciuni* or *vampascione* refer to wild grape-hyacinths whose small bulbs are called "wild onions."

Split Fava Beans

Fave spizzutate

Serves 4

This dish is made with fava beans that have been shelled and dried in the sun, but they shouldn't be aged for too long.

Ingredients

1 1/2 pounds (3 cups) split dried fava beans
1 onion, chopped
1 celery stalk, chopped
Sea salt
Pepper
Extra-virgin olive oil

With a knife, cut off the little piece of the beans that sticks out at the top of the fava skin. Fill a medium pan with water to cover the fava beans and cook them as you would any other type of bean, adding the onion, celery, and salt and pepper to taste. Simmer for a few hours, and then serve the dish with its broth (it should still be a little soupy) and drizzle some olive oil on top.

Toasted bread may be served alongside.

Fresh Fava Beans and Chicory

Fave fresche e catalogne

Serves 4

Ingredients

1 pound chicory, preferably a red variety
3 1/2 pounds shelled fresh young fava beans
Sea salt
Extra-virgin olive oil

Clean the chicory thoroughly. In a large pan, cook the fava beans and the chicory together in a large amount of boiling salted water. Serve piping hot and drizzle with a little olive oil.

These may be served cold, but in that case add some wine vinegar.

Fried Fava Beans

Fave soffritte

Serves 4

Fava beans cooked this way make a meal when served over some slices of crusty semolina or country bread with a sprinkling of grated Parmigiano-Reggiano *on top. Without the bread, this makes a nice side dish.*

Ingredients

2 3/4 pounds (5 1/2 cups) shelled fresh young fava beans
1/2 cup extra-virgin olive oil
1 large onion, thinly sliced
Sea salt
Pepper

Rinse the beans. In a pan with a lid, fry the beans in the olive oil with the onion. Season with salt and pepper. Cover the pan and cook over high heat, then simmer. Add water occasionally to keep the beans from sticking to the skillet until the beans are cooked through.

Fava Bean and Pea Soup

Minestra di fave e piselli

Serves 4

Ingredients

2 3/4 pounds (5 1/2 cups) shelled fresh young fava beans
1/2 cup extra-virgin olive oil
1 large onion, thinly sliced
2 3/4 pounds shelled peas
3 to 4 leaves lettuce, minced
Sea salt
Pepper

Rinse the beans. In a pan with a lid, fry the beans in the olive oil with the onion, peas, and lettuce. Season with salt and pepper. Cover the pan and cook over high heat, then turn down to low heat and simmer. Add water occasionally to keep the mixture from sticking to the skillet, until the beans are cooked through.

VIEW OF OSTUNI

WEEKLY ROUTINES

CALENDARIO GASTRONOMICO

Above: favas

THE DIET of those who lived out in the country was fairly monotonous—an interminable series of dishes of fava beans and chicory and other legumes, interrupted only by pasta on Sundays. The diet of those who lived in town was also fairly repetitive, though their meals were richer and larger.

The days of the week were marked by a recurring routine. Monday, the first day of the week, was marked by the bubbling sounds of simmering broth. Light food such as broth was considered appropriate after the rich food eaten on Sunday, and cooking broth—which didn't require a lot of watching—gave the lady of the house time to take care of the laundry. Tuesday and Wednesday meant legumes, minestrone, potatoes, and so forth; Thursday, pasta; Friday, legumes again. Saturday brought broth again, followed by pasta and meat on Sunday.

MONDAY was laundry day, and laundry was the most difficult and time-consuming task of the week. Washing machines were still a dream far in the future then, and in the present there were mountains of clothing to wash, rinse, wring, hang, and iron. Only the wealthiest families could afford to pay a laundress who, with her assistant, would wash the family's sheets. Laundry was done in a large rectangular cement tub or a wide wooden washtub. Clothes were rubbed vigorously on a washboard (a wooden board with grooves that was about sixteen inches wide and two feet high) after they had been thoroughly soaped up with hard soap that at the time was purchased in big dark yellow blocks that are still available today. Delicate items were washed with a special soap that came in the form of a dark burnt sienna colored cream.

Once the clothes were rinsed and wrung out they were placed in a large ceramic tub called a *crasta*. The *crasta* was flared at the top and more than three feet tall, with openings on the side. The clothes were spread out in the *crasta* and covered with a very thick piece of white cotton canvas that had been made by hand. Ashes and sprigs of aromatic herbs like thyme and bay leaves were spread out over the top of the canvas, and then boiling water was poured slowly over the entire thing. The canvas was so thick and sturdy that only the water and soluble substances filtered through, which meant that the potassium hydrate from the ashes and the essences of the herbs made their way down to the clothing. This was left to rest overnight, and the following morning the holes in the tub were unplugged and the canvas was carefully removed. The laundry was then gloriously clean and could be hung in the sun to dry. The memory of the delicate scent that this process lent to our clothes is still strong in my mind—it's a scent that no maker of commercial detergents will ever be able to replicate.

That wasn't the end of our laundry ritual either. Dry clothes were moistened and then rolled up, and the following day they were ironed with either an iron heated with coals or something called *lu scarfalietto*. This was a copper pot with a very long wooden handle. It was filled with burning coals, and then two women held a sheet open, and a third moved the instrument over it in a circular motion. Shirts, tablecloths, and undergarments were smoothed only with an iron, and the temperature had to be regulated constantly, because if it was overloaded with coal it would burn the clothing, and if it didn't have enough coal it would leave the clothing wrinkled.

Keeping this type of iron at the right temperature—putting burning coals inside of it and distributing the heat evenly—required particular skill. The iron was held by its handle, and then the cover was lifted. In the most skilled hands, the iron was swung around in a complete circle, which never failed to elicit gasps of admiration from any children watching. The term *scarfalietto* indicates the original use of this contraption: in Salento dialect, *scarfà* means to heat up, so *lu scarfalietto* was a bedwarmer, an object that was treasured and indeed indispensable on winter evenings, when it was used to heat up the freezing cold sheets in houses where the only sources of heat were fireplaces and braziers.

IT WAS so cold that when we went to bed we put on more clothes rather than getting undressed: we wore long flannel nightgowns, pajamas, virgin wool jackets, and our grandparents even wore nightcaps made of hand-spun sheep's wool.

Fireplaces were usually located in rooms where guests would be received, while braziers were used to warm up bedrooms. These were very low containers made of brass or iron with two handles that were filled with *cinisa,* coal dust, that when lit in the morning stayed lit until the evening, as long as it was jogged every once in a while with a poker, which was also made of iron or brass. Each member of the family wanted to keep the brazier close, because it gave off heat immediately, which the fireplace could not do unless you were directly in front of it.

The brazier was the poor man's fireplace; any family that didn't have a fireplace gathered around the brazier. An iron brazier was placed in the middle of a circular platform about two and a half feet wide with a kind of cylindrical cage on it. A large blanket was placed on top of this so that it could also serve as a dining table. All members of the family sat around it and lifted the blanket and put their legs underneath for a pleasantly warm sensation. The price paid for that warmth, however, lay in the visible blotches on the legs of many women who got too close. The brazier was the family's winter gathering place, a short stop for young people, and the permanent station of the elderly. For all, it was a place to enter into dialogue with others. Dinner was eaten around the brazier, and then everyone ran to bed after the mother of the family had warmed all their sheets with a bedwarmer.

In many houses there was another item used to warm the bed. This was called a *monaca* and was shaped like a double wooden sled that could hold a copper pot full of charcoal. This was slipped under the sheets, and kept them apart. The warmth spread over the entire bed, and the *monaca* was removed only when its owner arrived to take its place in the bed.

THE COAL SELLER was a picturesque character whose black face and hands were the mark of his trade. He walked the streets of the town with a sack over his shoulder and shouted at the top of his voice, *Cinisa, ci vo' cinisa* ("Coal dust, who wants coal dust"), and he pronounced the words in a way that made them incomprehensible as words, but their sound was so characteristic that all the women knew to head out into the street to purchase the black substance that was indispensable for heating their homes.

Legumes I Legumi

The traditional weekly calendar called for legumes to be served on Tuesday, Wednesday, and Friday. In addition to fava beans, chickpeas, lentils, and other beans were common.

The woman of the house often let the family have the privilege of choosing which kind of beans they wanted the next day. Then she soaked them in salted water overnight. (Lentils do not need to be soaked—they are simply sorted, rinsed and cooked over low heat for a few of hours.) These legumes may be eaten simply with olive oil and salt or a dash of tomato sauce, but usually they are served with pasta. Beans and chickpeas match best with homemade pasta, while lentils are better with dried semolina pasta.

All the legumes were grown by our own local farmers and therefore tasted differently and had different monetary value depending on where they were grown. They were grown with natural fertilizer, which made them very flavorful. The crops were actually watered with rainwater at the time. Today, the water is supplied by artesian wells.

Legumes, and every other crop, looked less pretty then, but had more intense, fuller flavor. There were several types of beans grown. Cannellini beans were harvested after their pods had dried, and they were stored for the long term. Thin pods of "pinto" beans, as we called them, about eight inches long were a good deal smaller than cannellini. The beans were also darker in color, each with a small "eye" on the side. When these were picked young, they sold at a high price and were served as a side dish or sometimes with pasta. Dried "pinto" beans didn't taste as good as dried white beans, so there was little demand for them.

Chickpeas were the trickiest crop for farmers, because often an entire harvest didn't cook properly. Usually a woman would buy only enough chickpeas for one batch of soup, soak them overnight in salted water, and then the next day put them to the test. If they were soft and flavorful, she'd return to that same farmer and buy enough chickpeas for the winter, but if they didn't cook properly and came out *scrudievoli,* a word that means *raw* in dialect, she would move on to try the beans of a different farmer. Few areas could be counted on to provide chickpeas that cooked properly year in and year out, and so these higher quality chickpeas were expensive. The town of Ceglie Messapico produced excellent chickpeas.

In May, a common sight in town was a farmer coming from the countryside bearing sprigs with small pale green leaves and little hazelnut-like orbs of that same green color hanging from them—fresh chickpeas. These were a treat reserved for children. Eating them felt deliciously naughty. Since it was considered wasteful, they were harvested in small quantities.

Lupini beans were a pastime food. They weren't harvested in large numbers, and most of the farmers' harvest was sold to street vendors. Mothers would occasionally put up small amounts of *lupini* beans by curing them (soaking for several days in several changes of water and salting them when they were ready to be eaten). Not every home had *lupini* beans; they were considered an "extra" and not a necessity.

PEAS were preferably eaten fresh. The pods were picked when green and the very young peas shelled, as those offered the best flavor. Arguments routinely broke out when farmers brought peas to the landowners' houses that had surpassed a certain size.

The most beloved dish with peas was and still is pasta with peas. The type of pasta shape can be varied according to taste: broken spaghetti, *tubettini,* or tagliolini. Peas cooked on their own are eaten as a side dish. Dried peas are not very popular in the Murgia area of Puglia, but they are available in the Salento area, where they are an ingredient in a traditional dish of the poor called *ciatedda.*

When more peas were harvested than were needed (and since peas could only be sold for about one month at market), they were preserved in olive oil and used during the winter as a side dish for boiled meat or as in ingredient in salads.

The lentil was the legume that appeared most frequently on our tables. Rich in iron, it was prepared as a purée and served mostly to small children, as the beans are difficult for them to digest.

CAVATELLI WITH CHICKPEAS

Pasta e ceci

Serves 4

This is a fairly liquid soup, and the chickpeas and pasta all cook together.

Ingredients

3/4 pound (1 1/2 cups) chickpeas
Sea salt
1 stalk celery, chopped
1 clove garlic, chopped
1 3/4 cups flour (or 10 ounces dry *cavatelli*)
6 tablespoons extra-virgin olive oil
Pepper

Soak the chickpeas overnight in lukewarm salted water. Some people add a handful of flour to the soaking water. In the morning, drain the chickpeas, and rinse them. In a large pot, bring them to a boil in water to cover, then simmer over low heat (in an earthenware pot if you have one) with the celery, garlic, and some salt. The chickpeas will require at least 3 hours of cooking time.

Meanwhile, to make the homemade *cavatelli,* mound the flour on a smooth work surface and create a small well in the middle. Pour in a small amount of water. Combine the flour and enough water to create a soft dough. Knead until the dough it is no longer sticky. Working with small amounts of dough, roll out long, roughly shaped cylinders about 1/2 inch thick. Cut each cylinder into 1 inch pieces, and then make grooves around each piece with the tines of a fork.

When the chickpeas are cooked, add more water to the pot if necessary. Add the uncooked *cavatelli* to the pot and bring to a boil. When the pasta is cooked, transfer the soup to a tureen or serve it from the earthenware pot. Drizzle on the olive oil and sprinkle on a generous amount of pepper.

You can make *cavatelli* or purchase them for ease of preparation. If you do purchase them, make sure you buy them from an artisanal pasta shop and that they are freshly made in-house.

Cavatelli with Chickpeas and Tomato

Pasta e ceci al pomodoro

This is a version of Pasta with Chickpeas (Pasta e ceci) *recipe but the tomatoes give it a little added flavor, and it's denser as well.*

Ingredients

1 3/4 cups flour
3/4 pound (1 1/2 cups) chickpeas
Sea salt
1 stalk celery, chopped
2 cloves garlic, chopped
6 tablespoons extra-virgin olive oil
Peperoncino, hot red chili pepper, sliced [or dried flakes] to taste
3 to 4 canned peeled tomatoes
Pepper

Soak the chickpeas overnight in lukewarm salted water. Some people add a handful of flour to the soaking water. In the morning, drain the chickpeas, and rinse them. In a large pot, bring them to a boil in water to cover, then simmer over low heat (in an earthenware pot if you have one) with the celery, half the garlic, and some salt. The chickpeas will require at least 3 hours of cooking time.

Meanwhile, to make the homemade *cavatelli,* mound the flour on a smooth work surface and create a small well in the middle. Pour in a small amount of water. Combine the flour and enough water to create a soft dough. Knead until the dough it is no longer sticky. Working with small amounts of dough, roll out long, roughly shaped cylinders about 1/2 inch thick. Cut each cylinder into 1 inch pieces, and then make grooves around each piece with the tines of a fork.

You can make *cavatelli* or purchase them for ease of preparation. If you do purchase them, make sure you buy them from an artisanal pasta shop and that they are freshly made in-house.

When the chickpeas are cooked, add more water to the pot if necessary. Add the uncooked *cavatelli* to the pot, bring to a boil, and cook until al dente.

Heat the olive oil and chili in a skillet and brown the remaining garlic. Add the tomatoes, salt to taste, and cook over low heat until the tomatoes have thickened and all their liquid has evaporated. Add the cooked tomato mixture to the chickpeas and pasta. Transfer to a serving bowl.

PASTA AND BEANS WITH TOMATO SAUCE

Pasta e fagioli al sughetto di pomodoro

This is prepared like Cavatelli and Chickpeas with Tomato (Pasta e ceci al pomodoro), *using cannellini beans.*

CHICKPEA PURÉE

Passato di ceci

Ingredients

3/4 pound (1 1/2 cups) chickpeas
Sea salt
1 stalk celery, chopped
1 clove garlic, chopped
Thick slices semolina/country bread, cubed
Extra-virgin olive oil
Pepper

Soak the chickpeas overnight in lukewarm salted water. Some people add a handful of flour to the soaking water. In the morning, drain the chickpeas, and rinse them. In a large pot, bring them to a boil in water to cover, then simmer over low heat (in an earthenware pot if you have one) with the celery, half the garlic, and some salt. The chickpeas will require at least 3 hours of cooking time.

Purée the chickpeas through a food mill.

In a skillet, brown small cubes of bread in olive oil. Stir the bread into the chickpea purée, drizzle on olive oil, and sprinkle with pepper.

CHICKPEAS AND FRESH TAGLIATELLE

Ciceri e trie

Serves 4

Ingredients

- 10 ounces (about 1 1/4 cups) chickpeas
- 1 onion, chopped
- 1 stalk celery, chopped
- 1 clove garlic
- *Peperoncino*, hot red chili pepper, sliced [or dried flakes] to taste
- 1 3/4 cups flour

Soak the chickpeas overnight. Put them in a pot with the onion, garlic, and celery and about 2 quarts of water. Bring to a boil, then turn down to a simmer and cook for about 3 hours.

To make the tagliatelle, combine the flour and enough water to make a fairly stiff dough, roll out, and cut into tagliatelle. Place the noodles on a lightly floured tea towel and set them aside to rest.

In a large skillet, heat a generous amount of olive oil and add the garlic and chili. Add a handful of uncooked tagliatelle and fry until just browned. Remove from the heat. Bring a pot of salted water to a boil and cook the remaining tagliatelle. Drain the tagliatelle and add them to the pot with the chickpeas.

Stir in the cooked garlic and chili mixture with the browned tagliatelle. Serve piping hot.

Left: a wide variety of legumes are now available to Puglian shoppers

CHICKPEA SOUP

Zuppa di ceci

Serves 4

Ingredients

1 pound (2 cups) chickpeas
1 stalk celery, chopped
Sea salt
Thick slices semolina/country bread, cubed
Extra-virgin olive oil
Pepper

Soak the chickpeas overnight in lukewarm salted water. Some people add a handful of flour to the soaking water. In the morning, drain the chickpeas, and rinse them. Transfer the beans to a large pot (in an earthenware pot if you have one), add water to cover, bring to a boil, then turn down to a simmer and cook with the celery and some salt for about 3 hours.

Bake the bread cubes on a baking sheet for a few minutes to make croutons, then arrange them on the bottom of a serving bowl. Pour the chickpeas and their broth over the croutons, drizzle on olive oil, and sprinkle on a generous amount of pepper.

BEAN SOUP

Zuppa di fagioli

Serves 4

Ingredients

3/4 pound (1 1/2 cups) dried cannellini beans
Sea salt
1 stalk celery, chopped
1 clove garlic
Extra-virgin olive oil and pepper
Lemon juice

Soak the beans overnight in lukewarm salted water. In the morning, rinse them and transfer to a large pot, preferably earthenware. Add a generous amount of water to cover by a few inches then add the celery and garlic. Bring to a boil, then lower to a simmer and cook for 3 hours. If serving hot, drizzle on olive oil and sprinkle on pepper. If serving at room temperature, squeeze in a little lemon juice.

PASTA AND BEANS

Pasta e fagioli

Serves 4

Ingredients

3/4 pound (1 1/2 cups) cannellini or *borlotti* (cranberry) beans
Fresh flat-leaf parsley leaves, chopped
1 clove garlic
Sea salt
Peperoncino, strong red chili pepper, sliced [or dried flakes] to taste
1 tomato
1 stalk celery, chopped
1 1/2 cups flour
6 tablespoons extra-virgin olive oil

Soak the beans overnight. In the morning, drain them, rinse them, and put them in an earthenware pot with the parsley, garlic, salt, chili, tomato, and celery. Cover with about 4 quarts of water, bring to a boil, turn down to a simmer, and cook for 3 hours.

To make the homemade *cavatelli,* mound the flour on a smooth work surface and create a small well in the middle. Pour in a small amount of water. Combine the flour and enough water to create a soft dough. Knead until the dough it is no longer sticky. Working with small amounts of dough, roll out long, roughly shaped cylinders about 1/2 inch thick. Cut each cylinder into 1 inch pieces, and then make grooves around each piece with the tines of a fork.

You can make *cavatelli* or purchase them for ease of preparation. If you do purchase them, make sure you buy them from an artisanal pasta shop and that they are freshly made in-house.

When the beans are cooked, add the uncooked *cavatelli* to the pot. As soon as the *cavatelli* are cooked, removed the pot from the heat and set aside to rest for 5 minutes. Drizzle on 6 tablespoons olive oil and serve.

PASTA AND BEANS WITH GREENS

Pasta e fagioli con verdure

This dish can be made with dried beans or with fresh shelled borlotti *beans. Either way, the results should be fairly thick.*

Ingredients

2 1/4 pounds fresh *borlotti* (cranberry) beans in their pods
or 10 ounces (1 1/4 cups) dried *borlotti* beans
10 ounces (1 1/4 cups) carrots, diced
1 bunch celery, chopped (leaves included)
Basil leaves
2 cloves garlic, minced
Sea salt
6 tablespoons extra-virgin olive oil
Peperoncino, hot red chili pepper, sliced [or dried flakes] to taste
6 canned peeled tomatoes
8 ounces egg tagliatelle, crushed

If using fresh beans, shell them. If using dried beans, soak them overnight. Rinse and put the beans in a large pot, preferably earthenware, with the carrots, celery, basil, 1 clove garlic, and salt to taste. Add water to cover, bring to a boil, turn down to a simmer, and cook until the beans are soft.

In a small skillet, heat the olive oil, 1 clove garlic, chili, and tomatoes. Cook down to a thick sauce and add more basil leaves. Stir the tomato mixture into the beans and cook for 5 additional minutes.

Meanwhile, bring 2 quarts of salted water to a boil and cook the crushed tagliatelle until they are halfway cooked (still quite raw in the center). Drain the pasta and add it to the beans and continue cooking until the pasta is cooked through.

DRIED PEAS

Ciatedda

Serves 4

Ingredients

10 ounces (1 1/4 cups) dried peas
1 clove garlic, chopped
1 stalk celery, chopped
Fresh flat-leaf parsley, chopped
Extra-virgin olive oil
1 onion, thinly sliced
Peperoncino, hot red chili pepper, sliced [or dried flakes] to taste
1 pound broccoli rabe, boiled and drained
Slices of semolina or country bread, cubed

Soak the dried peas for several hours, then put them in a large pot with 2 quarts of water and the garlic, celery, and parsley. Bring to a boil, then turn down to a simmer and cook for 3 hours. The water should evaporate completely and the peas should break apart.

In a large pot, heat a generous amount of olive oil, then fry the onion and chili. Add the peas and cook until the peas have absorbed the flavor of the onion and chili. Add the cooked broccoli rabe.

In a skillet, brown the bread cubes in olive oil. Stir the bread into the peas and serve.

LENTIL SOUP

Zuppa di lenticchie

Serves 4

Ingredients

10 ounces (1 1/4 cups) lentils, sorted and rinsed
1 stalk celery, chopped
1 clove garlic, chopped
Fresh flat-leaf parsley, chopped
1 small onion, sliced
1 tomato, diced
Sea salt
Extra-virgin olive oil

Put the lentils in a pot, preferably earthenware, with the celery, garlic, parsley, onion, tomato, salt, and add water to cover. Simmer gently for about 2 hours, drizzle on olive oil, and serve piping hot.

DITALINI WITH LENTILS

Pasta e lenticchie

Serves 4

Ingredients

- 10 ounces (1 1/4 cups) lentils,sorted and rinsed
- 1 stalk celery, chopped
- 1 small onion, sliced
- 2 cloves garlic, chopped
- 6 tablespoons extra-virgin olive oil
- 5 canned peeled tomatoes, chopped
- Sea salt
- 1/2 pound spaghetti, broken, or 1/2 pound *ditalini*
- Pepper

Put the lentils in a pot, preferably earthenware, with the celery, onion, and half the garlic. Add water to cover by a few inches, bring to a boil, then turn down to a simmer.

In a skillet, heat the olive oil and add the remaining garlic and the tomatoes. When the tomatoes have thickened considerably, stir the tomato mixture into the pot with the lentils. Heat 2 quarts of salted water to boiling and cook the spaghetti or *ditalini* halfway. Drain the pasta and add it to the pot with the lentils. Cook until the pasta is cooked through. Add a generous amount of pepper and serve.

LENTIL PURÉE

Passato di lenticchie

Cook the lentils as above. When the lentils are cooked, pass them through a food mill. Serve with either croutons browned in olive oil or small pasta cooked in the purée itself.

Mixed Bean Soup

Zuppa Caterina

Serves 4

Ingredients

1 3/4 cups flour (or 10 ounces dry *cavatelli*)
8 ounces (1 cup) chickpeas
8 ounces (1 cup) dry beans, cannellini or *borlotti* (cranberry beans)
1 stalk celery, chopped
1 onion, chopped
1 pound *cardoncelli* mushrooms, trimmed and diced
Extra-virgin olive oil
1 clove garlic
Peperoncino, hot red chili pepper, sliced [or dried flakes] to taste
2 tablespoons tomato purée

If making homemade *cavatelli,* mound the flour on a smooth work surface and create a small well in the middle. Pour in a small amount of water. Combine the flour and enough water to create a soft dough. Knead until the dough it is no longer sticky. Working with small amounts of dough, roll out long, roughly shaped cylinders about 1/2 inch thick. Cut each cylinder into 1 inch pieces, and then make grooves around each piece with the tines of a fork.

Soak the beans (separately) overnight. Drain and then cook them in separate pots, adding water to cover, with celery and onion until soft.

In a skillet, cook the mushrooms in a generous amount of olive oil with the garlic and chili. Add the tomato purée and cook down.

Below: borlotti (cranberry) *bean pods*

Cook the *cavatelli* in a large pot of boiling salted water for a few minutes and drain. When the beans and chickpeas are cooked, combine them in an earthenware pot and add the mushroom sauce and the *cavatelli.* Bring to a boil, stirring occasionally, and serve hot.

PASTA AND PEAS

Pasta e piselli

Serves 4

Ingredients

1 onion, minced
2 ounces pork fat
1 1/2 ounces *prosciutto crudo*, diced
1 pound (2 cups) shelled peas
3/4 pound short pasta
Sea salt
Pepper

Chop and mix together the onion, pork fat, and *prosciutto crudo.* Put the mixture in a large pot and place over medium heat. Cook, stirring, for 5 minutes, then add the peas. When the peas have absorbed the flavor of the other ingredients, add enough water to cook the pasta, but not so much water that the resulting dish will be soupy. This should be more of a pasta dish than a soup. Add the pasta and cook until al dente. Season to taste with salt and pepper.

POTATOES LE PATATE

PUGLIA is both a major producer and consumer of potatoes. Because potatoes are starchy, they often take the place of bread or pasta. Potatoes could not be planted in the same plot every year—they needed to be rotated in order to produce a healthy harvest. Farmers who had land that was good for planting potatoes grew potatoes for themselves and also for sale.

Once harvested, potatoes were always stored on the floor under the bed. This might seem strange, but given how small the houses were at the time and how large the families that lived in them, it was the only option. That was the only space available that was big enough for the potatoes to be spread in a single layer. (Lying on top of each other, potatoes would rot.) Every once in a while all the potatoes were removed at once so the floor under the bed could be swept free of dust and bugs. Then the potatoes were returned to their spot.

THE SIMPLEST and tastiest salad imaginable was made by boiling potatoes and dressing them with olive oil, salt, and pepper. Even today there is a kind of potato minestrone served in the region that consists solely of potatoes, pasta, and celery. Indeed, potatoes still appear frequently on the tables of Puglia, either cooked in sauce, roasted, mashed, or fried.

Fried potatoes were a classic accompaniment to meat, but the large amount of olive oil needed to fry them made this dish a privilege of the wealthy, while the poor had to settle for frying, boiling, or baking them without meat.

Another delicious tradition was a dish of lamb or chicken served *assutto assutto* with potatoes. When brought to the table, a dish described as *assutto assutto* ("dry dry" in dialect) appeared dry and even a little burned. The chicken or lamb was cut into pieces, combined with cubed potatoes, and then roasted slowly, preferably in a wood-burning oven.

Potatoes are served with many different meat dishes: stew with potatoes, mutton with potatoes, tripe with potatoes. They are also made into gnocchi. Fried potato croquettes were once quite popular. Potatoes cooked in ashes have already been mentioned. Potatoes were also used in fava bean purée and in the dough for focaccia. When potatoes reached the size of a walnut, some of them were harvested and sold as "new potatoes." These are baked whole with their peels. They are delicious and are available only for a short time.

ROASTED POTATOES

Patate al forno

Serves 4

This is the traditional accompaniment to roasted meat.

Ingredients

1 1/2 pounds potatoes, peeled and cut into large pieces
1/4 cup extra-virgin olive oil
Sea salt
Pepper
Fresh rosemary

Put the potatoes in a baking dish with the other ingredients, to taste. Pour in 1 cup water and stir to combine. Roast in a preheated 475° oven until the potatoes are easily pierced with a knife or fork and are browned on top.

POTATO STEW

Spezzatino di patate

Serves 4

Ingredients

1/3 cup extra-virgin olive oil
1 clove garlic
1 1/2 pounds potatoes, peeled and cut into large pieces
1 cup white wine
2 canned peeled tomatoes, chopped
4 fresh bay leaves
Sea salt
Pepper

Put the olive oil and garlic in a pot. Brown the garlic, then remove and discard. Add the potatoes. Cook them for a few minutes, then add the wine. When the wine has evaporated, add the tomatoes, bay leaves, and salt and pepper to taste. Stir to combine thoroughly and add water to cover. Cook until the potatoes begin to break apart. [Remove bay leaves if not fresh.]

POTATOES AND ARTICHOKES

Patate e carciofi

Serves 4

Ingredients

1 1/2 pounds potatoes, peeled and thickly sliced
6 artichokes, trimmed, cut in half, "chokes" removed, and thickly sliced
1 clove garlic, minced
Fresh flat-leaf parsley, chopped
Sea salt
Pepper
4 tablespoons grated pecorino
3 tablespoons bread crumbs
Extra-virgin olive oil

Arrange alternating layers of potatoes and artichokes in a baking dish. On top of each layer, sprinkle some garlic and parsley, and season with salt and pepper. Sprinkle the pecorino and bread crumbs on top. Drizzle with olive oil, then pour 1/2 cup of water around the edge of the dish. (The idea is for the water to collect on the bottom of the pan but not disturb the ingredients.) Bake in a preheated 400° oven for about 1 hour.

POTATOES IN BROTH

Patatine in brodo

Serves 4

This is a quick soup, perfect for cold winter evenings.

Ingredients

2 quarts vegetable broth (using a bouillon cube is acceptable)
1 pound potatoes, peeled and diced
4 tablespoons grated pecorino
4 tablespoons grated *Parmigiano-Reggiano*

Bring the broth to a boil and add the potatoes. Cook until potatoes are soft, then serve with sprinkled pecorino and *Parmigiano-Reggiano* on top.

POTATO CROQUETTES

Crocchette di patate

Serves 4

Ingredients

2 1/4 pounds potatoes
4 tablespoons butter
2 eggs, lightly beaten
Fresh flat-leaf parsley, chopped
5 tablespoons grated *Parmigiano-Reggiano*
Sea salt
Pepper
Flour for dredging
Bread crumbs for dredging
1 cup extra-virgin olive oil

Clean the potatoes and boil them unpeeled. Drain the potatoes, and as soon as they are cool enough to touch, peel them. Then pass them through a potato ricer, letting them fall into a large bowl. Add the butter, eggs, parsley, and *Parmigiano-Reggiano.* Season with salt and pepper. Mix to combine thoroughly. Set out plates of flour and bread crumbs for dredging.

Oil your hands lightly and create stick-shaped croquettes. Dredge the croquettes in flour and then in the bread crumbs. Add olive oil to a skillet and fry a few croquettes at a time. Remove with a strainer and drain.

POTATO PUDDING

Sformato di patate

Serves 4

Ingredients

5 pounds potatoes
3 eggs, lightly beaten
2 cups milk
4 tablespoons butter
10 ounces mozzarella, diced
4 tablespoons grated pecorino
4 tablespoons grated *Parmigiano-Reggiano*
2 1/2 ounces (1/4 cup) mortadella, diced
Sea salt
Pepper
Grated nutmeg
Bread crumbs

Clean the potatoes and boil them unpeeled. Drain the potatoes, and as soon as they are cool enough to touch, peel them. Then pass them through a potato ricer, letting them fall into a large bowl. Add the eggs, 1 1/2 cups milk, 3 tablespoons butter, mozzarella, pecorino, *Parmigiano-Reggiano*, and mortadella. Season with salt, pepper, and nutmeg. The mixture should be very soft. If it feels too stiff, add a little more milk.

Butter and flour a baking dish, then pour the potato mixture into the dish, smooth the top, and pour the remaining milk over the top. Sprinkle on the bread crumbs and dot the top with the remaining tablespoon butter, cut into small pieces. Bake in a preheated 475° oven until the top is browned and crusty.

Potato Salad

Insalata di patate

Serves 4

In Puglian tradition, any vegetable preserved in olive oil could be added to this salad.

Ingredients

2 1/4 pounds potatoes
3 anchovies, rinsed, boned, and minced
1 can Italian tuna in olive oil, drained
4 salad tomatoes, diced
1 tablespoon capers
2 hard-boiled eggs, diced
2 to 3 marinated artichoke hearts, drained and minced
Sea salt
Extra-virgin olive oil

Clean the potatoes and boil them unpeeled. As soon as they are cool enough to touch, peel the cooked potatoes and cut them into medium dice. In a large bowl, combine the diced potatoes, anchovies, tuna, tomatoes, capers, hard-boiled eggs, and artichoke hearts. Season to taste with salt and olive oil and mix to combine.

Potato Cake

Tortino di Patate

Serves 4

Ingredients

2 1/4 pounds potatoes, peeled and thinly sliced
6 slices aged provolone
2 tablespoons butter
Sea salt
Pepper
5 tablespoons grated *Parmigiano-Reggiano*
About 3/4 cup milk

Butter a baking dish. Arrange a layer of potato slices on the bottom, topped with a layer of cheese slices. Dot the cheese with butter and season with salt and pepper. Repeat until you have used up all the potatoes and cheese slices. Sprinkle the *Parmigiano-Reggiano* on top and dot the surface with additional butter. Pour in enough milk to come halfway up the side of the pan, then bake in a preheated 400° oven for about 1 hour.

POTATOES COOKED IN HOT ASH

Patate sotto la cenere

These taste best when eaten close to the fireplace where they were cooked. They aren't part of a meal, but more of a combination snack and leisure activity.

Ingredients

Small potatoes
Sea salt
Extra-virgin olive oil or butter

Rub the potatoes vigorously with a dish towel to eliminate all traces of soil. Move any embers away from the fire so that only hot ash remains in the fireplace. Place the potatoes under the ashes and cover them with more hot ash. Arrange a few pieces of burning embers around the potatoes. Cook for at least 30 minutes, but keep a close watch on the potatoes, because cooking time can vary widely, depending on the intensity of the heat and the size of the potatoes.

Pull the potatoes out of the ashes and clean them thoroughly with a damp dish towel. Split the potatoes in half and sprinkle on salt and drizzle on olive oil or place a bit of butter on top. The potatoes are eaten in their peels and should be served very hot.

VEGETABLES GLI ORTAGGI

VEGETABLES and fruits are major crops in the Salento area. In fact, vegetables grow so abundantly in Puglia that it's very common to serve a large basket of raw fennel, celery, radishes, lettuce, and chicory in place of dessert at the end of a meal, even after having eaten all the same vegetables in cooked form as side dishes or part of pasta dishes.

Many country festivals are dedicated to vegetables and fruit. Farmers, locals, and tourists often get together to celebrate to the sounds of local bands and drink excellent local wine. There is a celebration of artichokes in San Ferdinando di Puglia, one for cherries in Conversano, and there are festivals for figs, grapes, and peaches in other towns. Legend has it that Greek mathematician Archytas of Taranto taught the people of what was then Apuli the art of cultivating the fields, giving rise to the region's flourishing agriculture, as well as several offshoot industries that developed to process the resulting products. Until the 1960s, over fifty percent of the workers in the region were involved with agriculture in one way or another.

The Salento area has rocky soil in some parts and finer volcanic soil in other parts. The area from the Murgia plain to the coast is almost all limestone with sinkholes of reddish soil. The red soil that came from volcanic soil and glacial deposits remains cool and therefore is suited to growing vegetables.

In Puglia, it's not uncommon to see row after row of green, neatly laid out fields that look like gardens rather than farms. Indeed, in earlier times, small and medium-sized pieces of land were used to grow vegetables and were called (in dialect) *lu sciardino,* or "the garden."

These pieces of land yield crops from the beginning to the end of the year, because growing periods are cyclical. Zucchini give way to artichokes, eggplant give way to peppers, which give way to tomatoes and then to cabbage, broccoli rabe, chard, lettuce and other greens, and so on. One area that always has vegetables growing is the Fasano plain. Another is the Metaponto plain along the Basilicata border. Since ancient times, many vegetables have been prepared as a first course: peppers, eggplant, and zucchini are found in every farmer's garden. Lacking anything better, a big batch of peppers or a soup of eggplant and zucchini could be cooked up and served with thick slices of semolina or country bread. Such a meal was lunch or dinner for many families. Any vegetables that couldn't be eaten were preserved in oil.

TOMATOES were dried in the sun and then made into jarred tomato purée that would last through the winter and was a key ingredient in *ragù*. But tomatoes were also picked in small bunches and threaded on string in order to make wreaths (called *pennule*) that were then hung inside in well-ventilated areas. Tomatoes stored in this way remained fresh and could be eaten with bread and used atop focaccia. For centuries, farmhands and shepherds subsisted on bread and tomatoes. These two basic foodstuffs were also breakfast for children and dinner for adults.

Another way to preserve tomatoes was to cut them in half and let them dry on *cannizze,* mats made by weaving reeds together with wire. Tomatoes dried this way were salted and then stored in *capase* (wide-mouthed ceramic containers); they could be dressed with extra-virgin olive oil and served with bread or fava beans. Peppers, eggplant, and zucchini were handled the same way in certain parts of the Salento area. In winter, these vegetables were soaked for a few hours to rehydrate them and then cooked with the vegetables that were then in season to create delicious and satisfying soups. Peppers, eggplant, and cucumbers were also pickled and served with boiled meat and white fava bean purée.

ROASTED EGGPLANT

Melanzane arrostite

Serves 4

This makes an excellent side dish for meat and fish courses, but it may also be served as a light appetizer.

Ingredients

1 1/2 pounds eggplant (3 small), sliced 1/2 inch thick
2 to 3 cloves garlic, minced
Fresh flat-leaf parsley, chopped
Sea salt
Pepper
Extra-virgin olive oil

Make small slits in each slice of eggplant and insert garlic and parsley into the slits. Heat a griddle and cook the eggplant slices, turning them frequently. When they are blackened and cooked through, place them on a serving platter. Season the eggplant slices with salt and pepper to taste and drizzle them with olive oil. Let rest for at least 4 hours before serving.

These can be served either hot or cold. If serving them cold, drizzle a little white wine vinegar on them.

[Eggplants are produced in a variety of shapes and sizes so be sure to weigh them.]

EGGPLANT MEDALLIONS

Medaglioni di melanzane

Ingredients

Eggplant, sliced into rounds about 1/2 inch thick
Mozzarella, sliced
Tomatoes, sliced
Sea salt
Basil or oregano leaves

Arrange the eggplant slices in a single layer on a baking sheet. Top each eggplant slice with a slice of mozzarella, a slice of tomato, salt, and basil or oregano. Bake in a preheated 400° oven for 30 minutes or until the eggplant is cooked through.

BAKED EGGPLANT WITH OLIVES

Melanzane al forno con olive

Serves 4

This may be served as a side dish or as an appetizer and also makes a nice small dish between courses.

Ingredients

1 1/2 pounds eggplant (3 small), sliced 1/4 inch thick
Sea salt
Mint leaves
1 clove garlic, minced
Black olives, pitted and chopped
Capers
Extra-virgin olive oil
White wine vinegar

Arrange the eggplant slices in slightly overlapping layers in a baking dish. Sprinkle on some salt, mint, garlic, olives, and capers. Drizzle on olive oil and wine vinegar and bake in a preheated 400° oven for 30 minutes or until the eggplant is cooked through.

EGGPLANT ROLLUPS

Involtini di melanzane

Serves 6

Ingredients

1 onion, minced
Extra-virgin olive oil
2 cups fresh tomato purée or 2 8-ounce cans
Basil leaves
3 1/4 pounds eggplant (6 small)
2 eggs
Sea salt
Flour for dredging

Stuffing

6 ounces ground meat, any combination of lamb, veal, and pork
2 tablespoons grated *Parmigiano-Reggiano*
2 slices day-old country bread (remove crusts, soak in water, squeeze dry, and tear into small pieces)
1 egg yolk
2 ounces mozzarella, diced
Fresh flat-leaf parsley, chopped
Salt
Pepper

To make the tomato sauce, in a skillet, fry the onion in olive oil and then pour in the tomato purée and add some basil. Continue cooking until thickened.

Cut the eggplants lengthwise, about 1/4 inch thick. Lightly beat 2 eggs and salt them. Set out a plate of flour. Dredge the eggplant slices first in the beaten egg and then the flour. Fry them in a generous amount of olive oil in a large skillet.

Meanwhile, make the stuffing. Combine the ground meat, the *Parmigiano-Reggiano*, bread, egg yolk, mozzarella, parsley, and salt and pepper to taste. Put a small amount of this stuffing on top of each slice of eggplant and roll up the eggplant.

Spread about 1/2 cup of the tomato sauce in the bottom of a baking dish and place the eggplant rolls in rows in the dish, sides touching, seam-side down. (You shouldn't need toothpicks to hold them closed.) Pour more sauce over the eggplant and top with some torn basil leaves. Cook in a preheated 350° oven for 30 minutes. Serve lukewarm or cold as a main dish or part of a buffet.

Fresh tomato purée: blanch and peel tomatoes, then purée them through a food mill.

FRIED EGGPLANT

Melanzane fritte

Serves 4

This is a good side dish to serve with more complex meat dishes, as well as game.

Ingredients

1 1/2 pounds eggplant (3 small), sliced 1/4 inch thick
Extra-virgin olive oil
1 clove garlic, minced
Sea salt
Mint leaves
White wine vinegar

In a large skillet, fry the eggplant in a generous amount of olive oil. As the slices are cooked, transfer them to a serving dish in layers. Sprinkle garlic, salt, mint leaves, and a small amount of wine vinegar between each layer of eggplant. Mix the eggplant and set aside. Serve cold. If the eggplant becomes soggy, transfer it to a dry serving dish.

EGGPLANT "MEATBALLS"

Polpette di melanzane

Serves 6

Ingredients

2 1/4 pounds eggplant (3 medium)
2 eggs, lightly beaten
4 tablespoons grated pecorino
1 clove garlic, minced
Fresh flat-leaf parsley, chopped
Sea salt
Pepper
2 to 3 tablespoons bread crumbs, if needed
Extra-virgin olive oil
1 onion slice
2 cups fresh tomato purée or 2 8-ounce cans
Basil leaves

In a large pot, boil the eggplants whole in salted water for about 10 minutes, then wring them out and set them in a colander to drain. Remove and discard eggplant skins.

Fresh tomato purée: blanch and peel tomatoes, then purée them through a food mill.

Transfer the eggplants to a mixing bowl and use a wooden spoon to break them down into pulp. Stir the eggs, pecorino, garlic, and parsley into the eggplant pulp, and season with salt and pepper to taste. Mix until the ingredients are well combined and the mixture is dense enough to shape into balls. If it seems too liquid, add bread crumbs, about 1 tablespoon at a time, until you achieve the right consistency. Make hazelnut-sized balls of the eggplant mixture and fry them in olive oil in a skillet.

Meanwhile, make the tomato sauce. In a skillet large enough to hold the "meatballs," fry the slice of onion in a small amount of olive oil, then add the tomato purée and basil. Cook 10 minutes. Add the fried eggplant "meatballs." Cook an additional 5 minutes.

You can also serve these fried without tomato sauce, and without the sauce they may be eaten cold as well.

EGGPLANT MUSHROOM-STYLE

Melanzane al funghetto

Serves 4

This is a classic side dish.

Ingredients

- 2 1/4 pounds eggplant (3 medium)
- 5 tablespoons extra-virgin olive oil
- 1 clove garlic
- 3 to 4 fresh tomatoes, diced
- Sea salt
- Basil leaves

Cut the unpeeled eggplant into thick slices, then cut the slices into strips. Put 5 tablespoons of olive oil and the garlic in a large skillet. Brown the garlic, then remove and discard it. Add the eggplant to the pan. Cook over high heat until the eggplant has softened, then add the tomatoes and season with salt. Cook for about 30 minutes. If the tomatoes do not produce enough liquid and it seems as if the eggplant might burn, add water in small amounts. But once the eggplant is almost cooked through, allow most of the liquid to evaporate, as the resulting dish is meant to be rather dry. When the eggplant is cooked, add basil leaves and transfer to a serving dish.

EGGPLANT CUTLETS

Cotolette di melanzane

Serves 4

These are good for a buffet.

Ingredients

Filling

6 ounces ground meat, any combination of lamb, veal, and pork
2 tablespoons grated pecorino
1 egg yolk
2 slices day-old semolina/country bread, (remove crusts, soak in water, squeeze dry, and tear into small pieces)
Fresh flat-leaf parsley, chopped
1 clove garlic, minced
Sea salt
Pepper
2 ounces mozzarella, diced

Flour for dredging
2 eggs
4 medium eggplants, sliced 1/4 inch thick
Extra-virgin olive oil

To make the filling, combine the ground meat, pecorino, egg yolk, bread, parsley, garlic, salt and pepper to taste, and mozzarella in a mixing bowl.

Set out a plate of flour for dredging. In another bowl, beat the 2 eggs lightly and set aside. Dredge the eggplant slices in flour.

Spread a walnut-size piece of the filling on top of one slice of eggplant then top with another slice of eggplant. Press down hard to hold the eggplants and filling together. Dredge the eggplant "sandwiches" in the egg and fry both sides in a generous amount of olive oil in a skillet. Transfer to paper towels to drain. (Work in batches if necessary.) Serve at room temperature or cold as a second course or as part of a buffet.

ZUCCHINI STUFFED WITH RICE

Zucchine ripiene di riso

Serves 4

Ingredients

6 zucchini, bulbous and not too long
2 cups fresh tomato purée or 2 8-ounce cans
1 onion, minced
Basil leaves
1 clove garlic
Extra-virgin olive oil
4 tablespoons Arborio rice
3 tablespoons grated *Parmigiano-Reggiano*
4 tablespoons bread crumbs
1 canned peeled tomato, crushed
1 clove garlic, minced
Fresh flat-leaf parsley, chopped
1 egg
Sea salt
Pepper

Cut the zucchini in half the long way and scoop out some of their pulp with a corer. Reserve pulp. Set aside hollowed out zucchini.

Prepare a tomato sauce with the tomato purée, onion, and basil.

In a skillet, brown the garlic in olive oil. Remove and discard the garlic, then add the zucchini pulp to the pan and fry. Set aside to cool, and as soon as it is cool, add the rice, *Parmigiano-Reggiano*, bread crumbs, peeled tomato, garlic, parsley, egg, and salt and pepper to taste. Stir to combine. Use a spoon to fill the hollowed out zucchini with this mixture.

The rice may be replaced with ground meat.

Spread about 1/2 cup of tomato sauce on the bottom of a baking dish and arrange the zucchini in it. Pour on additional tomato sauce, add 1 cup of water by pouring it slowly around the zucchini (you don't want to disturb them), and bake in a preheated 350° oven for 45 minutes. Serve at room temperature as a light second course.

Fresh tomato purée: blanch and peel tomatoes, then purée them through a food mill.

MARINATED ZUCCHINI

Zucchine scapece

Serves 4

This is a delicious side dish for complex meat preparations or game.

Ingredients

1 1/4 pounds zucchini (3 medium)
Extra-virgin olive oil
1 clove garlic, minced
2 to 3 mint leaves, torn
Sea salt
3 tablespoons white wine vinegar

Slice the zucchini into rounds. If possible, dry them in the sun for a few of hours. If that's not possible, set them on a cotton canvas for a couple of hours to drain. In a skillet, fry the zucchini slices in olive oil then transfer them to a serving bowl in layers. Make several layers of zucchini distributing garlic, mint, salt, and wine vinegar over each layer. Stir occasionally as the dish is cooling and serve cold.

ZUCCHINI FRITTATA

Frittata di zucchine

Serves 4

Ingredients

1 clove garlic
1/2 cup extra-virgin olive oil
1 1/4 pounds zucchini (3 medium), thinly sliced into rounds
Sea salt
Pepper
Fresh flat-leaf parsley, chopped
5 eggs
4 tablespoons grated *Parmigiano-Reggiano*
2 tablespoons grated pecorino
2 tablespoons bread crumbs (optional)

In a large skillet, brown the garlic in 1/4 cup olive oil. Remove and discard the garlic then add the zucchini slices. Season with salt and pepper and cook over low heat. If necessary, add a little water to the skillet. When the zucchini are cooked, sprinkle them with parsley, and set aside to cool.

Beat in the eggs in a large bowl. Stir in the *Parmigiano-Reggiano* and pecorino. Remove the zucchini from the skillet with a slotted spoon, draining their cooking oil briefly as you do, and stir them into the egg mixture. Stir in bread crumbs, if you wish.

In a skillet with low sides or an omelette pan, heat the remaining olive oil and pour in the zucchini and egg mixture. Turn the heat to low, cover the pan, and cook for a few minutes, being sure the frittata doesn't brown too much. Turn the frittata over and turn the heat to high. After 1 minute, turn the heat down to low and cook 4 to 5 minutes uncovered. Serve either hot or cold.

FRIED ZUCCHINI

Zucchine fritte

Serves 4

These are usually served with other fried vegetables, mozzarella, and croquettes, as a second course.

Ingredients

- 1 1/4 pounds zucchini (3 medium), cut into 1/2 inch thick matchsticks
- Sea salt
- Flour for dredging
- 2 eggs
- Pepper
- Extra-virgin olive oil

Salt the zucchini and let them rest for about 1 hour. Set out a plate of flour for dredging. In a bowl, lightly beat the eggs and add a little pepper. Dredge the zucchini in flour, then in the beaten eggs. Coat the bottom of a large skillet with olive oil and fry the zucchini. These should be eaten piping hot.

SWEET AND SOUR PEPPERS

Peperoni in agrodolce

Serves 4

This is a wonderful side dish and matches well with meat.

Ingredients

1 clove garlic
1/4 cup extra-virgin olive oil
1 1/4 pounds yellow bell peppers (3 medium), seeded and cut into strips
Sea salt
1 tablespoon capers
2 teaspoons sugar
4 tablespoons white wine vinegar

In a wide skillet with low sides, fry the garlic in the olive oil. As soon as the garlic is browned, add the peppers and season them with salt. After 10 minutes, remove and discard the garlic, and add the capers, sugar, and wine vinegar. Cook, stirring frequently. Add 1 cup water if necessary to keep the peppers from sticking before they are cooked. Serve cold.

FRIED PEPPERS

Peperoni fritti

Serves 4

Fried peppers make an excellent side dish or may be served with white fava bean purée.

Ingredients

1 pound thin green peppers
Extra-virgin olive oil
Sea salt
1 clove garlic, minced

In a large skillet, fry the peppers whole—without cutting off their stems or removing their seeds—in olive oil. Transfer the fried peppers to a serving dish. Season them with salt and sprinkle with minced garlic.

These are also delicious with a few drops of white wine vinegar and some mint leaves. You can also fry larger green peppers, but quarter them and remove their seeds first.

Roasted Peppers

Peperoni arrostiti

Serves 4

Ingredients

3 large yellow bell peppers
Extra-virgin olive oil
Sea salt
Pepper
Fresh flat-leaf parsley, chopped
1 clove garlic, minced
2 tablespoons white wine vinegar

Wash and dry the peppers and roast them in a preheated 400° oven. When the skin of the peppers begins to brown, turn them so that they cook evenly all over. Remove from the oven and peel. This has to be done when the peppers are still hot or the skin won't come off. Cut the peppers, seeded, into thin strips and combine them with olive oil, salt, pepper, parsley, chopped, garlic, and wine vinegar. Arrange them neatly on a serving dish.

Peppers with Bread Crumbs

Peperoni ammollicati

Serves 4

This serves equally well as an appetizer or as a second course.

Ingredients

Bread crumbs
Fresh flat-leaf parsley, chopped
1 clove garlic, minced
Sea salt
Pepper
4 to 5 black olives, pitted and chopped
4 medium yellow bell peppers, halved and seeded
Extra-virgin olive oil

In a mixing bowl, combine the bread crumbs, parsley, garlic, salt, pepper, and chopped olives. Put the peppers in one layer in a baking dish and sprinkle the bread crumb mixture over them. Drizzle with a little olive oil and pour 1/2 cup of water around the peppers into the dish. Bake them in a preheated 400° oven for 30 minutes.

STUFFED PEPPERS

Peperoni ripieni

Serves 4

These work well as a second course.

Ingredients

8 medium green bell peppers, roasted, peeled, halved, stemmed, and seeded
3/4 cup bread crumbs
2 tablespoons grated pecorino
1/4 cup water-cured black olives, pitted and chopped
Fresh flat-leaf parsley, chopped
1 clove garlic, minced
2 tablespoons capers
3 anchovies, rinsed, boned, and chopped
Sea salt
Pepper
2 tablespoons extra-virgin olive oil

Wash and dry the peppers and roast them in a preheated 400° oven. When the skin of the peppers begins to brown, turn them so that they cook evenly all over. Remove from the oven and peel. This has to be done when the peppers are still hot or the skin won't come off.

In a mixing bowl, combine the bread crumbs, pecorino, olives, parsley, garlic, capers, and anchovies. Season to taste with salt and pepper and moisten with olive oil. Stir to combine.

Stuff the peppers carefully with the breadcrumb mixture. Arrange the stuffed peppers in a baking dish and bake in a preheated 400° oven for 20 minutes.

SUMMER CAPONATA

Caponata estiva

Serves 6

This makes a good first or second course in summer.

Ingredients

3/4 pound eggplant (2 small)
Flour for dredging
2 medium onions, sliced
2 cloves garlic, minced
7 tablespoons extra-virgin olive oil
1 large yellow bell pepper, diced
6 ounces green beans, chopped
10 ounces potatoes, peeled and thinly sliced
2 zucchini, thinly sliced
3/4 pound tomatoes, passed through a food mill
Basil leaves
Sea salt
Pepper

Cut the eggplant into rounds, then rinse them and let them rest. Set out a plate of flour for dredging.

In a heavy-bottomed casserole, cook the onions and garlic in olive oil briefly, then add the pepper and green beans. Cook for a few minutes, stir, then add the potatoes and zucchini. When the vegetables are incorporated, after about 15 minutes of total cooking time, add the tomatoes. Cover and cook for 30 minutes. Add about 1 cup of water if necessary to keep them from burning.

Meanwhile, dredge the eggplant in flour and fry in a skillet in olive oil. Add the fried eggplant to the casserole, together with basil. Season with salt and pepper 2 to 3 minutes before serving. Serve hot or cold.

PEPPERS AND TOMATOES

Scacchiata o scattiata

Serves 4

These are excellent as a side dish or light second course. In the Taranto area they are also served with pasta.

Ingredients

5 tablespoons extra-virgin olive oil
1 clove garlic, minced
Fresh flat-leaf parsley, chopped
1/2 onion, minced
2 1/4 pounds green bell peppers, torn in half and seeded
Sea salt
Pepper
6 fresh tomatoes, diced

Heat the olive oil in a skillet and add the garlic, parsley, and onion. Stir to combine and cook until just beginning to color. Add the peppers and season with salt and pepper. When the peppers are half-cooked, add the tomatoes and cook until the tomatoes give up all their liquid and the peppers are very soft.

SWEET AND SOUR ONIONS

Cipolle in agrodolce

Serves 4

Ingredients

1 1/4 pounds whole Acquaviva or Tropea [red] onions
1 tablespoon capers
4 tablespoons white wine vinegar
2 teaspoons sugar
1/4 teaspoon salt
1/4 cup extra-virgin olive oil

Put the peeled, sweet onions in a pot (preferably earthenware) and combine with the capers, wine vinegar, sugar, salt, and olive oil. Add enough water to cover and cook them until the water has evaporated. If desired, arrange the onions in a baking dish and place them in a preheated 400° until they brown on top. Serve at room temperature.

STUFFED ONIONS

Cipolle ripiene

Serves 4

These may be served as a second course.

Ingredients

6 ounces ground meat, any combination of lamb, veal, and pork
2 slices day-old semolina/country bread (remove crusts, soak in water, squeeze dry, and tear into small pieces)
1 egg yolk
Sea salt
Pepper
Fresh flat-leaf parsley, chopped
1/3 cup mozzarella, diced
2 tablespoons grated pecorino or *Parmigiano-Reggiano*
1 1/4 pounds medium peeled white or red onions
Extra-virgin olive oil

In a mixing bowl, make a mixture of the meat, bread, egg yolk, salt, pepper, parsley, mozzarella, and grated cheese as if you were making meatballs. Cut the onions in half. Carefully remove some of the central rings of the onions so that they are somewhat hollow shells.

Fill the onion halves with the meat mixture, then arrange the onions in a baking dish, drizzle with olive oil, and pour 1 cup of cold water around the onions so it fills the bottom of the dish.

Bake in a preheated 400° for 30 minutes or until the onions are soft.

ARTICHOKE FRITTATA

Frittata di carciofi

Serves 4

Ingredients

- 10 medium artichokes
- Lemon juice
- 1 clove garlic, minced
- Extra-virgin olive oil
- Sea salt
- Pepper
- Fresh flat-leaf parsley, chopped
- 5 eggs
- 2 tablespoons grated *Parmigiano-Reggiano*
- 2 tablespoons grated pecorino

Trim the artichokes, removing and discarding all their hard leaves until you have only those that are light-colored and tender. Cut off the sharp tips of the artichokes. You may use their stems as long as they are meaty, but peel them, being sure to remove any fibrous parts. Cut in half and remove the "chokes." Cut both the artichokes and their stems into thin slices and put them in a bowl with water and lemon juice to keep them from turning brown.

In a large skillet, brown the garlic in 1/4 cup olive oil. Remove and discard the garlic then add the artichoke slices. Season with salt and pepper and cook over low heat. If necessary, add a little water to the skillet. When the artichokes are cooked, sprinkle them with parsley, and set aside to cool.

Beat the eggs in a large bowl. Stir in the *Parmigiano-Reggiano* and pecorino. Remove the artichokes from the skillet with a slotted spoon, draining their cooking oil briefly as you do, and stir them into the egg mixture. Stir in bread crumbs, if you wish.

Coat the bottom of a skillet with low sides or an omelette pan with olive oil and heat, then pour in the artichoke and egg mixture. Turn the heat to low, cover the pan, and cook for a few minutes, being sure the frittata doesn't brown too much. Turn the frittata over and turn the heat to high. After 1 minute, turn the heat down to low and cook 4 to 5 minutes uncovered. Serve hot or cold.

STUFFED ARTICHOKES

Carciofi ripieni

Serves 4

Ingredients

- 8 artichokes
- Lemon juice
- 6 tablespoons bread crumbs
- 2 tablespoons grated pecorino
- 2 salted anchovies, rinsed, boned, and chopped
- Fresh flat-leaf parsley, chopped
- 1 clove garlic, minced
- Sea salt
- Pepper
- Extra-virgin olive oil

Trim the artichokes, removing and discarding all their hard leaves until you have only those that are light-colored and tender. Cut off the sharp tips of the artichokes. Put them in a bowl with water and lemon juice to keep them from turning brown.

In a bowl, combine the bread crumbs, pecorino, anchovies, parsley, and garlic. Season with salt and pepper and moisten with a small amount of olive oil.

Holding the artichokes by their stems, hit them vigorously against a cutting board to open their leaves. Remove the "chokes," then cut off the stems so the artichokes will stand upright.

Fill the artichokes from the top with about 1 tablespoon of the bread crumb mixture each and arrange them upright in a baking dish so they are touching one another on all sides. Drizzle on some olive oil then pour 1/2 cup water into the baking dish around the artichokes.

Bake in a preheated 400° oven for about 45 minutes. Serve at room temperature.

ARTICHOKE GRATIN

Carciofi gratinati

Serves 4

Serves as a light second course.

Ingredients

16 artichokes
Lemon juice
Extra-virgin olive oil
Fresh flat-leaf parsley, chopped
1 clove garlic, minced
Sea salt
Pepper
Bread crumbs

Trim the artichokes, removing and discarding all their hard leaves until you have only those that are 2/3 light-colored and tender. Cut off the sharp tips of the artichokes (you may use their stems as long as they are meaty, but peel them, being sure to remove any fibrous parts). Cut in half and remove the "chokes."

Cut the artichokes and their stems into slices about 1/4 inch thick. Very lightly oil a baking dish then layer the artichoke slices, overlapping them slightly. Top each row of artichoke slices with some parsley, garlic, salt, and pepper. Sprinkle bread crumbs over the top and drizzle on olive oil. Pour 1/2 cup of water around the artichokes so it sits at the bottom of the dish and bake in a preheated 400° oven until the top is browned, about 30 minutes.

CARDOON GRATIN

Cardi gratinati

Serves 4

This can be either a side dish or a light second course.

Ingredients

3 1/4 pounds cardoons*
1 clove garlic, minced
Fresh flat-leaf parsley, chopped
Sea salt
Pepper

Extra-virgin olive oil
Bread crumbs
Grated pecorino (optional)

Discard any hard or damaged ribs from the cardoons and remove the fibrous parts that run along the ribs. Cut the most tender cardoons into pieces about 8 inches long. Boil the cardoons in a large pot of salted water then arrange them in layers in a baking dish without draining too much water out of them. Sprinkle on the garlic and parsley, season with pepper, then drizzle on olive oil. Sprinkle on bread crumbs (mixed with pecorino, if using). Bake in a preheated 400° oven for 20 minutes.

*Only the ribs of the cardoons are edible. Remove and discard any leaves.

CAULIFLOWER SALAD

Insalata di cavolfiore

Serves 4

This is excellent as a side dish or as a salad.

Ingredients

1 head cauliflower, about 2 1/4 pounds
5 tablespoons extra-virgin olive oil
1 tablespoon white wine vinegar
2 tablespoons capers
7 tablespoons water-cured black olives, chopped
4 anchovy filets, rinsed and chopped
1 clove garlic, whole
Sea salt
Pepper

Trim the cauliflower and cut it into florets. Boil the florets in a large amount of salted water for 20 minutes. Drain well.

While the cauliflower is cooking, combine the olive oil, wine vinegar, capers, olives, anchovies, and peeled garlic in a large bowl. Season with salt and pepper and stir to combine thoroughly. When the cauliflower has cooled to room temperature, remove the garlic from the bowl and add the cooked cauliflower.

BAKED CHICORY

Catalogne racanate

Serves 4

Ingredients

2 1/2 pounds chicory, tops only
Sea salt
1 clove garlic, minced
Capers
2 fresh or canned tomatoes, chopped
Bread crumbs
Extra-virgin olive oil

In a large pot, blanch the chicory tops in a generous amount of salted water. Drain, then arrange them in a baking dish and sprinkle on the garlic, capers, and tomato. Sprinkle on bread crumbs and drizzle on olive oil. Bake in a preheated 400° oven until the bread crumbs brown.

FENNEL GRATIN

Finocchi gratinati

Serves 4

Ingredients

4 large fennel bulbs
1 clove garlic, minced
Fresh flat-leaf parsley, chopped
Extra-virgin olive oil
Bread crumbs
Pepper

Trim any leaves from the fennel bulbs. Cut the bulbs lengthwise, about 1/2 inch thick, and rinse out any grit. In a large pot, blanch the fennel in boiling salted water. Then, with a strainer or skimmer, transfer them with some of their cooking liquid (don't drain them completely when you remove them) to a baking dish. Sprinkle on some garlic and parsley and season with salt and pepper. Sprinkle on bread crumbs and top with a little more garlic, parsley, and salt and pepper to taste. Drizzle some olive oil over the top and bake in a preheated 400° oven for 20 minutes.

Casseroles provide another way to use vegetables. These preparations are rich and elaborate and have become known in Puglia as "Le parmigiane."

EGGPLANT PARMIGIANA

Parmigiana di melanzane

Serves 6

This is usually served as a second course and is always served either cold or at room temperature, never hot.

Ingredients

3 1/4 pounds eggplant (4 medium)
Flour for dredging
4 eggs
1/4 teaspoon sea salt
Extra-virgin olive oil
1 onion slice
2 1/4 pounds fresh tomatoes, puréed through a food mill
Basil leaves
12 ounces mozzarella, sliced
Hard-boiled eggs, sliced (optional)

Meatballs

6 ounces ground meat, veal and pork
7 tablespoons grated *Parmigiano-Reggiano*
2 slices day-old country bread (remove crusts, moisten with water, squeeze dry, and tear into small pieces)
1 egg yolk
Fresh flat-leaf parsley, chopped
Sea salt
Pepper

Slice the eggplants about 1/4 inch thick and set aside to rest for 1 hour. Set out a plate of flour for dredging. Beat the 4 eggs with salt. Dredge the eggplant slices first in flour, then in the beaten eggs. In a large skillet, fry them in a generous amount of olive oil. Drain well on paper towels.

In a pot, heat 3 tablespoons of olive oil with

the onion. Once the onion has browned, remove and discard it and add the puréed tomatoes. Cook the sauce for 10 minutes. Do not allow it to thicken too much. Add basil leaves to the sauce.

To make the meatballs, combine the ground meat, about 2 tablespoons of the *Parmigiano-Reggiano,* the bread, egg yolk, and parsley in a mixing bowl. Season with salt and pepper. Mix with your hands to combine thoroughly then make meatballs the size of hazelnuts. Fry the meatballs in olive oil then set aside.

Spread about 1/2 cup of the tomato sauce on the bottom of a baking dish and arrange some eggplant slices in a single layer, overlapping slightly. Add a layer of mozzarella, meatballs, *Parmigiano-Reggiano,* and sliced hard-boiled eggs if using.

Spread 1/2 cup of tomato sauce on top. Repeat for 2 or 3 layers, ending with a layer of eggplant and sauce. Tear some basil leaves and spread them on top. Bake in a preheated 350° oven for 45 minutes.

ZUCCHINI PARMIGIANA

Parmigiana di zucchine

Serves 6

This may be eaten cold or at room temperature as a second course.

Ingredients

- 3 1/4 pounds zucchini (about 6 medium)
- Sea salt
- 5 tablespoons extra-virgin olive oil
- 1 onion slice
- 2 1/4 pounds fresh tomatoes, puréed through a food mill
- Basil leaves
- Flour for dredging
- 2 eggs
- 3/4 pound mozzarella, diced
- 3 1/2 ounces mortadella, cut into strips
- 2 hard-boiled eggs, sliced
- 6 tablespoons grated *Parmigiano-Reggiano*

Trim the ends of the zucchini, wash them, and cut them the lengthwise about 1/4-inch thick. Salt the zucchini slices and let them rest for about 1 hour.

To make the tomato sauce, heat the olive oil and fry the onion slice. When the onion begins to brown, remove and discard it and add the puréed tomatoes, then tear and add a few basil leaves. Cook for 10 minutes.

Set out a plate of flour for dredging. Then lightly beat 2 eggs with a pinch of salt. Dredge the zucchini slices in flour, then in the eggs. In a large skillet, fry them in a generous amount of olive oil. Drain on paper towels.

Spread 1/2 cup of the tomato sauce on the bottom of a baking dish and arrange some zucchini slices on top of it in a single layer, overlapping slightly. Add a layer of mozzarella, a layer of mortadella, and slices of hard-boiled eggs. Sprinkle with *Parmigiano-Reggiano* and spread about 1/2 cup of tomato sauce on top.

Repeat layers until you have used up all the zucchini. Cover with *Parmigiano-Reggiano*, tomato sauce, and a few basil leaves. Bake in a preheated 350° oven for 30 minutes.

Artichoke Parmigiana

Parmigiana di carciofi

Serves 4

Ingredients

- 16 artichokes
- Extra-virgin olive oil
- 1 onion slice
- 1 pound fresh tomatoes, puréed through a food mill
- Basil leaves
- Flour for dredging
- 2 eggs
- 3/4 pound mozzarella, sliced
- 3 1/2 ounces mortadella, sliced
- 2 hard-boiled eggs, sliced
- 4 tablespoons grated *Parmigiano-Reggiano*

Trim the artichokes, removing and discarding all their hard leaves until you have only those that are light-colored and tender. Cut off the sharp tips of the artichokes (you may use their stems as long as they are meaty, but peel them, being sure to remove any fibrous parts). Cut in half and remove the "chokes." Cut into slices. Then, in a large skillet, fry them in olive oil.

To make the tomato sauce, heat the olive oil and fry the onion slice. When the onion begins to brown, remove and discard it and add the puréed tomatoes and tear and add a few basil leaves. Cook for 10 minutes.

Set out a plate of flour for dredging. Then lightly beat 2 eggs with a pinch of salt. Dredge the artichoke slices in flour, then in the eggs. In a large skillet, fry them in a generous amount of olive oil. Drain on paper towels.

Spread 1/2 cup of the tomato sauce on the bottom of a baking dish and arrange some artichoke slices on top of it in a single layer, overlapping slightly. Add a layer of mozzarella, a layer of mortadella, and slices of hard-boiled eggs. Sprinkle with *Parmigiano-Reggiano* and spread about 1/2 cup of tomato sauce on top.

Repeat layers until you have used up all the artichoke pieces. Cover with *Parmigiano-Reggiano*, tomato sauce, and a few basil leaves. Bake in a preheated 350° oven for 30 minutes.

CARDOON PARMIGIANA

Parmigiana di cardi

Serves 4

This works as either a first or second course.

Ingredients

4 pounds cardoons
1 egg
Sea salt
Flour
2 tablespoons extra-virgin olive oil
1 onion, sliced
10 ounces fresh tomatoes, puréed through a food mill
4 hard-boiled eggs, diced
3/4 pound mozzarella, diced
6 tablespoons grated *Parmigiano-Reggiano*

Meatballs

6 ounces ground meat, veal and pork
2 slices day-old country bread (remove crusts, moisten with water, squeeze dry, and tear into small pieces)
2 tablespoons grated pecorino
1 clove garlic, minced
Fresh flat-leaf parsley, chopped
1 egg yolk
Sea salt
Pepper

Trim away any hard ribs or soft spots on the cardoons. Remove the leaves and the fibrous part along the ribs. Cut into pieces about 8 inches long and boil in a large pot of salted water. Drain thoroughly. In a bowl, mix 1 egg, a little water, 1 pinch of salt, and enough flour to make a thick batter. Dip the cardoons in the batter. In a large skillet, fry them in a generous amount of olive oil. Drain on paper towels.

To make the meatballs, combine the ground meat, bread, pecorino, garlic, parsley, and 1 egg yolk in a bowl. Season with salt and pepper. Form the mixture into hazelnut-size meatballs and fry them in olive oil.

To make the tomato sauce, heat olive oil and the onion in a pot. Once the onion has browned, remove and discard it. Add the puréed tomatoes and cook the sauce 10 minutes. Do not allow it to thicken too much.

Spread a small amount of tomato sauce on the bottom of a baking dish. Cover with a layer of fried cardoons, then top the cardoons with some of the diced hard-boiled eggs, mozzarella, meatballs, *Parmigiano-Reggiano*, pepper, and a small amount of tomato sauce. Make at least 3 layers like this and end with some tomato sauce. Sprinkle on more *Parmigiano-Reggiana*. Bake in a preheated 400° oven for 30 minutes.

"Le Tielle"

These layered casseroles are named for the special dish used to make them, which is a legacy of the Spanish rule of Puglia.

A *tiella* is always a dish of various ingredients in layers and always includes potatoes and a sprinkling of grated cheese, but other than that there are no set rules for making them. Each home cook uses her imagination and the vegetables she has on hand.

THESE dishes were first made for farmers. They were created during an era when women worked in the fields alongside men, and since women not only worked in the fields but did the cooking, too, they had to have in their repertoires nutritious dishes that could be prepared quickly when they got home. A *tiella* could be made by simply layering everything in the house in a single dish.

The casseroles used to be cooked in the fireplace with "flames above and below." That expression refers to an arrangement that was an early predecessor to the oven. A pan was set in the fireplace on a small tripod with embers burning beneath it. The pan was covered with an old iron lid, and more embers were placed on top of that. In this way, the dish cooked as if it were in an oven, with heat coming from all sides.

Traditionally, there has been a difference between the way the peasantry and the way wealthy and middle-class families cooked.

HOUSES of farmers in the country had only one source of heat, the fireplace, which was also used for cooking. At dawn, the lady of the house got out of bed to light the fire. Once the fire was roaring, she set a tripod in it and set a cauldron of water on the tripod.

This cauldron sat in the fire the entire day. Heated water was used for doing housework— washing, laundry, and cooking food. As the day wore on, cold water was added. When it was time to eat, the

same water was used to cook pasta or boil potatoes. Another small tripod was added to heat up sauces or cook other dishes.

Usually in winter, upon returning from the fields, people gathered around the fireplace, where it was warm, to eat the evening meal. At the end of the meal the largest chunks of log were taken out of the fireplace so they could be used the next day, and the fire was allowed to die out slowly, so that it continued to give off some heat late into the night.

In middle-class and wealthy homes, cooking was done in a corner where a cooking area was made out of stone with some firebricks. This was usually a rectangle or semicircle about twenty-eight inches high. At about fourteen inches off the ground sat two small iron doors where firewood was loaded. A few inches below them were two openings where ashes fell. The ashes were removed and discarded every morning. On the cooking surface, over one of the little doors for loading wood, was a griddle, and over the other little door was a large circular hole. An iron cauldron with a large red copper lid sat in the hole.

The cauldron served the same purpose as the one in a more rustic kitchen—it was always full of hot water. Legumes, vegetables, and anything else that was to be served for lunch was cooked on the griddle. The embers would be placed underneath the griddle.

A grate was sometimes placed in the griddle area for cooking meat or sausage. Meat cooked this way absorbed the delicious flavor of wood smoke. The grate was also used for roasting fish, eggplant, peppers, and bread. Bread toasted over a wood fire, the predecessor of today's *bruschetta,* was spread with *ricotta forte* or flavored with raw tomatoes, olive oil, salt, pepper, and oregano. It also was served underneath chickpeas and beans. Before a ladleful of chickpeas was poured into a bowl, pieces of toasted bread were set in the bottom of the bowl. This way they were moistened by the liquid of the legumes and the olive oil that was drizzled over them. The resulting dish is as beautiful to look at as it is delicious to eat.

ONLY a few wealthy homes had wood-burning stoves because these were true luxuries. A wood-burning stove was an iron contraption about four feet long, two and one-half feet deep, and two and one-half feet high. It was truly an aesthetically beautiful object, and even today in older houses where the kitchens have been remodeled—sensibly enough—a wood-burning stove sometimes still sits happily in its corner, a relic of bygone days. A wood-burning stove had three or four little doors for inserting wood that heated the cast iron plates on the upper part of the stove, as well as, of course, a pot of water that had a special insert, a sort of colander of the same size and shape as the pot that fit inside it. This was used to cook pasta, and then the colander was lifted out and the water could drain from it right over the stove.

A wood-burning stove was actually very similar to a modern electric stove, though it took up a little more space and had an iron pipe that wrapped around it. Because a wood-burning stove had two or three plates, plus the water pot, it could be used to cook several dishes at the same time.

TARANTO-STYLE CASSEROLE

Tiella tarantina

Serves 4

This can be served hot or cold.

Ingredients

- 2 onions, thinly sliced
- 2 medium zucchini, thinly sliced
- 1 pound potatoes, peeled and thinly sliced
- 2 1/4 pounds mussels, shelled, juices strained and reserved*
- 10 ounces (1 1/4 cups) rice
- 1 pound tomatoes, sliced
- 1/4 cup grated *Parmigiano-Reggiano*
- Basil leaves
- Extra-virgin olive oil

Arrange the onion slices in a layer on the bottom of a baking dish, then cover with the zucchini slices. Top the zucchini with a layer of potato slices, then arrange the mussels over the potatoes. Sprinkle the rice over the mussels, and then pour the juices from the mussels over them. Layer the tomato slices over the rice. Sprinkle on the *Parmigiano-Reggiano* and top with a few basil leaves. Drizzle on olive oil. Bake for 45 minutes in a preheated 350° oven.

MUSSELS AND RICE CASSEROLE

Tiella di riso e cozze

Serves 4

This may be served as a first or second course and may be served warm, at room temperature, or even cold.

Ingredients

- 1 pound cherry tomatoes, halved
- 2 large onions, sliced
- 2 cloves garlic, minced
- Fresh flat-leaf parsley, chopped
- Sea salt
- Extra-virgin olive oil
- 1 pound potatoes, peeled and thinly sliced
- 2 1/4 pounds mussels, shelled, juices strained and reserved*
- 3 tablespoons grated pecorino
- 1 cup rice
- Pepper

In a baking dish, arrange about half the tomatoes in 1 layer and top with the onion slices. Sprinkle about 1/3 of the garlic and parsley over them. Salt lightly and drizzle on some olive oil. On top of the onions place a layer of about half the potatoes and then a layer of the remaining tomatoes. Arrange the mussels neatly in a layer on top of the tomatoes. Sprinkle the pecorino and another third of the garlic and parsley over the mussels.

*For best results, the [rinsed and cleaned] mussels should be shelled by hand; reserve any liquid that comes out of them as you're doing so and strain it.

If you're not comfortable shelling raw mussels, cook them briefly over high heat until they open and remove them from their shells. Strain and reserve any liquid.

In doing this, however, you will deprive yourself of the wonderful whiff of the sea that raw shellfish give off when opened by hand.

Then sprinkle on the rice and top with a neat layer of the remaining potato slices. Add the remaining garlic and parsley, a pinch of salt, a generous amount of pepper, and pour any liquid from the mussels over the top. Drizzle on some olive oil and bake in a preheated moderate oven at 350° for 35 minutes.

CASSEROLE OF MIXED VEGETABLES

Tiella capricciosa

Serves 4

This makes a first or second course and is also suitable for a buffet.

Ingredients

1 pound "wild onions"*
3/4 pound tomatoes, sliced
1 bunch fresh flat-leaf parsley, minced
1 clove garlic, minced
Sea salt
Pepper
Extra-virgin olive oil
3/4 pound potatoes, peeled and sliced
1 1/4 pounds mushrooms, preferably pezza or cardoncelli mushrooms, brushed clean
Bread crumbs
2 tablespoons grated pecorino (optional)

Peel the onions. Trim away the roots at their bases, then cut an X into the flat base of each onion. In a large pot, boil the onions in salted water for about 30 minutes. Slice the onions.

In a large baking dish, make a layer of the onion slices, then top with a layer of half the tomato slices. Sprinkle on some parsley and garlic. Season with salt and pepper, and drizzle on a little olive oil. Top with a layer of the potato slices, then a layer of the mushrooms, and end with the remaining tomatoes, sprinkling each layer with parsley and garlic, seasoning with salt and pepper, and drizzling on a little olive oil. Sprinkle bread crumbs on the top layer and the pecorino, if using.

Pour about 1/2 cup water around the sides of the dish so it runs to the bottom. Bake in a preheated 350° oven for 30 minutes. Serve at room temperature or cold.

**Lampasciuni* or *vampascione* refer to wild grape-hyacinths whose small bulbs are called "wild onions."

MUSHROOM CASSEROLE

Tiella di funghi carduncidd

Serves 4

Ingredients

1 large onion, thinly sliced
1 clove garlic, minced
1 bunch fresh flat-leaf parsley, minced
Sea salt
Pepper
Extra-virgin olive oil
3/4 pound potatoes, peeled and thinly sliced
1 1/4 pounds *cardoncelli* mushrooms, cleaned
Bread crumbs

In a baking dish, make a layer of the onion slices, then top with a little garlic and parsley. Season with salt and pepper and drizzle on a little olive oil. Repeat with the potatoes and then the mushrooms, topping each layer with garlic and parsley, seasoning with salt, and drizzling on a little olive oil. Sprinkle bread crumbs over the top layer and drizzle a little more olive oil.

Pour about 1/2 cup water around the sides of the dish so it runs to the bottom. Bake in a preheated 400° oven for 30 minutes. Serve at room temperature.

POTATO AND RICE CASSEROLE

Tiella di patate e riso

Serves 4

This is usually served as a first course.

Ingredients

4 tablespoons grated pecorino
1 clove garlic, minced
1 bunch fresh flat-leaf parsley, minced
2 1/4 pounds potatoes, peeled and thinly sliced
2 large onions, thinly sliced
10 ounces (1 1/4 cups) tomatoes, diced
3/4 pound (1 1/2 cups) Arborio rice
Sea salt
Pepper
Extra-virgin olive oil

In a small bowl combine the pecorino, garlic, and parsley. Set aside.

In a large baking dish, arrange half the potatoes in a layer. Top with a layer of half the onions. Cover with half the diced tomatoes. Sprinkle half the rice on top, and then sprinkle on the pecorino mixture. Season with salt and pepper, and drizzle with olive oil.

Layer the remaining potatoes, onions, rice, and sprinkle on the remaining pecorino mixture. Top with the remaining tomatoes and season with salt and pepper. Pour about 1/2 cup water around the sides of the dish so it runs to the bottom. Bake in a preheated 350° oven for 40 minutes. Serve at room temperature.

MOTHER-IN-LAW'S CASSEROLE

Tiella della suocera

Serves 4

Ingredients

- Extra-virgin olive oil
- 10 ounces (1 1/2 cups) fresh or canned tomatoes, diced
- 1 pound potatoes, peeled and thinly sliced
- 2 medium eggplants, thinly sliced
- 2 yellow bell peppers, seeded and thinly sliced
- 1/2 pound mozzarella, diced
- Sea salt
- Pepper
- Basil leaves
- 4 tablespoons grated pecorino
- 4 tablespoons bread crumbs
- Fresh oregano

Lightly oil a large baking dish and arrange a layer of half the tomatoes in it. Then layer half these ingredients in this order: potatoes, eggplant, peppers, and mozzarella. Occasionally season with salt and pepper and toss in a few basil leaves as you go. Repeat the layers in the same order, finishing with the mozzarella, then the remaining half of the tomatoes.

In a small bowl, combine the pecorino and bread crumbs with fresh oregano, salt and pepper to taste. Sprinkle the mixture over the tomatoes and drizzle on some olive oil. Cook in a preheated 400° oven for about 1 hour.

The following recipes for marinated vegetables are used as side dishes and accompaniments to first courses.

*CANNING NOTE

Follow safe preserving procedures when making these recipes. Always put ingredients in sanitized, dry glass jars (boiled or put through a dishwasher). Cover jars using airtight, hermetically sealed lids. After opening the jars, always refrigerate them.

MARINATED MUSHROOMS

Funghi sott'olio

Ingredients

- Sea salt
- White wine vinegar
- 2 1/4 pounds mushrooms, preferably *ascuanti, amaretti*, and *chiodini* variety
- Mint leaves
- 1 clove garlic, minced
- *Peperoncino*, hot red chili pepper, roughly chopped
- Extra-virgin olive oil

In a large pot, prepare a mixture that's 1 part salted water for every 2 parts wine vinegar. Bring to a boil and boil the mushrooms for 2 to 3 minutes. Drain thoroughly. It's helpful to leave them weighted down for a few hours to get them to release every drop of liquid. Then

Prepared in this way, the mushrooms will keep for several months.

Tomatoes drying in the sun

transfer the mushrooms to glass jars with mint leaves, garlic, and a few pieces of chili. Add olive oil to cover* and let sit for a few days before eating.

*See Canning note

MARINATED TOMATOES
Pomodori sott'olio

Ingredients

- 2 1/4 pounds tomatoes
- Sea salt
- White wine vinegar
- Anchovies, rinsed, boned, and chopped
- 1 clove garlic, minced
- Capers
- *Peperoncino,* hot red chili pepper, roughly chopped
- Extra-virgin olive oil

Cut the tomatoes in half, sprinkle them with salt, and put them in the sun to dry for 5 days. Be sure to bring them in the house at night so that they don't acquire moisture overnight. Submerge the sun-dried tomatoes in a bowl of lukewarm wine vinegar and leave them there for 20 minutes.

Drain the tomatoes and arrange them in glass jars, interspersing the anchovies, garlic, capers, and chili. Add olive oil to cover.* Allow to rest 10 days before serving.

*See Canning note

MARINATED RAW EGGPLANT
Melanzane sott'olio crude

In earlier times, these eggplants were used to make very flavorful sandwiches, but today they are also served as side dishes for boiled meats or in mixed salads. They will keep a long time.

Ingredients

- 4 1/2 pounds eggplant (8 to 10 small), peeled and thinly sliced
- 1/2 pound (1 cup) sea salt, coarse ground
- White wine vinegar
- Mint leaves
- *Peperoncino,* hot red chili pepper, roughly chopped (optional)
- 1 clove garlic, minced
- Extra-virgin olive oil

If you get serious about preserving vegetables in olive oil, you'll need to amass a collection of 1 inch-thick wooden disks of various diameters that can be used for this purpose. [Now plastic is being used.]

Arrange the eggplant slices in layers in a large earthenware container that is tall but not very wide. Between every 2 or 3 layers, sprinkle 1/4 cup or so of sea salt. When all the slices have been layered, cover with an earthenware plate or a wooden cover that fits inside the mouth of the container and place a weight on top to press down to release their liquids. A pot of water works as a weight.

Set aside for 24 hours, then drain off all the liquid the eggplants have released and pour in wine vinegar to cover, all without disturbing the eggplant in the container. Replace the cover and the weight and set aside for an additional 12 hours. Then pour off all the wine vinegar and, working quickly to avoid the eggplant turning brown, remove and press the slices so they are as dry as possible, and then arrange them in wide-mouthed glass jars in layers, distributing mint leaves, chili (if using), and garlic between the layers.

Add enough olive oil to come to the mouth of the jars and cover.* Allow to rest for 15 days before serving.

*See Canning note

MARINATED COOKED EGGPLANT

Melanzane sott'olio cotte

Like the marinated uncooked eggplant, these are excellent as a side dish for boiled meats or as an ingredient in mixed salads. These are softer than the uncooked version, but they also keep for a shorter period.

Ingredients

- 2 quarts white wine vinegar
- 3 tablespoons sea salt, coarse ground
- 4 1/2 pounds eggplant (8 to 10 small), peeled and sliced about 1/4-inch thick
- Mint leaves
- 1 clove garlic, minced
- *Peperoncino,* hot red chili pepper, roughly chopped
- Extra-virgin olive oil

In a large pot, combine the wine vinegar and salt with 1 quart of water. Bring to a boil and submerge the eggplant for about 5 minutes. (If the pot is too crowded to cook all the eggplant slices at once, cook them in batches in the same liquid.) Remove the cooked eggplant with a strainer or skimmer and transfer to a colander to drain. It's helpful to weigh them down with something in order to release their juices thoroughly.

Arrange the cooked and drained eggplant slices in glass jars roughly the same diameter as the eggplants, interspersing the mint, garlic, and chili between the layers. Add enough olive oil to cover completely.* Allow to rest for at least 2 days before serving. *See Canning note

MARINATED RAW PEPPERS

Pilacca cruda

These are excellent as a side dish with boiled meats or as an accompaniment to fava bean purée.

Ingredients

4 1/2 pounds red bell peppers, stemmed, seeded, and diced
1 pound large spicy red peppers, stemmed, seeded, and diced, *or* 6 to 7 *peperoncino*, hot red chili peppers, dried and crushed (optional)
4 1/2 pounds celery, diced
2 cloves garlic, minced
1/2 pound (1 cup) sea salt, coarse ground
Extra-virgin olive oil
White wine vinegar

Put the peppers—either the spicy peppers or chili peppers if you prefer a hotter taste—and celery in an earthenware container with the garlic and salt.

Set aside to rest for 24 hours, stirring occasionally. Drain the mixture in a colander, then transfer it to a container large enough to hold it all. Add a little wine vinegar. Cover or place a weight on top to release their liquids, and allow to rest.

Drain off the wine vinegar and transfer the mixture to glass jars, then add olive oil to cover.* Allow to rest 10 days before serving.

*See Canning note

MARINATED COOKED PEPPERS

Pilacca cotta

This very spicy mixture is served with boiled meats. It is also good for adding a little flavor to a salad of air-dried tomatoes. A mere teaspoon will do the trick.

In earlier days, this was used in the sandwiches that farmers ate at around 9 a.m. A good glass of wine and some spicy sauce helped perk them up so they could perform another half-day of work.

Ingredients

2 1/4 pounds large spicy red peppers, stems removed, but peppers left whole
Extra-virgin olive oil
Sea salt
1 clove garlic, minced

Fry the peppers in olive oil and drain them. When the peppers have cooled, mince them in a food processor. Transfer the peppers to a large bowl and mix in a little salt and some garlic. Add olive oil and set aside for several days. Stir frequently with a wooden spoon. The peppers will ferment and their volume will increase.

When the fermentation process has stopped, transfer the peppers to glass jars and add enough olive oil to cover, but without allowing the oil to come all the way up to the mouths of the jars.*

*See Canning note

red chili peppers

Marinated Green Beans
Fagiolini sott'olio

These go well with any type of meat.

Ingredients

2 quarts white wine vinegar
3 tablespoons sea salt
2 1/4 pounds young tender green beans, trimmed
Mint leaves
2 cloves garlic, minced
Extra-virgin olive oil

Combine the wine vinegar, salt, and 1 quart of water in a large pot and bring to a boil. Add the green beans and cook 5 minutes. Remove the green beans and drain thoroughly. Transfer the cooked green beans to glass jars and intersperse them with mint leaves and garlic. Add olive oil to cover* and set aside to rest at least 10 days before eating.

*See Canning note

Marinated Artichokes
Carciofi sott'olio

Ingredients

Artichokes
Lemon juice
2 quarts white wine vinegar
3 tablespoons sea salt
Mint leaves
1 clove garlic, minced
Extra-virgin olive oil

Trim the artichokes, removing and discarding all their hard leaves until you have only those that are light-colored and tender. Cut off the stems and sharp tips of the artichokes, and then cut them in half and remove the "chokes." Cut the artichokes into quarters and place them in a bowl of acidulated water—made by adding lemon juice to water.

In a large pot, combine the wine vinegar and salt with 1 quart of water. Bring to a boil, then add the artichokes. Cook them in batches using the same liquid until tender, 4 to 5 minutes. Drain the artichokes in a colander with a weight (a pot of water, for example) resting on top of them to release their liquids.

Transfer the drained artichokes to glass jars, interspersing the mint leaves and garlic. Add olive oil to cover.*

*See Canning note

Marinated Mixed Vegetables

Giardiniera sott'olio

This is good as part of a vegetable salad, a rice salad, or as a side dish for boiled meats.

Ingredients

- 2 1/4 pounds eggplant, peeled and cut into matchsticks
- 2 1/4 pounds yellow bell peppers, seeded and cut into strips
- 2 1/4 pounds celery, diced
- 1 pound carrots, peeled and diced
- 1/2 pound (1 cup) sea salt
- White wine vinegar
- 2 cloves garlic, minced
- *Peperoncino*, hot red chili pepper, roughly chopped
- Mint leaves
- Extra-virgin olive oil

In an earthenware container, combine the eggplants, peppers, celery, and carrots. Stir in the salt and set aside for 12 hours, stirring occasionally. Drain the vegetable mixture then cover it with wine vinegar.

Set aside to rest another 6 hours, then drain again and place a weight on top of the mixture to release their liquids. Drain off any liquid that gets squeezed out, then transfer the vegetable mixture to a glass jars, interspersing the garlic, chili, and mint leaves, then cover with olive oil.* Allow to rest for at least 10 days.

*See Canning note

Marinated Fava Beans

Fave sott'olio

These are excellent with all kinds of meat and with insalata russa, *which is similar to coleslaw.*

Ingredients

- 2 1/4 pounds young fava beans
- 1 quart white wine vinegar
- 2 tablespoons sea salt, coarse ground
- Mint leaves
- *Peperoncino*, hot red chili pepper, minced [or dried flakes] to taste
- 1 clove garlic
- Extra-virgin olive oil

Shell the fava beans. Combine the wine vinegar, salt, and 2 cups of water in a large pot. Bring to a boil, then add the fava beans and cook 3 to 4 minutes. Drain well and transfer the fava beans to glass jars, interspersing the mint leaves, chili, and garlic. Add olive oil to cover* and allow to rest at least 10 days before serving.

*See Canning note

Marinated Peas

Piselli sott'olio

Prepare the peas exactly as you prepared the Marinated Fava Beans *(Fave sott'olio)* above and use them in the same way.*

*See Canning note

Evening Pastimes CIBI PASSATEMPO 

THE HOUSES of the wealthy had fireplaces, but they were not used for cooking. Instead, the whole family gathered around the fireplace in the evening to chat and to snack on what we might call "leisure foods." For example, in late autumn many houses had baskets of pinecones collected from the pine trees that graced their villas.

I remember very festive times —it really took very little to make us happy—when we went into the pantry and brought out pinecones and arranged them where they would feel the heat of the fireplace. That heat melted their pitch, and the pinecones began to crackle and open up to reveal their pine nuts. When this happened, they were removed from the heat of the fire and allowed to cool so the pine nuts could be harvested and distributed among everyone present.

First we shelled them with our incisors, and then we ate them greedily. Sometimes we were so anxious to eat the pine nuts that we didn't give them enough time to cool off and we burned our thumbs opening them. It was terribly disappointing to come across a pine nut with a hard shell, because you had to get up and use the nutcracker, and so you lost the magical rhythm of the moment, as well as the chance to feel the soft meat of the nut between your teeth.

We also cooked potatoes in the fireplace in the evenings by burying them under the ashes. And the supplies that the farmer brought to the "big houses" weekly always included fresh eggs. Some eggs were rinsed and then buried under hot ash. After five to six minutes they were ready to be eaten soft-cooked, and after fifteen minutes they were hard-cooked. There were actually "fireworks" of a sort when the eggs were cooking. Most of the time the eggshell couldn't take the heat and exploded, making an extremely loud noise. At least half the eggs placed under the ashes exploded and couldn't be eaten, because they were contaminated with ash. But the taste of a hard-cooked egg prepared in this way was so delicious that the idea of it being wasteful never occurred to us, despite the high number of fatalities.

When shelled, roasted eggs had a brownish color, like other roasted foods, and they gave off a whiff of smoke, which made them unique. Eggs boiled on the stovetop have a completely different taste.

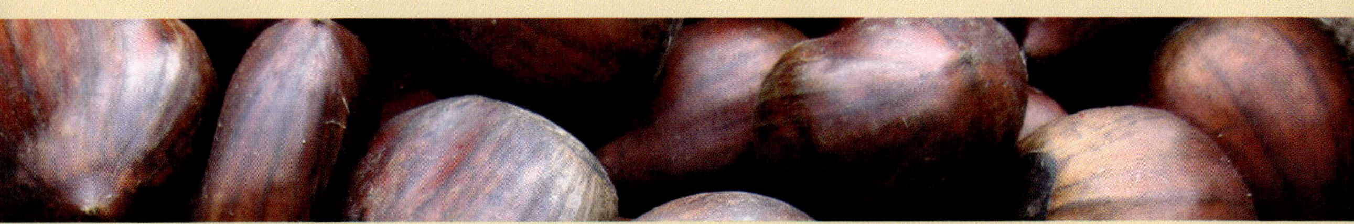

ANOTHER WAY to pass the time was to cook chestnuts. Some embers were gathered under a tripod, and then the chestnut pan—which had holes punched in the bottom—was balanced on the tripod. Older people patiently cut an X into the bottom of each chestnut so that they wouldn't explode when cooking. The chestnut ritual was just as carefully defined as the ritual for roasting and eating pine nuts.

Sometimes children were so eager that they would not wait for them to be cooked, and would grab a chestnut as soon as the shell began to curl back where the X had been cut.

That was how we passed our winter evenings, gathered around the fireplace with relatives and friends, telling each other stories. A good glass of red wine was the perfect accompaniment to our chatter.

Above: chestnuts

PUGLIAN TOWN NIGHT SCENE

Field Greens *Erbe Campestri*

MUCH of Puglia's cooking tradition includes greens that grow in the wild, such as *ciucredde* or *cicuredde* (chicory), traditionally served alongside fava beans. In Grottaglie they eat *zunguni,* which in Martina Franca are known as *sevòne* (barberry). These are greens with thick stems and fringed leaves that are cooked in broth or served with a drizzle of olive oil.

Senàpe, or mustard greens, have a spicy bite and are served with olive oil and lemon, or fried in oil with some garlic. *Prugghiàzza* (purslane) is a kind of lettuce with shiny oval leaves that are quite fleshy.

Lampasciuni or *vampascione* refer to wild grape-hyacinths whose small bulbs are called "wild onions," which are boiled, roasted, or cooked in sauce. Wild arugula, known in dialect as *rucòla* or *rûchele,* is a slightly spicy green that is eaten raw in salad, usually mixed with other greens, or is tossed with pasta.

Carduncieddi or *carduncidde* are dialect names for the Latin *cynara carduncultus;* these are wild cardoons with spiny leaves. Once the leaves have been removed, they're boiled and dressed with olive oil, or they may be fried with olive oil or butter. They are also prepared *arracanati,* or gratin-style, meaning they're sprinkled with bread crumbs and baked.

Wild asparagus has a very delicate, subtle taste. The tops are picked when very young and thin, and then boiled. They also make a wonderful frittata.

Wild fennel is used to flavor *taralli* as well as cured olives. *Marogghiele* are members of

Above: wild fennel

the dandelion family and quite bitter. Oregano can be found in the wild and is a necessary component of tomato salad. Capers, which go into a variety of dishes in Puglia, can also be foraged. Finally, *ciocce* or *apûdde,* or white wallrocket, is one of the least used of the field greens, which I find a great oversight. Boiled and dressed with oil and lemon or fried in olive oil, it is truly excellent.

Chicory Timbale

Timballo di cicuredde

Serves 4

This is a first course.

Ingredients

3 1/4 pounds wild chicory
Sea salt
Extra-virgin olive oil
1 onion slice
2 16-ounce cans tomato purée
6 ounces mozzarella, diced
2 hard-boiled eggs, diced
1/3 cup mortadella, diced
1/2 cup grated pecorino

Meatballs

6 ounces ground meat, veal and pork
1 egg
1 slice day-old country bread (remove crust, sprinkle with water, squeeze dry, and tear into small pieces)
1 tablespoon grated pecorino
Sea salt
Pepper

Wash the greens carefully, cook them al dente in a large pot of salted water, and drain well.

Meanwhile, in a skillet, heat the olive oil and fry the onion slice, removing and discarding it when it browns. Then add the tomato purée and cook until thick.

To make the meatballs, combine the ground meat, egg, bread, and pecorino in a mixing bowl and season with salt and pepper. Mix with your hands to combine thoroughly. Make hazelnut-size meatballs, then fry them in oil in another skillet and set aside.

Fresh tomato purée: blanch and peel tomatoes, then purée them through a food mill.

In a bowl, combine the cooked greens with about 1 cup of the tomato sauce and abundant pecorino. Spread about 1/2 cup of tomato sauce on the bottom of a baking dish, then spread half the greens evenly over it. Top the greens with half the mozzarella, 1 diced egg, and half the mortadella. Arrange half of the meatballs on top, and then sprinkle on some pecorino and spread on additional tomato sauce. Make another layer of the remaining greens. Top with the remaining mozzarella, egg, and mortadella. Top that with the remaining meatballs, and then sprinkle on pecorino and top with the remaining tomato sauce.

Bake in a preheated 400° oven until the top is nicely browned, about 30 minutes. Serve warm, but not piping hot.

VEGETABLE SOUP

Minestra maritata di verdure

Serves 4

Ingredients

3 pounds wild chicory or wild chicory tops, trimmed and rinsed
Sea salt
1 1/2 tablespoons butter
1 clove garlic
1 cup diced tomatoes
2 cups broth
4 slices semolina/country bread
2 tablespoons grated *Parmigiano-Reggiano*
3 tablespoons extra-virgin olive oil

Boil the greens in a large pot of salted water. Drain well. In a wide earthenware pot, melt the butter and then cook the garlic. As soon as the garlic begins to brown, remove and discard it, then add the tomatoes. Cook the sauce until it is very thick, and then add the cooked greens. Cook an additional 10 minutes. Bring the broth to a boil.

Toast the bread slices and place them on the bottom of 4 soup bowls. Spoon some greens and tomato sauce over the bread, then ladle boiling broth into each bowl. Sprinkle with *Parmigiano-Reggiano* and drizzle with olive oil.

Layered Chicory Soup

Ciucredde azzise

Serves 4

The word azzise means "seated down" in dialect and refers to placing the ingredients in layers.

Ingredients

2 1/4 pounds wild chicory or barberry (or cultivated escarole if these aren't available), trimmed and rinsed
6 cups beef broth
4 tablespoons grated pecorino
2 ounces mortadella, diced
1 slice semolina/country bread, cubed
Extra-virgin olive oil

Meatballs

6 ounces ground meat, veal and pork
1 egg yolk
Sea salt
Pepper

To make the meatballs, combine the ground meat and egg yolk in a bowl using your hands and season with salt and pepper. Form into hazelnut-sized meatballs and set aside.

Cook the greens in a large pot of boiling salted water until al dente. Drain the greens well. Pour the broth into a pot and bring to a boil.

Meanwhile, in a heavy-bottomed casserole, make a layer of the cooked greens. Top with some of the pecorino, some mortadella, and some uncooked meatballs. Continue to layer the greens with the other ingredients in this order until you have used them up. Pour in the boiling broth, and cook 10 minutes.

Brown the cubes of bread in olive oil in a non-stick skillet. To serve, put a few croutons in each soup bowl, then ladle the soup over the bread. Season with pepper and serve piping hot.

ROASTED "WILD ONION" BULBS*

Lampascioni alla pignatta

Serves 4

Ingredients

2 1/4 pounds "wild onion" bulbs
Extra-virgin olive oil
Sea salt
Pepper

Cut off the roots of the onion bulbs and wash them without peeling them. Dry the onions and put them in an earthenware pot. Plug the mouth of the pot tightly with a large crumpled brown paper bag and place the pot in the oven, preferably a wood-burning oven, upside-down. Roast for at least 2 hours. When the onions are easily pierced with a fork, take them out of the oven, peel them, and season with olive oil, salt, and pepper. Eat piping hot.

**Lampasciuni* or *vampascione* refer to wild grape-hyacinths whose small bulbs are called "wild onions."

SWEET AND SOUR "WILD ONION" BULBS

Lampascioni agrodolci

Serves 4

Ingredients

2 1/4 pounds "wild onion" bulbs
Sea salt
6 tablespoons extra-virgin olive oil
1 clove garlic
3 tablespoons white wine vinegar
2 teaspoons sugar
2 tablespoons capers

Peel the bulbs, cut off their roots, and cut an X into the base of each onion. Boil them in a large pot of salted water for about 45 minutes. Drain well. Add the olive oil to a large skillet and brown the onions and the garlic, removing the garlic when browned. Then add the wine vinegar, sugar, and capers. Cook until the wine vinegar has completely evaporated. Roast in a hot oven for a few minutes, if desired.

"WILD ONION" BULB FRITTATA

Frittata di lampascioni

Serves 4

Ingredients

1 1/4 pounds "wild onion" bulbs
Sea salt
5 eggs
2 tablespoons grated *Parmigiano-Reggiano*
2 tablespoons grated pecorino
Fresh flat-leaf parsley, chopped
Pepper
5 to 6 tablespoons extra-virgin olive oil

Peel the bulbs and trim away their roots. With a paring knife cut an X in the base of each onion. Boil in a large pot of salted water for 45 minutes.

Beat the eggs together with the *Parmigiano-Reggiano*, pecorino, and parsley. Season with salt and pepper.

When the onions are cooked and have cooled, drain them and transfer them to a bowl, then mash them roughly with a fork. Stir them into the egg mixture.

Heat the olive oil in a skillet with low sides or an omelette pan and pour in the egg mixture. Cook over high heat for 1 minute, then turn the heat down and cover the pan with a lid. Cook 4 to 5 minutes, making sure that the bottom of the frittata browns nicely. (Check by lifting the edge with a fork occasionally.) Flip the frittata, return it to the pan, and cook for 1 minute over high heat, then turn the heat down and cook 4 to 5 minutes, uncovered. Serve at room temperature.

"WILD ONION" BULBS* IN SAUCE

Lampascioni al sugo

Serves 4

These work as either an appetizer or a side dish.

Ingredients

2 1/4 pounds "wild onion" bulbs
Sea salt
6 tablespoons extra-virgin olive oil
1 clove garlic
6 ounces (about 3/4 cup) tomato purée
Peperoncino, hot red chili pepper, sliced [or dried flakes] to taste
2 tablespoons capers

Peel the bulbs. Trim away their roots and with a paring knife cut an X into the base of each onion. Rinse them and boil them in a pot of salted water for 45 minutes. Drain well.

In a large skillet, heat the olive oil and add the garlic. When the garlic just begins to brown, remove it and add the onions. Brown them well, then add the tomato purée, chili, and capers. Cook 15 additional minutes.

**Lampasciuni* or *vampascione* refer to wild grape-hyacinths whose small bulbs are called "wild onions."

WILD ASPARAGUS FRITTATA

Frittata di asparagi di campo

Serves 4

This can be either a light second course or an appetizer.

Ingredients

10 ounces wild asparagus tips
5 eggs
5 tablespoons grated pecorino
Sea salt
Pepper
4 tablespoons extra-virgin olive oil

Boil the asparagus tips in a pot of salted water for 3 to 4 minutes. Drain thoroughly. In a bowl, beat the eggs with the pecorino and season with salt and pepper. Stir in the cooked asparagus.

Heat the olive oil in a skillet with low sides or an omelette pan and pour in the egg mixture. Cook over high heat for 1 minute, then turn the heat down to low and cook 3 to 4 additional minutes. Flip the frittata, return it to the pan, and cook over high heat for 1 minute, then turn the heat down to low and cook 3 to 4 additional minutes. Serve immediately.

Keep in mind that you will lose much of the asparagus when you clean it, as the stems are basically useless. You should have 10 ounces of asparagus after cleaning them. Use your hands, rather than a knife, to trim them and snap off any part that doesn't feel tender.

WILD ASPARAGUS WITH EGGS

Uova con asparagi di campo

Serves 4

This is a second course.

Ingredients

10 ounces wild asparagus tips
Sea salt
2 tablespoons extra-virgin olive oil
1 tablespoon butter
Pepper
4 eggs

Boil the asparagus tips in a pot of salted water for 3 to 4 minutes. Drain thoroughly.

In a rectangular baking dish with a lid, fry the asparagus tips in the olive oil and butter and season with pepper. Arrange the asparagus tips in a single layer using a spoon to arrange them so there are 4 small empty spaces between groups so you can see the bottom of the dish. Crack an egg into each of these empty spaces, taking care not to break the yolk. Season with salt and cover for 2 or 3 minutes. Serve piping hot.

Mushrooms I Funghi

Numerous types of mushrooms grow in the woods in the southern part of Puglia. The most common are called *funge asckuante*. In local dialect this means "burning mushrooms" because these mushrooms have a bitter and slightly spicy flavor. In order to tame that flavor, they are boiled and then water-cured for a few of days, at which point they can be prepared in any number of ways.

Expert mushroom gourmets prefer to place them uncooked, stem side up, on large unglazed ceramic plates and then roast them. The unglazed ceramic material absorbs the bitter liquid from the mushrooms, and once the mushrooms are cooked they are served hot with olive oil, salt, and pepper—truly delicious.

Other mushrooms found in this area include *palummini*, which are beautiful to look at because their brightly colored caps range from yellow to red to purple. There isn't much demand for these, and yet when cooked in tomato sauce they have a delicate flavor which enhances spaghetti. There are also *cardilli* (chanterelles), *cappellacci*, and *spugnette* (morels), which are small and look like clusters of yellowish coral.

Amaretti mushrooms taste very similar to *funge asckuante,* but are smaller. They are best marinated in olive oil. *Chiodini* mushrooms, so-called because they take the shape of a nail, *chiodo,* grow profusely in pine woods in the area. They are found in large numbers and are not much appreciated by gourmets, but when marinated in olive oil they make an excellent side dish. Brown-capped *menetole* (boleti) grow in those same pine woods. The spongy yellow substance hidden under their caps needs to be removed before they are cooked. They're somewhat soft and are best fried or used in risotto.

Cuppetedde is a white, medium-sized mushroom that can be cooked using any method and is loved for its delicate flavor and meaty texture. The most highly valued mushroom is the *fungo di pezza,* which is brownish. These grow in plowed fields and have a firm texture. They are usually sliced thinly and fried with garlic and parsley, but they also make a sauce that is excellent with spaghetti. Another highly valued mushroom is the *u carduncidd* or *cardoncello,* which is similar to the *fungo di pezza.*

In earlier times, mushroom hunters gathered to sell their wares at sundown, usually in a small piazza close to the town market. Putignano, Turi, Alberobello, Locorotondo, and, of course, Martina Franca were a source for high-quality mushrooms. Buyers came from surrounding towns and picked up enough mushrooms to last through the winter. There is still great demand for mushrooms today, but much fewer are available, and prices are sky-high.

Today, the woods are invaded not only by professional mushroom hunters but also those who use mushroom hunting as an excuse to relax in the open air. Their enthusiasm is understandable as mushroom hunting is fun. The hunter carries a stick and moves it around among the leaves that collect at the base of trees and in the bushes, inspecting every inch of earth. When an entire family of mushrooms, all joined together, is discovered, there is much celebration as the hunter grabs for them.

Foraging for field greens is another useful excuse for escaping from the house. On holidays and Sundays, hundreds of people can be seen along the sides of roads in the countryside, in the woods, and in fields—all gathering chicory, arugula, barberry, and other wild edibles. Once home, foragers begin the ritual of cleaning greens and the delicate work of removing any grit or soil from the mushrooms. Very elite mushroom hunters will even dedicate themselves to the painstaking work of removing every speck of dirt from their mushrooms by hand rather than rinsing them in order not to dilute their flavor.

In the days before freezers, when mushrooms were truly abundant, they could be kept in ceramic containers, with a large amount of sea salt sprinkled over them. They kept for a long time this way. When you wanted some mushrooms, you took out as many as you needed, boiled them, and then cooked them any way you liked. Another classic method for preserving mushrooms was to boil them in a mixture of salted water and white wine vinegar. The mushrooms were then drained and marinated in oil.

ROASTED MUSHROOMS

Funghi asckuanti arrostiti

Serves 4

Ingredients

1 1/4 pounds *asckuanti* mushrooms
1/2 cup extra-virgin olive oil
Sea salt
Pepper

Arrange the mushrooms on their caps on unglazed ceramic plates and bake in a preheated 425° oven for about 30 minutes.

Meanwhile, pour the olive oil into a bowl and season with salt and pepper. When the mushrooms are wrinkled but still meaty, remove them from the oven, then quickly dice them (they cool quickly). Toss them with the olive oil mixture. Serve hot.

MUSHROOM GRATIN

Funghi arracanati o ammollicati

Serves 4

Ingredients

1 1/4 pounds *coppetelle or* May mushrooms
7 tablespoons fine bread crumbs
2 ounces grated pecorino
1 clove garlic, minced
Fresh flat-leaf parsley, chopped
Sea salt
Pepper
Extra-virgin olive oil

For this dish you can use *coppetelle*, May mushrooms, *asckuanti* mushrooms, or *amaretti*.

Clean the mushrooms and remove and discard their stems. Arrange the mushrooms upside down in a baking dish. In a small bowl, combine the bread crumbs, pecorino, garlic, and parsley and season with salt and pepper. Sprinkle this mixture over the mushrooms. Drizzle with olive oil and bake in a preheated 425° oven for about 30 minutes.

STUFFED MUSHROOMS

Funghi ripieni

Serves 4

These may be served as a second course or intermediate course.

Ingredients

1 1/4 pounds *coppetelle or* May mushrooms
6 ounces ground lean meat, veal and pork
1 egg yolk
3 1/2 ounces mozzarella, minced
2 ounces *prosciutto cotto,* minced
2 tablespoons grated pecorino or *Parmigiano-Reggiana*
Fresh flat-leaf parsley, chopped
1 pinch grated nutmeg
2 slices whole wheat bread (remove crusts, moisten with water, squeeze dry, and tear into small pieces)
Sea salt
Pepper
Extra-virgin olive oil

Clean the mushrooms, then remove and discard their stems. In a bowl, combine the meat, egg yolk, mozzarella, *prosciutto cotto*, grated cheese, parsley, nutmeg, and bread. Season with salt and pepper. Fill the mushroom caps with this mixture and arrange the caps in a baking dish.

Pour about 1/2 cup of water around the edge of the dish so that the water runs to the bottom. Drizzle on olive oil and bake in a preheated 425° oven for about 30 minutes.

In Puglia, this dish is usually made with a variety called *coppetelle* or May mushrooms, and those are the best choice to obtain the best flavor.

If you can't find those, however, you can try using the caps of button mushrooms.

MUSHROOMS WITH EGGS

Funghi ripieni di uova

Serves 4

This makes an excellent light intermediate course.

Ingredients

1 1/4 pounds *coppetelle or* May mushrooms
3 eggs
4 tablespoons grated pecorino
Fresh flat-leaf parsley, chopped
Sea salt
Pepper
Extra-virgin olive oil

Clean the mushrooms and remove and discard their stems. In a small bowl, beat together the eggs, cheese, and parsley. Season with salt and pepper. This mixture should be relatively stiff. If it is too liquid, add some fine bread crumbs a little at a time.

Oil a baking dish and arrange the mushrooms upside down and very close to each other. There should be very little space between them. Pour the egg mixture over them and bake in a preheated 425° oven for about 30 minutes.

For this dish, too, *coppetelle* or May mushrooms are the best choice. Since these mushrooms are relatively sweet, they can be substituted—albeit inadequately—with cultivated mushrooms.

Flat-leaf parsley

MUSHROOMS WITH PARSLEY

Funghi trifolati

Serves 4

You can use any type of mushroom you like in this recipe, but the best results are achieved with *funghi di pezza* and *carduncidd/ cardoncello*. One nice variation calls for adding 2 or 3 cherry tomatoes when the mushrooms are halfway cooked.

Ingredients

1 pound mushrooms
2/3 cup extra-virgin olive oil
1 clove garlic
Sea salt
Fresh flat-leaf parsley, chopped

Clean the mushrooms and cut them into small pieces. In a skillet, heat the olive oil and add the garlic. When the garlic begins to color, remove and discard it. Add the mushrooms. Cook until the mushrooms have given up all their liquid and the liquid has evaporated. Season with salt and sprinkle on parsley.

MUSHROOMS WITH TOMATOES

Funghi al pomodoro

Serves 4

This can be served as a second course.

All kinds of mushrooms work here, although I'd go with *funghi di pezza* or *carduncidd/ cardoncello*.

Ingredients

1 1/4 pounds mushrooms
2/3 cup extra-virgin olive oil
1 clove garlic
About 10 fresh cherry tomatoes or air-dried tomatoes, chopped
Sea salt
Pepper
Fresh flat-leaf parsley, minced

Clean the mushrooms and chop them into small pieces. Heat the olive oil in a skillet and add the garlic. When the garlic begins to color, remove and discard it. Add the mushrooms and when they have given up all their liquid, add the tomatoes. Season with salt and pepper and cook until the mixture has thickened slightly. Add the parsley, then remove from heat.

MUSHROOM FRITTERS

Funghi in pastella

Serves 4

Ingredients

1 pound mushrooms
Extra-virgin olive oil
1 egg
1 1/2 cups flour
Sea salt
Pepper

Clean the mushrooms, removing any spongy substance under their caps if the variety you are using has any, then chop them roughly. Heat a generous amount of olive oil in a large pot. Meanwhile, in a mixing bowl, beat the egg with 3/4 cup water. Whisk in the flour a little at a time until you have a fairly runny batter (you may not use all the flour). Season with salt and pepper then toss the mushroom pieces into the batter. Drop the mushrooms about 1 teaspoon at a time into the oil. Serve hot.

For this recipe you can use any type of mushroom except *palummini (Russula), funghi di pezza,* or *carduncidd.* In Puglia, this is usually made with a variety known as *menetole.*

FRIED MUSHROOMS

Funghi fritti

Serves 4

Ingredients

1 pound mushrooms
Extra-virgin olive oil
2 eggs
Sea salt
Pepper
Flour for dredging

Clean the mushrooms well and chop roughly. Set out a plate of flour for dredging. In a mixing bowl, beat the eggs and season them with salt and pepper. Dredge the mushrooms first in flour, then in eggs. Heat a generous amount of olive oil in a large skillet. Fry the mushrooms in the olive oil and serve hot.

SNAILS PATEDDE E CUZZEDDE

SNAILS—gastropod mollusks—are a longstanding part of Puglia's culinary tradition. Small snails have variegated shells that range from gray to light brown and are very small, so much so that in the Salento area they are called a name I find truly funny—the same name they are given in English, "baby shells."

They cling in groups to the stalks of herbaceous plants. In the right climate, they proliferate rapidly. Their natural habitat in Puglia is extensive, but some say that the seashore climate produces the tastiest baby snails. In fact, those who sell small snails on street corners (there are still a few vendors dedicated solely to small snails, but fewer every year) often put special emphasis on their origin by shouting "sea snails!"

Children and adults are on a level playing field when it comes to collecting small snails. This activity requires neither knowledge nor ability. Everyone has the same opportunity to fill his or her basket or another container as quickly as possible.

TO BE CLEANED, small snails are placed in a covered container for a few days. A weight is placed on top of the cover—otherwise the animals escape and invade the house. When it's time to cook snails, they are rinsed in running water and then cooked over low heat in a pan of cold water. The pan is covered and cooked over low heat for about ten minutes after the water comes to a boil. Finally, the small snails are rinsed again in cold water and then boiled again in a saltwater. They then can be prepared in a variety of ways, with tomato sauce or with olive oil, garlic, and oregano.

Eating these requires experience and skill, as well as an eagle eye and perseverance. If the snail is already outside of the shell, it's easy to eat. All you have to do is bite down and it's all over. But if the snail has had a chance to withdraw back into its shell, the issue becomes more complicated. This is where a true snail aficionado earns his or her stripes. Here's what you do: pinch the snail between two fingers, move it close to your mouth, and put it as precisely as possible between your upper and lower incisors on one side. Apply light pressure, which should make two small holes in the shell without breaking it. Then all you

view of Gargano coast

have to do is suck on it, and the mussel meat will come out of the shell along with any sauce.

Of course, not everyone likes small snails, and some people outright refuse even to be present when they're being eaten. True lovers of small snails hear the loud sucking sound that consuming them requires as a kind of music. When several people are punching holes in the shells with their teeth and enjoying small snails it does seem like a concert, although I will admit that it's a performance of a type of music that can be a little disturbing for the first-time listener. In short, no matter how delicious, I suggest you do not include them on the menu of any kind of formal meal.

Large snails (called "earth snails" in Italian) on the other hand have found their way onto restaurant menus. They are available everywhere in Puglia throughout the year, as they are now cultivated on a grand scale. In the past, though, these brown-shelled gastropods were pretty rare, because it was hard to find them and hard to harvest them. In fact, they hid underneath brier bushes and other thorny bushes—and sometimes, instead of a whole big family of snails, one would find a wasps' nest! Snail harvesters carried cloves of garlic with them to rub on any insect stings.

When snails hide underground, they produce a protective *panna*, a white film. Snails covered in this film can be eaten without going through the lengthy cleaning process that they otherwise require. All you have to do to roast snails with film is place them directly on a grate over an open fire and salt them generously. Real snail lovers will even eat them raw. They're delicious in tomato sauce as well—but if freshwater snails are going to be cooked in sauce they will need the little lids *(opercolo)* that cover the shells' openings removed and be salted.

In early fall and right after summer storms, these snails wake from hibernation, leave behind their white film, and run (well, in a manner of speaking) for the fields. This is why they are also known as "running snails." Many people in Puglia used to spend half the summer season and much of the fall in the countryside. Each time the rain stopped, every member of the family—including children—put on old shoes and went out into the fields to gather snails. This was one of the rare moments when children could get covered in dirt without being punished for it.

I have a sharp memory of the wonderful smell of wet soil mixed with the smell of snails. Snails without film were cured for forty-eight hours in closed containers with large amounts of bran. They ate the bran, which didn't have a strong flavor, so when they were eaten they had an extra delicate flavor. The snails were carefully cleaned and rubbed with sea salt in order to eliminate any slime. In Puglia, snails are never served out of their shells the way they are in France and parts of northern Italy.

OLIVES LE OLIVE

ALTHOUGH the scarcity of water has always been a problem in Puglia, it has led to widespread farming of grapes and olives, since both adapt well to arid conditions. Today, about thirty percent of the olive oil produced in Italy comes from Puglia.

Large fields of olive trees are a constant everywhere in Puglia, but each part of the region has its own trees. In the Bari area, olive trees are pruned so that their branches grow downward, and the crown remains flat even as the trees grow in height and their twisted branches come to resemble wonderfully creative sculptures. This makes it easier to pick the olives and the distant branches allow the sun's rays to pass through easily and ripen the olives quickly.

In the southern part of the Murgia area and in the Salento area, branches are allowed to develop more naturally, so the tree crown is full and impressive. The crown of an olive tree is twenty to twenty-five feet in diameter. Before the invention of the net and mechanical shaker system, harvesting olives required months of work. Remember that olive trees were also planted in inaccessible areas, which was why women—women were the olive harvesters, because they could be paid much less than men—sometimes had to climb up on cliffs and precipices to reach them. Beginning in September, any women over the age of twelve could help out her family, first by picking grapes, and then by picking olives. If you asked a girl what her plans for the following day were, you were likely to hear *agghia scè all'alìe,* dialect for "I have to go pick olives."

These workers left home at dawn, wrapped in old winter coats, their legs covered in thick wool stockings, sturdy shoes on their feet. Each one wore one handkerchief tied on her forehead and another to protect her ears. Each carried a wicker basket (*lu panarieddo*) that was the tool of the trade. Olives were put in that basket, and then once the basket was full they were poured into burlap bags. For a very small amount of money, these women braved the cold of early morning. The sight of them was truly heart-wrenching. By the time they returned home in the evening their hands were red and their backs were aching, and usually they still had to do housework. Yet seeing them work like this was so normal to us that when the first attempts at "modernization" were introduced in the 1950s, some eyed them with barely concealed hostility. Women began to wear pants, jackets, plastic boots, gloves, and even sunglasses. Many interpreted these changes as early signs of the disintegration of the social fabric.

Unlike olives that were to be used to make oil, those that were intended to be eaten were not beaten free from the trees, but were picked by hand. First came the green olives that would be cured with caustic soda flavored with fennel seeds and bay leaves, and then preserved in brine. There is a wide variety of these available in stores today, but I've never found any that taste as good as those cured at home—bright green, just soft enough, but meaty, too, with a wonderful aroma and moderate saltiness.

Curing green olives wasn't easy; they went bad frequently, turning soft and smelly if they did not sit in the caustic soda solution for the right amount of time. I recall entire tubs of green olives that were thrown in the garbage, to the dismay of the whole family. At my house, we frequently messed up preparation of the olives. When that happened, we ate the olives cured by my maternal grandmother and my aunt Giuseppina—those were always perfect.

When green olives are fully ripe they become black olives, which can be pierced with a fork, salted heavily, and then left in the sun, where they shrivel up. This has also earned them the name *olive morte*, "dead olives." This process can be accelerated by putting them in the oven for a few hours at a low temperature.

As unripe or ripe as they are, olives can never be eaten right off the tree because of their natural bitterness. There is one exception to this rule—what we call "bruised olives," meaning those that fall off the tree by themselves and sit on the ground for a while. As these olives sit, the wind and sun dry them out and make them sweet. You won't find them for sale in any store, because they are eaten by the olive pickers or the people who own the land. We even have a saying based on them. We say, *s'è spiritoso come n'alìa maccata,* or "you're as witty as a bruised olive," meaning dried up and not witty at all.

Olives are eaten in large quantities in Puglia, where they add their punchy flavor to many dishes. Many types of olives are used, including those usually grown for extra-virgin olive oil. Small yellowish green olives and dark purple olives in brine are found for sale everywhere in Puglia.

Every house in Puglia, especially farmers' houses and those of landowners, is equipped with a *capasone,* a big clay jar with a wide mouth that is used to store water-cured black olives. The supply lasts all year.

Olives are left to rest for about fifteen days in fresh water that is changed several times a day, then they are transferred to the *capasone* and covered with salted water with a few lemon wedges and bay leaves. It takes at least two months for them to ripen completely. During that time they get even sweeter and take on a slightly acidic taste.

Olives will always have a faint bitter edge to them, but if they're really well-prepared they will be excellent both in a variety of dishes and eaten out of hand. They pair especially well with fava beans.

Another method for preparing olives is to blanch them in boiling water, then dry them and fry them with a little extra-virgin olive oil and salt. They shrivel up and have an extra-sharp bitter edge. These are known as "fried olives."

Aunt Giuseppina's Olives

Olive di zia Giuseppina

Ingredients

10 ounces caustic soda
22 pounds large green olives

Brine

1/4 cup fennel seeds
3 sprigs myrtle
20 fresh bay leaves
4 teaspoons salt

Fill a small plastic container with warm water and use a wooden spoon to stir in the caustic soda until it has dissolved. Fill a glazed ceramic container with 10 quarts cold water, then add the mixture. Set aside until the liquid has cooled completely, then add the olives, stirring frequently with a wooden spoon.

Soak the olives 3 to 4 hours, depending on their size. To test whether the olives have soaked long enough, scoop one out with a wooden spoon and pierce it with your fingernail. When the olives are ready, the olive flesh should come away from the pit easily.

At this point, drain off the liquid and keep the olives in fresh cold water for about 1 week, changing the water at least twice a day.

To prepare the brine, combine in a stockpot 5 quarts of water, the fennel seeds, myrtle, bay leaves, and salt, then bring to a boil. Boil for a few minutes and set aside to cool.

When the brine is cool, transfer the olives to [sanitized] glass jars and strain the brine over them. Hermetically seal the jars and let the olives rest for at least 10 days before eating them.

Left: olive grove

GREEN OLIVE SALAD

Insalata di olive verdi

Ingredients

1 pound large green olives in brine, pitted
1 bunch celery, minced
3 anchovies, rinsed, boned, and minced
1 tablespoon capers
2 *peperoncini*, hot red chili peppers, chopped, to taste
1 clove garlic, minced
Sea salt
1 tablespoon white wine vinegar
Extra-virgin olive oil

In a large bowl combine the olives, celery, anchovies, capers, chili, and garlic. Season with salt, the wine vinegar, and a generous amount of olive oil. Stir to combine thoroughly then set aside to rest for at least 2 hours before serving.

Olives at market

OLIVE ROLLS

Uliate (pane con olive)

Ingredients

3/4 cup small black olives, pitted and chopped
1 cake yeast [or 1 package active dry yeast]
3 cups flour
1 tablespoon salt

Toss the olives with about 1 tablespoon of the flour and set aside. Dissolve the yeast in 3/4 cup of lukewarm water. Make a dough with the remaining flour, the dissolved yeast, and the salt. Knead in the olives. Divide the dough into small pieces, shape into rolls, and place the rolls on a greased baking sheet. Cover and set aside to rise for 1 hour. Bake in a preheated 475° oven until golden brown.

If at all possible, bake in a wood-burning oven. It gives the bread much better flavor.

BLACK OLIVES WITH ANCHOVIES

Olive nere con acciughe

Ingredients

1 pound Greek-style black olives (in brine), pitted
4 anchovies, rinsed, boned, and minced
2 *peperoncini,* hot red chili peppers, chopped, to taste
1 clove garlic, minced
1 tablespoon white wine vinegar
Extra-virgin olive oil

Prick the olives with a fork and put them in a large bowl. Add the anchovies, chili, and garlic. Dress with the wine vinegar, drizzle on some olive oil, and stir vigorously. Set aside to rest 12 hours before serving.

ONION, TOMATO, AND OLIVE ROLLS

Pucce

Ingredients

5 tablespoons extra-virgin olive oil
3 scallions, cut up
3 ripe tomatoes, peeled and chopped
3/4 cup water-cured black olives, pitted and chopped
Sea salt
1 cake yeast [or 1 package active dry yeast]
3 cups flour

In a pan, heat the olive oil and fry the scallions. Add the tomatoes. Cook, stirring constantly, then add the olives and a pinch of salt. Cook for a few minutes, then set aside to cool.

Meanwhile, dissolve the yeast in 3/4 cup lukewarm water and make a dough of the flour, yeast mixture, and some salt. Knead the cooled vegetable mixture into the dough. Divide the dough into small pieces, shape into rolls, and place the rolls on a greased baking sheet. Cover and set aside to rise for at least 1 hour. Bake in a preheated 475° oven until golden brown.

If possible, bake in a wood-burning oven. Sometimes zucchini slices are included in the vegetable mixture.

TOMATO AND OLIVE SALAD

Insalata di pomodori e olive

Ingredients

1 pound salad tomatoes, sliced
10 ounces Greek-style black olives (in brine), pitted and halved
1 clove garlic, minced
Peperoncino, hot red chili pepper, sliced, to taste
Sea salt
Extra-virgin olive oil
Fresh oregano

In a serving bowl combine the tomatoes, olives, garlic, and chili. Season with salt, drizzle on some olive oil, and add a small amount of oregano. Mix to combine.

OLIVES AND CACIORICOTTA

Olive e cacioricotta

Ingredients

10 ounces Greek-style black olives (in brine), pitted
10 ounces *cacioricotta,** crumbled
Peperoncino, hot red chili pepper, chopped, to taste
Fresh oregano
Sea salt
Extra-virgin olive oil

In a serving bowl combine the olives, cheese, and chili. Season with oregano and salt, then drizzle on some olive oil. Mix to combine thoroughly and set aside to rest for a few minutes before serving.

*A local cheese (see page 16). A bright white farmer's "basket" cheese hard enough for grating is an alternative.

Olive Oil L'olio

Today, olives for making olive oil are either hand-picked, shaken off, or beaten off the trees. With any method, the ground around the bottom of the tree, equivalent in diameter to its crown, is first lined with plastic sheets or tight-knit nets.

The best method for picking olives is still picking them by hand, which allows one to select only the ripest and healthiest looking olives and then place them carefully into a basket so as not to squash them. In some places olives are picked by hand and dropped onto a sheet or raked up off the branches, but those methods don't keep as many olives intact as hand-picking does.

Other methods, such as shaking or beating the trees, can be performed by people or machinery. These methods are less costly, but they also risk bruising or damaging olives and, worse, they result in a harvest of olives at all different levels of ripeness, which means the resulting olive oil is of lesser quality.

In Puglia, the *Coratine* and *Frantoio* olive varieties are most commonly used to make extra-virgin olive oil. The olives must be processed as quickly as possible after being picked, or they begin to ferment and their taste changes. The most common types of olive mill are roller mills and hammer mills. A roller mill, by far the most common, consists of a tub that holds the olives and two rolling stone or granite pieces that crush them.

The resulting olive paste, or "olive must," as it is called, is spun, clarified, and filtered, and the result is extra-virgin olive oil. The best extra-virgin olive oil is no more than one degree oleic acid, but oils that go as high as three degrees can still be quite good.

Extra-virgin olive oil is judged also by color and clarity. Green extra-virgin olive oil deserves mention, too. Green extra-virgin olive oil is made by pressing olives grown mainly in the Bari area. It has a strong and bitter flavor and some find it hard to swallow—literally—but it is considered a very special olive oil to be used raw on legumes and bruschetta. Despite its strong flavor, it is not particularly acidic.

In Puglia, every family acquires olive oil, flour, legumes, and wine by going directly to the

source. To purchase extra-virgin olive oil, they go to the mill and pick an oil after tasting it with a spoon or drizzled on a piece of bread. Everyone exits the mill smelling strongly of olive oil; indeed, it's hard to shake the smell of oil and olive residue that permeates such mills.

Extra-virgin olive oil is more expensive than other oils, but it is much preferred in Puglia. It is even used for frying, which can seem like an expensive proposition, since such a large amount of oil is used. It is actually cost-effective in the end, however, as extra-virgin olive oil can be used for frying two or three different times without its flavor being affected. Foods fried in extra-virgin olive oil taste the same whether eaten hot or cold, whereas foods fried in seed oils tend to develop an unpleasant smell and taste as they cool. Olive oil is used in large quantities in Puglia for bottling and jarring foods.

Because extra-virgin olive oil is undeniably expensive, in earlier times it was sometimes replaced with pork fat or lard, but never with butter. Today, however, these animal fats are rarely used and when they do appear it is mainly in baked goods.

Tops of trulli

TRULLI I TRULLI

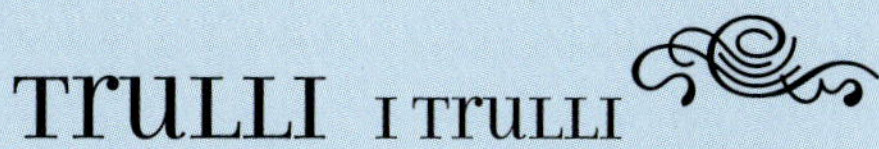

THE OLIVE TREE has been considered sacred since ancient times. No wonder, then, that men built their first homes in olive groves, in order to protect themselves from bad weather and to store their tools and the items they'd harvested.

Naturally, when it was time to build these structures, they relied on the most abundant material around them. The calcareous rock common in Puglia is often stratified and therefore can easily be divided into slabs. That's the source of creation of the *trullo* (*trulli* is the plural), a quadrangular structure with a cupola roof. The slabs of rock (called *chianche*) were arranged without any plaster or plaster-type substance to hold them together. They were placed in concentric circles that formed the conical roofs of the buildings.

The perimeter of a *trullo* was painted inside and out with a paste of *grosello*, calcareous rock powder, and a small amount of thin straw. Finally, its walls were painted white with lime, both for sanitary reasons and to keep out parasites and other insects, especially ants. Only the slabs on the outside remained the natural color of the stone. On top of every roof was a pinnacle, usually topped with a ball. Painted on the outside of each *trullo* in lime was a large symbol—a cross, a circle, vertical lines, and so forth. These very ancient structures—descendants of the mysterious truncated cone-shaped monuments that date back to the stone age—were sparsely distributed at first, but soon they could be found in the whole southern part of the Murgia area.

THE GREATEST concentration of *trulli* outside the city of Alberobello is found in Valle d'Itria, which stands as an example of orderly, thoughtful, and rational use of every inch of land. The division of land into small plots has its roots in the needs of large landowners, who recognized that tilling the land and then planting crops was an expensive proposition. It was more economically advantageous for them to rent portions of their land to farmers. The farmers needed houses in which to live with their families while working the land. [See page 170 for a sample farmer's lease contract.] For social reasons, these houses were built close to one another, and so *frazioni*, or villages, began to form. Such communities were fairly self-sufficient. Families lived on what they grew in the

fields, and for raw materials they could turn to the local store in their village. Each group of houses had a small church where a priest celebrated Mass every Sunday.

When a lease—which usually had a term of twenty-nine years—was up, the farmer had to return the land to its owner in decidedly better condition than he'd received it, and he turned over any improvements to the landowner as well.

As these large pieces of land were split up, it became necessary to build a system of roads that allowed each farmer to access his own fields without crossing someone else's. That's why the Valle d'Itria and the southern part of the Murgia area have the most extensive network of roads in the whole region of Puglia.

Each road is lined on both sides with low dry stone walls that give the countryside a neat and harmonious look. Like the *trulli*, these walls were built out of materials that farmers had available, and as they tilled the land they turned up an abundance of stones.

When these walls had been built, *specchie* were built using the leftover stones. These consisted of stones arranged in a circular pattern that also helped the land look neat and tidy. Even the landowner made a contribution to clearing the land of stones, sending women and children to clear the fields at his own expense. Oddly, the owner established which stones to remove by weight: only those that weighed less than five hundred grams [about one pound] could remain.

Some landowners preferred to farm at least some of their land themselves. To do so, they needed employees who would be there while the work was being done and take care of tasks like hiring, supervising work, and paying workers. This person was known as a *fattore*, or overseer. The landowner put much power in the hands of the overseer, who was responsible for all the work done on the land. This figure became the subject of much jealousy and gossip.

SOME TIME AGO I found an unsigned letter in the pages of a book that describes better than I ever could the relationship that existed in these communities.

Dear Madam,
I am writing without putting a date on this letter because I wish to get down on paper quickly what is happening on your land. Dear lady, since you have a good heart and descend from honest and well-mannered people, surely you can't even imagine what is happening on your property. People steal from you and take everything copper sulfate, powdered sulfur, and sulfur, and if you want proof you'll find it in the tower of the person in charge of the fruit.

There is still dust and some other coal products there, and now I will explain it all. I will begin by telling you the truth. Just last year a quintal of copper sulfate was missing and it wasn't sold to anyone but instead was taken and divided between the overseer and the person in charge and now that is still not enough. This year, too, they robbed from you, during the work on the olive trees the overseer gathered many stakes meant for the vineyard and sold them to tenant farmers. Also, when he went in the morning and took ricotta and sold it in Grottaglie he kept some of the cheese and it's true that he offered it to his friends when they went to his house for cheese and wine and even the person in charge of the fruit had cheese that the overseer had given him that is now gone and also you should take a look in the wine cellar. See how much white wine has been taken and they may still have some white wine from the year before, meaning the overseer and the person in charge of the fruit. Dearest mother of us all, you and your family are in our prayers and will always be in our prayers, but do me a favor and come out to the countryside and see what they are doing in the morning at ten and at half past three in the afternoon because that's when they steal and if you want proof you can come out and search the tower. Look in the right place and you will find the stakes that they plan to divide among themselves, meaning the person in charge of the fruit and the overseer, and then it will all be clear.

We all live together and we pay you honestly, dear lady. In the evening you can come to the house as they're leaving, about quarter after four you should come out here and then you will see his cart and you will see how much they take from you and grab them by the collar and you will catch these thieves, these robbers who are not worthy of being on your property, so I recommend that you come see and observe and then you will see and you can kick them out if you wish.

You should come soon, and then you will see what they steal.

Sincerely and wishing you fruitful observation.

The Farmhouse La masseria

To appreciate the economic history of Puglia, we need to understand the division of its people into social classes and, in turn, the distribution of labor among those classes for many centuries.

The economy revolved around agriculture and much of it was based on a landowner/tenant farmer system. Industry arrived in this region relatively recently. While some of the land had been broken up into small parcels and leased, most wealthy landowners kept their large holdings intact over centuries. [See page 170 for a sample tenant farmer contract.] The estates usually held several farmhouses, surrounded by dozens of hectares [2 1/2 acres] of land. Each farmhouse itself was a large complex, often built to resemble a castle, and included a watchtower. The owner's living quarters were usually found on the second floor of the main farmhouse. The tenant farmer lived on the ground floor. Also on the ground floor were the grain deposits and, removed slightly from the living quarters, stalls for animals, living quarters for shepherds, and often a small church. Many farmhouses were fortified, and there are several splendid examples of these in the Murgia area and along the Adriatic coastal road.

You could even say that all the farmhouses were fortified, if by fortified you mean that they were designed to defend their inhabitants from people with bad intentions. Only the farmhouses along the coast played a truly active defensive role, because they protected their inhabitants from potential enemies arriving by sea. Farmhouses inland might have needed to fend off thieves and brigands at most.

If all the watchtowers, with arrow slits in their parapets, had been guarded by people ready to confront the enemy, there would have been very few farmers and shepherds to work in the fields and pastures! Back then as today, a tenant farmer or someone hired by him would patrol the property in the evening and during the night to guard against unpleasant surprises, not the least of which might have been poachers.

Along the coast, on the other hand, fortified farmhouses often resembled actual castles. They were large and could be occupied by a large group of people. These medieval fortifications were often outfitted with watchtowers and trapdoors, for defense purposes, and arrow slits so the inhabitants could shoot to defend themselves from approaching forces. There were also farmhouses with *trulli* built around their perimeters that were used as stalls or to store equipment.

Some small parcels of estates were leased to farmers for three-, four-, or nine-year terms. The duration of the lease and the terms of the contract were directly proportional to the value of the farm.

In the 1600s and 1700s, contracts were signed that were not advantageous, to say the least, for the poor farmers who got very little in return and had to work from morning to night. The leases were in effect from August 15 of one year to August 15 of the expiration year. That date could not be changed, and the rent paid consisted of a fee that the farmer had to pay the owner, who in return asked that his land be improved and that all inventory present at the time the land was delivered be returned in pristine condition. This included items that could not be removed (equipment, walls, small buildings, *trulli,* doors, and so on). A long and detailed list was made up at the start of the lease and then consulted again as it expired. If anything had deteriorated or been destroyed or disappeared, it had to be replaced by the farmer, while anything new became the exclusive property of the owner.

Gradually, the farmers' leases began to change. Eventually, the farmer was assigned certain

SAMPLE TENANT FARMER CONTRACT

Duration 2 years from August 15 of the year in which the contract is signed to August 15 of the year in which it expires.

Landowner will manage technical and administrative activities.

Tenant farmer is responsible for all that is necessary to grow crops.

Threshing: divided equally.

All inventory from the farm must be returned in equal number upon expiration of the contract; any animals born in the interim are to be divided equally.

If animals die due to the negligence of the farmer, damage is divided equally.

If animals do damage to the neighbors, the farmer is responsible.

Products divided in half.

The landowner will pay the property taxes.

Benefits to workers, livestock taxes, seeds, shoeing of horses plus servicing of animals, divided equally.

The tenant farmer has the right to 20 quintals of wood.

SAMPLE FARMER'S LEASE

Rent in cash + rent in kind: 4-year duration.

Rent in cash: 50,000 annually to be paid on August 15 each year.

Rent in kind: fava beans, wheat, barley, every year at the end of July; lambs in December; turkeys and capons at Christmas; pigs in January; cheese by August 31; fowl; one thousand eggs annually, one hundred of them at Easter; *cacioricotta*.
Mature lambs in mid-May. *Ricotta forte* and fresh ricotta. Vegetables.
Wool in June. Goats, potatoes, tomatoes, melons, fruit, and oil to be shared 50/50.
Milk at Ascension Day.

The landowner is responsible for pruning the woods and will give the farmer solely the amount needed to meet the needs of the farm.

Remove stones and keep up walls annually with expenses divided equally.

The farmer's other responsibilities include bringing household goods to the landowner's house, tending the fields, and pruning fruit and olive trees. Resulting wood divided equally. Grafting pear trees. He is not allowed to graze goats among the trees. Paint *trulli* and other buildings. Pay taxes.

If the farmer fails to fulfill one of these duties, he will pay a fine to the landowner.

duties, the owner certain obligations. For example, responsibility for repairing walls around the property or distributing the animal and/or human waste used as fertilizer was divided equally. The harvest was also divided fifty/fifty. The owner received extra in the form of weekly deliveries to his home of produce and the farmer received firewood.

NATURALLY, the items due depended on the size of the farm and the types of products grown there. For example, in the Murgia areas of Grottaglie, Manduria, Monteiasi, and Francavilla Fontana where the soil is rich and flat, there were valuable crops compared to Martina Franca, Villa Castelli, Ceglie Messapica, and Ciesternino where the soil was rocky and inhospitable and only animals were raised.

Wooded areas were pruned on a rotating basis and the wood was a major source of revenue. The value of a piece of property did not depend solely on the contract, but also on the relationship that the farmers had with landowners. If they were especially kind, farmers didn't stick closely to the lease or tenant farming contract, but instead brought the owners the best of everything. That's why in addition to eggs, ricotta, *pampanelle* (curdled whey wrapped in green fig leaves, a dairy product with an extremely delicate flavor), young cheese, fruit, and poultry, they brought whatever else grew on the land spontaneously and according to the seasons. This meant they might bring wild asparagus, field greens, or mushrooms that the shepherds found during their long workdays following their flocks.

There is an interesting social phenomenon to note here. At one time, whatever the shepherds found in the fields was brought to the owners. A farmer wouldn't have dreamed of eating asparagus or mushrooms, but instead brought these to "his" landowner, as if by birthright landowners were the only ones worthy of such delicacies. Gradually, though, things changed. Landowners began to remark to each other, "The farmers have wised up and now they eat the mushrooms and asparagus themselves!"

This was due to the eventual emancipation of the farming class. They became disaffected with landowners for a number of reasons, but mostly it was just a natural evolution. In earlier times, the pace of life was slow. A farmer went into town only once a week, to let the owner know what was going on out in the country on his land, and they made decisions together. [Many landowners had moved into towns.] The farmer arrived at the owner's house dragging behind him a *traino*, a cumbersome cart on two wheels that consisted of a piece of wood with two side panels and was pulled by a strong horse. A farmer's wife went into town only on the occasion of their town's protector saint's feast, followed by a gaggle of children. Their children didn't attend school at all, but instead lived out in the country with their parents and did whatever work they could handle, according to their age and strength.

Living in these isolated conditions, farmers weren't very shrewd and were always amenable to what landowners wanted. But a farmer's only contact with social life was through the landowner, whom he came to see as a charismatic, even beloved, respected, and honored figure. On Sunday, the farmer's wife did everything in her power to send the landowner's wife special homemade foods. These might be bread cooked in a wood-burning oven, or cookies, or *taralli* made with eggs, cooked, and then frosted. Sometimes they were small forms of *scamorza* shaped like animals for the landowner's children.

The farmer had a wonderful phrase for offering these items to the landowner's wife. I still remember hearing *Signù, quisto t'lu manna la massara* ("My lady, the farmer's wife sends you all of this"). The farmer's wife was certainly never mentioned by name—not by her husband and not by the landowner. She was the farmer's wife and that was all, and that title conveyed a special dignity. As time passed, the farmer's rudimentary cart was replaced by a *sciarabà*, a small carriage drawn by a young horse that made the trip much faster.

NATIONAL school reforms made during the twentieth century required children to go to elementary school. The farmer's family reluctantly went without the help of young children, who walked several miles every day to reach the nearest schoolhouse. The *masseria*, which until then had been an isolated and tranquil fortress, slowly began to change. The farmer's wife found more reasons to go into town, perhaps to buy shoes or clothing for her children, as they couldn't show their faces at school wearing the torn clothing that had been used for working out in the country. In most cases, however, the farmer's wife continued to make the children's clothing. Inhabitants of the country began to cross paths with those in town. Slowly, the farmers' horizons widened, and soon the landowner was no longer their only contact with "civilization." As a result, he lost some of his magic in their eyes. He was still respected, but no longer idolized. That's why all the attention that had been given him was now given to a number of other people who became important to the farmers.

Children now brought wild delicacies to their teachers, principals, or doctors. These people appreciated the gifts and—to insure that they would keep coming—talked about how wonderful they were. The farmers themselves became curious. They realized that those bitter wild asparagus, tossed with some beaten eggs and grated cheese, made for a delicious frittata, and those mushrooms made a wonderful side dish when roasted or cooked in tomato sauce. Why give all these things to the landowners if the lease didn't mandate it? They might as well take advantage of them. So the landowners no longer received these gifts. There's an old saying that still rings true: "Don't let the farmer know how good cheese tastes with pears."

Farm animals

Animali da cortile

During Puglia's long history of leased farming, wealthy landowners received eggs, milk, ricotta, and fruit on Sundays, while meat arrived more intermittently. There were chickens and rabbits weekly, every fifteen days, or even once a year. And an Easter lamb and a Christmas capon were included in the contract.

A capon is a chicken that's castrated when it's sixty days old and then ready to be eaten when it is seven months old. Castration helps give the animal evenly distributed fat, so capon meat is tender and delicate. Tradition called for serving capon broth on Christmas with homemade egg *tagliolini*, or sometimes a kind of pasta fritter. Very often the boiled capon was cut into pieces, tossed with olive oil or pork fat, and then roasted. It could also be roasted without being boiled first, and in those cases it was cooked whole, sometimes stuffed, and accompanied by the ever-present potatoes.

Chicken was prepared in the same manner, but a distinction must be made between a hen and a rooster. A male chicken or rooster was used mainly for reproduction and a hen for laying eggs. After a couple of years, these animals could no longer perform their primary functions, and they were slaughtered. Their meat, however, was very tough. A rooster was roasted in the oven, but a hen was boiled. The resulting broth was very flavorful, hence the saying *gallina vecchia fa buon brodo* ("an old hen makes good broth"). A chicken tastes its very best when it is ten months old. Of course, I'm talking only about chickens that are allowed to roam the barnyard. Anyone from Puglia will tell you that a chicken that walks around has a completely different flavor from one raised in a cage.

Furthermore, animals raised in cages are much better these days than they were in those early days of industrial farming and they're also fairly priced. It's not difficult, however, to buy free-range chickens these days, and the farmhouses and *trulli* in the Puglia countryside still raise poultry. These birds are fed industrial feed, but while roaming around they also eat what they find in the fields. When cooked their flesh is firm, elastic, and difficult to remove from the bone. Their skin is crunchy and unmistakable. These chickens are priced accordingly, however. The same is true of rabbits. We have access to rabbits of excellent quality, and most butchers stock animals that have been raised in relatively "free-range" conditions.

In earlier times, meat was considered the food of the wealthy few. Poor people ate it only on very special occasions and in many cases when meat appeared on the table it was a generous gift from a wealthy family. Not even the wealthy could afford to eat much of meat, especially beef. Chickens, rabbits, lambs, and goats appeared on their tables more frequently (though still not that often). This wasn't because the meat of those animals was preferred, but because they were raised and butchered on their farms and therefore didn't need to be purchased.

Currency didn't circulate much—only on rare and special occasions like fairs. Farmers used chickens, rabbits, and turkeys to barter or as payment for the services of a lawyer or doctor, or perhaps to repay a favor. Eggs were used in the same way. They were actually eaten in a farmer's home fairly infrequently, though occasionally a raw egg was fed to a malnourished child, or a few eggs were cooked into a frittata with vegetables. The birth of a child was always a special occasion, marked by the slaughter of a hen or pigeon, because it was believed that the tender meat of those birds would give the weak mother strength and vitality and help her produce milk.

Pigeons were not found for sale in any store. Anyone who needed a pigeon had to get one directly from a breeder. They were raised in huts—buildings that usually sat next to farmhouses or landowners' villas and contained small cages in which the birds lived and laid their eggs. They acted like free birds and even built nests when it was time to lay their eggs. During the pigeons' hatching period, the farmer would sprinkle corn and other grains around the coop to help the birds and would leave them drinking water as well. Even in town, anyone who had a garden kept a small pigeon shack in it. These were both a burden and a delight. It was lovely to see a flock of pigeons flying around (and they reproduced easily), but their excrement had to be removed daily from the tiled paths that ran through the gardens.

STUFFED CHICKEN

Pollo ripieno

Serves 4

Ingredients

1 young chicken, preferably free-range, cleaned and innards reserved
Bread crumbs
1 tablespoon capers
1/2 clove garlic, minced
Fresh flat-leaf parsley, chopped
2 ounces spicy salami, diced
1 tablespoon grated pecorino
1 egg, lightly beaten
1 cup white wine

Mince the chicken innards and then combine them with the bread crumbs, capers, garlic, parsley, salami, pecorino, and egg. Stuff the chicken with this mixture, sew up the opening, then put the chicken in a baking dish. Drizzle olive oil over the chicken and roast for about 30 minutes in a preheated 375° oven. Pour the wine over the chicken, then roast for an additional 30 minutes.

CHICKEN WITH RAGÙ

Pollo al ragù

Serves 4

This chicken will only come out well if the chicken you use is truly "free-range."

Ingredients

3/4 cup extra-virgin olive oil
1 clove garlic, minced
1 onion, diced
1 free-range chicken, cut into pieces, rinsed with water and white wine vinegar
1 cup red wine
6 ounces (about 3/4 cup) tomato purée, diluted with water
Sea salt
Pepper

Fresh tomato purée: blanch and peel tomatoes, then purée them through a food mill.

Heat the olive oil in a large skillet. Brown the garlic and onion, then add the chicken pieces and brown them. Pour in the wine and, when the wine has evaporated, add the diluted tomato purée a little at a time. Simmer over low heat for at least 2 hours. Season with salt and pepper.

Chicken and Potatoes

*Pollo assutto assutto**

Serves 4

Ingredients

2 1/4 pounds potatoes, peeled and cut into large dice
5 tablespoons extra-virgin olive oil
Sea salt
Pepper
1 young free-range chicken, rinsed and quartered
Fresh flat-leaf parsley, chopped
1 clove garlic, minced

Put the potatoes in a baking dish and season with some of the olive oil, salt, and pepper. Set the chicken pieces on top of the potatoes and season the chicken with the remaining oil, salt, pepper, parsley, and garlic. Bake in a preheated 475° oven for about 1 hour. Halfway through the cooking time, turn the chicken so it browns all over.

*The word *assutto* is dialect for *asciutto*, dry.

Rabbit with Vegetables

Coniglio alle verdure

Serves 4

This may also be prepared with pheasant or free-range chicken.

Ingredients

1 young rabbit, cut into pieces
White wine vinegar
6 carrots, diced
1 bunch celery, diced
1 onion, diced
3 ripe tomatoes diced
2 ounces rolled pancetta, diced
4 bay leaves
Fresh rosemary
1/4 cup extra-virgin olive oil

4 tablespoons butter
1 clove garlic
1 small package dried mushrooms, soaked for 30 minutes, then drained
1 cup white wine
1 bouillon cube
Sea salt
Pepper

Marinate the rabbit in water and wine vinegar for about 3 hours. Drain the pieces, then transfer to a large bowl and combine with the carrots, celery, onion, tomatoes, pancetta, bay leaves, and rosemary.

Heat the olive oil and butter in a heavy-bottomed casserole. Brown the garlic, then remove and discard it. Add the rabbit pieces and ingredients of the bowl. Cook over high heat until the rabbit is browned. Add the mushrooms and the wine. When the wine has evaporated, add the bouillon cube and enough lukewarm water to cover. Cook until the water has evaporated completely. Season with salt and pepper. Remove the rabbit to a serving platter and set aside. Purée the remaining vegetable mixture through a food mill. Pour the purée over the rabbit and serve hot.

RABBIT WITH PEPPERS

Coniglio ai peperoni

Serves 6

This recipe also works well with not-so-young chickens or hens.

Ingredients

1 young rabbit, cut into pieces
1 cup milk
2 tablespoons butter
6 tablespoons extra-virgin olive oil
1 spring onion, minced
Sea salt
Pepper
6 green peppers, seeded and quartered

Soak the rabbit in the milk for 1 hour. In a heavy-bottomed casserole, heat the butter and 3 tablespoons of the olive oil. Add the onion and brown. Add the rabbit and cook until all the pieces are browned and cooked through. Season with salt and pepper. In a skillet, heat the remaining olive oil. When hot, add the peppers and cook until soft, about 30 minutes, then add the peppers to the casserole. Stir to combine thoroughly and cook over low heat for about 30 minutes. Add a little broth or warm water to keep the rabbit from sticking to the pot.

Rabbit with "Wild Onion" Bulbs*

Coniglio con lampascioni

Serves 6

Ingredients

1 rabbit, cut into pieces
White wine vinegar
2 1/4 pounds "wild onion" bulbs
Sea salt
Extra-virgin olive oil
Pepper

Marinate the rabbit pieces in water and wine vinegar for about 3 hours. Peel and rinse the onion bulbs, then boil them in a pot of salted water until al dente. Drain the onion bulbs and arrange them in a roasting pan. Season with olive oil and pepper. Drain the rabbit and arrange the pieces on top of the onions. Season with additional olive oil, salt and pepper, then bake in a preheated 475° oven for at least 1 hour.

**Lampasciuni* or *vampascione* refer to wild grape-hyacinths whose small bulbs are called "wild onions."

Marinated Thrushes

Tordi al solso (turde 'nsulsze)

Ingredients

Thrushes
Sea salt
Bay leaves
Dry white wine, with a high alcohol content

Pluck and gut the thrushes. Boil them in a generous amount of salted water for a few minutes, then set aside on a plate to cool. Cut off their heads and discard. Put the thrushes in sanitized, dry glass jars, layering bay leaves between the birds. Add dry white wine to cover. Cover jars using hermetically sealed lids and set aside to marinate for at least 1 week.

PORK IL MAIALE

ANOTHER farm animal raised during Puglia's tenant farming period was the pig. Pigs weren't raised in large numbers; as few as twenty would have been considered a more than respectable number for a large farm. Some of the pigs went to the farmer and the landowner, while the others were sold for butchering and were usually reserved in advance. Pig is the only animal that man uses completely, consuming its flesh, head, trotters, fat, blood, skin, innards, and bristles.

The back ribs were cooked and eaten. Usually they were cooked over an open fire. Pig muscles were used to make meatballs, cut into chops, or stewed. The rest of the meat was used to make various kinds of cold cuts. The pork fat attached to the pig's hide was salted and smoked and used as a flavoring; when sliced thinly it was even eaten raw. The softest part of the fat, the part that touched the flesh, was used to make lard, once a common ingredient in various sauces and sweets, although today lighter vegetable oils are preferred. Even the cracklings, the little pieces that remained after lard was made, were used in making excellent focaccia.

IN PUGLIA, people still make salami and other cold cuts at home, and so do small artisanal companies. Someone who doesn't have a pig of his own buys one live from a farm, and the farmer makes the pig into salami.

The Martina Franca area was known for producing the best cold cuts in Puglia— so much so that in areas around Taranto and the Salento, people were hired from Martina Franca. They came to live in homes to make the cold cuts. I remember two women from Martina Franca who came to my house. They were expert, and they had to be reserved each year in advance.

They would sit around a large marble table and, with their knives, make quick work of cutting up quintals [about 220 pounds] of meat that then was stuffed into casings.

The ritual of preparing pork products was a cheerful one, and it was the opportunity to taste in the best way each part of the pig. The pig was butchered at the farmhouse, then brought to the landowner's house. There these women cut it up and separated it into the various parts that would then be used in different ways. There we'd light a fire, and lunch would always consist of ribs cooked over a grill. I'll never forget the taste of that meat; I persist in buying pork ribs and smouldering them in the fireplace at my own house today, hoping to recreate the flavor, but always in vain.

ANIMALS RAISED in non-industrial settings yielded a great deal of meat. The saying *purpo e vaccina svrigogna ci la cucina* ("octopus and beef shame the cook") means that these shrink markedly when cooked. That's even more true today, because farm animals are raised mostly on artificial feed and therefore their meat has a higher water content. They yield much less than their ancestors, who lived in a sort of semi-wild state. This is particularly true of pigs, which were looked down on because they ate scraps. Today's pigs, raised in cages, certainly taste differently than those earlier pigs that subsisted on table scraps and mash enriched with bran and whey. There were small muscles at the edge of the rib cages of those pigs that made a succulent *ragù,* which was the perfect match for the wonderful *orecchiette di grosso.*

On the days when a pig was being cut up, a friend of the family would receive a gift of ribs to grill or a piece of loin for that Sunday's pasta sauce. The neediest received any rind that the family didn't need, after as much of the white fat as possible was melted off. While that fat was still liquid, it was poured into glass or earthenware jars, or sometimes stored in the entrails of the very animal that had produced it. In the latter case, pieces of intestine were filled until they swelled big and round, and then they were hung from hooks in the ceiling of the storeroom. As the melted fat cooled, it became solid and white as snow, and the whiter it was the more valuable it was.

Obviously, pork products like salami were a major attraction. These included tightly rolled pancetta stuffed into the largest section of the intestine; *capocollo*, which takes its name from the part of the animal between the neck and the ribs; *soppressata*, which is made with hand-cut meat and stuffed into large pieces of intestine; and finally the most common type of salami, which was made using thin casings about two feet long. (One thing missing from the list of Puglia's pork products is prosciutto, because the region doesn't have the right climate for it.)

Once the salami were made, they were hung from wire attached to the walls of an aging room. They were left there to age until the following Easter, but first they were smoked. Smoking was key to preserving these products. The floor of the salami room was covered with a carpet of green branches from aromatic plants like thyme, myrtle, and bay. These were lit on fire, with care taken that they didn't burst into uncontrollable flames. Instead, the goal was for them to burn as slowly as possible to give off smoke. This was the most delicate part of the process and required experience in order to be done properly. The smoking plants had to be watched carefully and new branches added constantly in order to avoid the fire burning too hard and fast. The room was soon impregnated with the scent of aromatic smoke, and then it was shut tight overnight. The next day, the aging process began.

The blood of a freshly slaughtered pig was used in two ways. First, it could be fried with some olive oil in a pan, like a frittata, along with a little onion and salt. But the best way to use pig's blood was to make a *sanguinaccio,* or blood pudding, which in many parts of southern Puglia is considered a refined and even fancy dessert. Aside from pig's blood, the ingredients in blood pudding differs from place to place and family to family.

GRANDMOTHER VENANZIA'S BLOOD PUDDING

Sanguinaccio di nonna Venanzia

This recipe was my grandmother Venanzia's. She made the best blood pudding I've ever tasted.

Ingredients

- 1 quart pig's blood
- 1 quart milk
- 2 cups sugar
- 1 cup cooked wine must [juice from pressed wine grapes before fermentation]
- 1 cup unsweetened cocoa powder
- 1 pound walnuts, crushed
- 7 tablespoons dark chocolate, chopped
- Ground cinnamon
- Zest of 1 lemon
- Zest of 1 orange

In a stockpot, combine the blood, milk, sugar, wine must, and cocoa powder. Cook over medium heat, stirring constantly in one direction with a wooden spoon. When the mixture begins to thicken, add the walnuts, dark chocolate, cinnamon, and the citrus zests. Continue stirring constantly until the mixture comes to a boil; it should have the consistency of custard. Pour the mixture into small glass bowls or small tinfoil cups. Set aside to cool, then refrigerate. Blood pudding may be refrigerated 4 to 5 days. Serve cold.

This was a traditional *Carnevale* dessert.

FRIED OFFAL BITS

U campanele

These were eaten as Carnevale *snacks, though the tradition has almost completely died out.*

Ingredients

- Pork offal
- White wine
- *Peperoncino,* hot red chili pepper, sliced [or dried flakes] to taste
- Semolina/country bread, sliced

Cut the pork offal into small pieces. In a skillet or sauté pan with a lid, cook them in their own fat. Add a generous amount of wine, then cover the pan and cook for a long time. Add a large amount of chili. The strong taste of the pork fat should be covered up by the spiciness of the chili. Serve with slices of semolina or country bread.

PORK COOKED IN MILK

Maialino al latte

Serves 4

Ingredients

- 1 1/2 pounds lean pork in a single piece
- Sea salt
- Pepper
- 1/4 cup extra-virgin olive oil
- 4 tablespoons butter
- About 6 cups milk
- 5 to 6 sage leaves
- 1 clove garlic, unpeeled

Season the pork with salt and pepper. In a heavy-bottomed casserole, heat the olive oil and butter in a pan with fairly high sides. Brown the pork on all sides, then add enough milk to cover the pork completely. Add the sage leaves and the garlic. Cook for about 2 hours, watching to be sure that the liquid doesn't boil over. Turn the pork occasionally, and remove from heat once the sauce has thickened. Cut the meat into slices, arrange them on a serving dish, then pour the hot sauce over the meat.

This same recipe works wonders on a turkey breast.

PORK ROLLS

Involtini al latte

Serves 4

Ingredients

4 tablespoons butter
3 tablespoons flour
4 cups milk
Sea salt
Grated nutmeg
3 tablespoons extra-virgin olive oil
1/4 pound ground pork
Pepper
1 1/4 pounds veal scaloppine, slices pounded thin
3 1/2 ounces mortadella, sliced

In a sauté pan or skillet, make a béchamel sauce. Melt the butter and then whisk in the flour. When the flour and butter are combined, pour in about 1 cup of milk, whisking a little at a time. Season with salt and nutmeg and cook over medium heat, stirring, until the mixture thickens to the consistency of a custard. Remove from the heat and allow to cool.

In another skillet, heat the olive oil and cook the ground pork. Season with salt and pepper. When the meat is cooked through, set it aside to cool. Once the pork and béchamel sauce have cooled, combine them.

Meanwhile, lay one of the veal slices on a work surface. Put 1 slice of mortadella on top of each veal slice. Spread about 1 teaspoon of the pork and béchamel mixture over each of the mortadella slices. Roll up the veal slices, closing them with skewers or toothpicks, making sure no filling is leaking out. Put the veal rolls in a large skillet fitting them tightly. When all the rolls are in the pan, pour the remaining 3 cups of milk over them. Cook over medium heat until the sauce thickens and veal is cooked through.

Baked Sausage

Cervellata (salsiccia)

Serves 4

Ingredients

1 1/4 pounds *cervellata* (sausage)
Red wine (optional)

Bake the sausage in a pan, preferably in a wood-burning oven (though an electric oven is acceptable) with no seasoning. Or, prick the sausage all over with a fork, place it in a pan, and pour in enough red wine to cover. Bake until the wine evaporates completely.

Cervellata is a thin sausage made with fairly large chunks of meat ground by machine. It may be either all pork or a mixture of pork and veal.

Hand-Chopped Sausage

Salsiccia a punta di coltello

Serves 4

Ingredients

1 1/4 pounds hand-chopped sausage
Red wine

Put the sausage in a pan and pour in red wine to cover. Cook the sausage, preferably in a wood-burning oven, but an electric oven is also acceptable.

Hand-chopped sausage is usually made solely of pork. To make your own sausage, cut the meat into small pieces with a sharp knife and season with salt, pepper, and red wine. Stuff into casings about 1 inch in diameter and tie off in segments.

SHEEP AND GOATS GLI OVINI

AS FAR back as the Middle Ages, the plains of Puglia were home to more than four million head of sheep and goats. This tradition of raising animals is still with us today, if on a smaller scale, and continues to provide top-quality meat and cheeses.

Until about fifty years ago, just outside towns in Puglia, one saw small goat-pens. The owners of these structures descended from generations of goatherds who sold goat milk to consumers. At daybreak, one could see a small flock guided by a goatherd and his faithful mixed breed dog walking through town and hear the ringing of little bronze bells. Women came out to their doorsteps holding containers. The herder would milk his goats one at a time, giving the milk to each woman, measuring it with a little zinc cylinder. He put his payment in his pocket and moved onto the next house.

Certainly there were none of the controls and inspections that are so prevalent today—though the milk was always boiled for safety's sake—but there's no doubt that the taste of that milk was far superior to that of the pasteurized milk from today's large farms. In any case, goat's milk has become close to impossible to find today.

Milk was delivered to landowners on the days and in the amounts agreed upon contractually. Sometimes a family had more milk than it needed, and the milk would then be boiled in order to extract the cream that was often poured into glass jugs and given to friends and relatives as gifts, or sometimes to a doctor or lawyer. This cream tasted best when stirred into coffee, or whipped with a little sugar, but it could also be enjoyed in its natural state. Countless generations of children in Puglia enjoyed dinners of fresh milk soup.

At one time when milk was to be fed to an infant, the herder was careful to collect the milk from the same animal every day, since its digestibility had already been tested. If that particular goat happened to become pregnant, however, her milk would acquire different characteristics, and the tiny customer had to turn to another goat. This might seem odd to us today, but obviously it was quite logical. Before the advent of modern nutrition, if a mother was unable to breastfeed and her family couldn't afford the luxury of a wet-nurse, she gave her infant goat's milk with a little barley water or plain water added to it.

THE MURGIA area of Puglia is known for its lamb and goats—components of the culinary masterpiece known as *gnummaridd,* which are rolls of grilled offal. Their preparation requires very specific techniques and calls for liver, lungs, and neck sweetbreads or thymus tied together with the intestines of the same animal, rinsed in warm water. These are threaded onto long skewers and cooked in wood-burning ovens fueled with olive and almond wood, grilled, or even fried with a few bay leaves.

In the *trulli* area of the region, almost every butcher shop is equipped with a good oven used to cook this specialty to order twice a week. Customers arrive bearing earthenware pots to collect the cooked food so it is still warm and fragrant when set on the table. Pieces of lamb or goat as well as *cervellata* are added to *gnummaridd*. They are seasoned solely with salt.

A popular dish, though less well-known, is *gnommerelli di trippa,* a specialty of Locorotondo butchers. This is made with sheep tripe, cleaned with a tablespoon of quicklime and sea salt. It is then cut into strips that are used to make rolls that look like skeins of wool. Inside these bundles are pieces of pecorino and some parsley.

Another specialty is *marro* or *marretto* or *cazzmarre,* a big roll of lamb or goat innards that is tightly wrapped in intestines from the same animal and then roasted with diced potatoes. A similar dish is *capuzzelle,* lamb or goat heads cut in half and roasted in the oven. These are an Easter treat in Puglia. Basically, all parts of young sheep and goats are used, including lamb cutlets roasted, with tomato sauce or in brine. Even mutton is cooked in Puglia, despite its strong flavor and toughness. There are still traditional restaurants today that have mutton on their menus, usually stewed with a lot of onion. Frankly, it's not bad.

Tripe Bundles

Gnemeriidde di trippa

Serves 4

The dialect word gnemeriidde *means skeins of yarn, because that's what these bundles resemble. This is a specialty of Locorotondo. Any good butcher in Puglia will sell these to you already made, but in case you want to make them at home, here is the recipe. This dish is usually served on its own, or at most with a selection of cheese or a small mixed salad.*

Ingredients

2 1/2 pounds sheep tripe
Intestines
Parsley sprigs
Pecorino shavings
1 large white onion, sliced
3 ripe tomatoes, chopped
1 large piece of pecorino crust
1/2 bouillon cube
Sea salt
Pepper
4 slices semolina/country bread, toasted
Grated pecorino

Wash the tripe and intestines or purchase them prewashed from a reputable butcher (just be sure they're not bleached). Cut the tripe into squares about 3 inches by 3 inches. Arrange two squares one on top of the other with two parsley sprigs and a few pecorino shavings between them, then tie them with by wrapping intestines around them three times. Rinse under running water and transfer to a heavy-bottomed casserole along with any water remaining on them. (Don't drain them or let them drip dry.) Add the onion, tomatoes, pecorino crust, and 1/2 bouillon cube to the pot. Season with salt and pepper. Fill an earthenware pot with warm water and set it on top of the pot with the tripe in it.

Cook for at least 2 hours on a very low flame. Do not add water to the pot with the tripe. Divide the toasted bread among four individual dishes.

Top each slice of bread with tripe, 1/2 cup or so of any broth in the pot, and a generous amount of grated pecorino.

The best tripe to use for this is sheep tripe, but veal tripe will also work.

LAMB CASSEROLE

Spezzato di agnello

Serves 6

This dish is traditionally prepared for the day after Easter.

Ingredients

- 1 pound wild chicory
- 1 pound cardoons
- 1 pound wild cardoons
- 8 artichokes, trimmed down to their edible centers
- 3/4 cup extra-virgin olive oil
- 1 clove garlic
- 2 1/2 pounds lamb or goat, cut up into cubes
- 1 cup white wine
- 3/4 cup grated pecorino
- Sea salt
- Pepper
- 7 eggs
- Fresh flat-leaf parsley, chopped

Clean the chicory, cardoons, wild cardoons, and artichokes and boil each one separately. Heat the olive oil in a heavy-bottomed casserole and fry the garlic (then remove and discard) and brown the lamb on all sides. Add the white wine and cook, turning the meat, until the wine has evaporated. Arrange one of the boiled vegetables in a layer in the bottom of a large baking dish. Top with a layer of meat. Sprinkle with a little pecorino (you should have a fair amount left over at the end) and season with salt and pepper. Continue, alternating layers of vegetables with layers of meat and sprinkling each layer with cheese and seasoning with salt and pepper until you have used up all the vegetables and all the meat.

Cook on the stovetop for 15 minutes. Beat the eggs with the remaining pecorino and the parsley. (This mixture should be fairly thick.) Pour over the ingredients in the pan and bake in a preheated 350° oven until the eggs are firm.

Breaded Lamb

Agnello impanato

Serves 4

Ingredients

- 1 3/4 pounds leg of lamb
- 1 egg
- Bread crumbs
- 1 clove garlic, minced
- Fresh flat-leaf parsley, chopped
- Sea salt
- Pepper

Cut the lamb into slices. In a large bowl, beat the egg and season with salt and pepper. Dredge the lamb chops in the beaten egg, turning to coat all sides, then set them aside in the egg to rest 2 to 3 hours.

About 1 hour before you plan to serve the lamb, combine the bread crumbs, garlic, and parsley in a low wide bowl or on a large plate. One at a time, remove the lamb pieces from the egg mixture and dredge them in the bread crumb mixture, then transfer to an ungreased roasting pan. Place on the lowest shelf of a preheated 450° oven and bake. When the lamb is nicely browned underneath, turn and cook until browned on the other side. Serve piping hot.

Tripe with Potatoes

Trippa con patate

Serves 4

Ingredients

- 1 clove garlic
- 5 tablespoons extra-virgin olive oil
- 2 1/4 pounds tripe, preferably mutton tripe, cleaned and cut into strips
- 1 pound potatoes, peeled and diced
- 2 canned peeled tomatoes
- Sea salt
- Pepper

In a heavy-bottomed casserole, cook the garlic in the olive oil. When the garlic is browned, remove and discard it, then add the tripe to the pan. Brown the tripe, then add the potatoes. When the potatoes have browned, add the tomatoes, stir to combine and add water to cover. Season with salt and pepper and cook until all the liquid has evaporated.

Purchase cleaned tripe from a reputable butcher.

ROASTED LAMB AND POTATOES

*Agnello assutto assutto**

Serves 4

This dish should be very brown and dry when it is finished.

Ingredients

2 1/4 pounds potatoes, peeled and cut into large dice
5 tablespoons extra-virgin olive oil
Fresh flat-leaf parsley, chopped
Sea salt
Pepper
Grated pecorino
2 1/4 pounds lamb, goat, or mutton, cut up into cubes
1 clove garlic, minced

Toss the potatoes with about half of the olive oil, some parsley, and a small amount of water. Season with salt and pepper. Arrange the potatoes in a large roasting pan and sprinkle on the pecorino. Put the pieces of meat on top of the potatoes and sprinkle with garlic, additional parsley, and more pecorino. Drizzle with the remaining olive oil and season with salt and pepper. Bake in a preheated 400° oven for about 1 hour.

*The word *assutto* is dialect for *asciutto*, dry.

MUTTON IN THE POT

Callaredda

Serves 4

Ingredients

2 1/4 pounds wild chicory
1 pound wild fennel, sliced
1 1/2 pounds mutton, cut up
Peperoncini, hot red chili peppers, minced
Sea salt
Extra-virgin olive oil
Grated pecorino

Arrange some of the chicory in the bottom of an earthenware or copper pot. Arrange some of the fennel in a second layer on top. Top the fennel with some of the mutton and chili. Season with salt and drizzle with olive oil. Continue

This Puglian chicory is reddish in color and has a somewhat bitter taste.

to make alternating layers in the same order until you have used up the ingredients. Pour in enough water to cover and cook covered over very low heat, until mutton is cooked through. Sprinkle with pecorino just before serving.

LAMB OFFAL

Marretto

Serves 4

Ingredients

- Pluck of 1 suckling lamb, including the liver, lungs, thymus, caul, and intestines
- 1 ounce grated pecorino
- Fresh flat-leaf parsley, chopped
- Sea salt
- Pepper
- Extra-virgin olive oil
- 1 cup dry white wine

Wash the intestines with salted water, rinsing the insides as well (a funnel is useful for this). Cut the liver, lungs, and thymus (neck sweetbread) into 1-inch thick strips. Sprinkle with the pecorino and a generous amount of parsley and season with salt and pepper. Arrange the seasoned pieces of pluck in the intestinal caul and roll it up so that you have a cylindrical roll. Seal the ends well and tie tightly with the intestines, wrapping them around the cylinder several times.

Place this bundle, the *marretto,* in a heavy-bottomed casserole and drizzle on a little olive oil, then pour the white wine over it. Cook it over low heat on the stovetop until the wine has evaporated. Put the covered casserole into a 350° preheated oven and bake until the meat is cooked through. Serve this dish with roasted potatoes and pour any sauce from the pan over the potatoes.

Be sure the oven is at moderate heat so that a crust doesn't form on the outside of the *marretto*.

PLUCK BUNDLES

Gnemeriidde

Serves 4

Ingredients

Pluck of 1 suckling lamb, including the liver, lungs, thymus, and intestines
Sea salt
Pepper

Rinse the intestines with water, rinsing the inside as well with the help of a funnel. Cut the liver, lungs, and thymus (neck sweetbread) into 1-inch thick strips. Place 3 pieces together on a work surface and tie them with the intestines, winding the intestines around to make a bundle that resembles a small skein of yarn. Repeat with remaining pluck and intestines.

The most traditional cooking method for these is to thread them on a long skewer that is then arranged vertically near the heat from the fire in a wood-burning oven. However, they may also be grilled, or roasted in the oven at home (with salt and pepper only).

One other method for cooking these is to fry them in extra-virgin olive oil with sliced onion and then add some dry white wine.

ROASTED LAMB HEADS

Capuzzelle

Serves 4

Ingredients

1 1/2 pounds potatoes, peeled and diced
Extra-virgin olive oil
Sea salt
Pepper
2 lamb heads, halved
1 clove garlic, minced
Fresh flat-leaf parsley, chopped
2 tablespoons grated pecorino

Toss the potatoes with some olive oil and season with salt and pepper. Spread the potatoes in the bottom of a roasting pan. Place the halved heads on top of the potatoes and sprinkle with garlic, parsley, and the pecorino. Season with salt and pepper and drizzle on a little olive oil. Roast in a preheated 350° oven until the meat is cooked through, then serve hot.

STEWED MUTTON

Pecora in umido

Serves 4

Ingredients

1 1/4 pounds mutton, cut into 8 pieces
1/3 cup extra-virgin olive oil
4 large potatoes, peeled
4 onions, peeled
1/2 cup dry red wine
2 tablespoons tomato purée
Sea salt
Pepper

In an earthenware pan with high sides [or heavy-bottomed cassserole], brown the mutton in the olive oil. After 5 minutes add the whole potatoes and onions. Brown for 3 to 4 minutes, turning frequently. Pour in the wine. Cook until the wine has evaporated and then add the tomato purée. Turn the meat again, season with salt and pepper, and add water to cover. Simmer until the potatoes and onions have cooked down almost to a pulp.

Trulli steps

Horse IL CAVALLO

I am well aware that horsemeat, no matter how it is prepared, does not have a lot of fans today. But it's no surprise that in pre-World War II Puglia, when meat was a rarity and the poor, especially, could not afford much of it, people turned to horsemeat. It was eaten more commonly back then than you might think.

Not only was horsemeat inexpensive, but it was recommended for anemic children, because it contains protein and is easily digested.

That was also the era of the scourge of tuberculosis. A horse steak cooked on the grill was believed to "strengthen the blood," and it cost very little. That was enough to make it popular. The various attempts to make this meat appeal to fussy eaters gave rise to recipes that by now are classics in the Salento area. Those include recipes for horse meatballs and chops that call for a great deal of spices and herbs to cover up the somewhat excessively sweet taste of the meat.

In Italy, horsemeat is sold only by specialized butchers who are not permitted to sell any other types of meat.

MEAT ROLLS

Brasciole

Serves 4

Serve these with a salad or vegetables preserved in olive oil.

Ingredients

1 3/4 pounds horsemeat, cut into 8 slices
Sea salt
Pepper
1 clove garlic, minced
Fresh flat-leaf parsley, chopped
8 tablespoons capers
8 tablespoons grated pecorino
1/3 cup extra-virgin olive oil
1 onion, sliced
1 cup red wine
10 ounces (about 1 1/4 cups) tomato purée

Put the meat slices on a work surface and season with salt and a generous amount of pepper. Sprinkle each slice with garlic, parsley, 1 tablespoon capers, and 1 tablespoon grated pecorino. Roll up the slices of meat and close them with toothpicks. Heat the olive oil in a large skillet and brown the meat rolls with the onion. Add the red wine and cook until all the wine has evaporated. Add the tomato purée. Cook for about 2 hours.

This may be made with veal or pork. You may also leave the pecorino whole and cut it into small chunks and place one chunk on each slice of meat.

MEATBALLS

Pulupitt (polpette)

Serves 4

Ingredients

1/2 pound country bread, crusts removed
1 pound ground horsemeat
2 ounces grated pecorino
1 clove garlic, minced
1 egg, lightly beaten
Sea salt
Pepper
Extra-virgin olive oil
1 slice spring onion
1 16-ounce can tomato purée

Soak the bread in water, then squeeze it dry and tear into small pieces. In a bowl, combine the meat, the moistened bread, pecorino, garlic, egg, and salt and pepper to taste. Mix with your hands and form into hazelnut-sized meatballs. In a large skillet, fry the meatballs in a generous amount of olive oil and drain them. Meanwhile, prepare the sauce. In a large pot, fry the onion slice in 5 tablespoons of olive oil. When the onion begins to color, remove and discard, then add the tomato purée to the pan. Add about 1 cup water and cook thoroughly. Bring the sauce to a boil and add the cooked meatballs. Cook for 5 minutes and then remove from the heat and serve.

These meatballs may also be made with various types of meat or with ground pork.

Fresh tomato purée: blanch and peel tomatoes, then purée them through a food mill.

Beef I BOVINI

ONLY in the last few decades has beef come to be a major source of nutrition in Puglia. Beef was eaten very rarely in earlier times, especially in towns and villages when farming was the main occupation, and usually on holidays and other special occasions. Cows were raised mostly for milking or for working in the fields, so no one would have dreamed of butchering a calf or even a cow—that would have been incredibly wasteful.

Society has changed drastically, though, and today there are few traditional farms left. Consumerism—including spending plenty of money on food—has spread to all economic classes, even those that once considered frugality a great virtue.

TODAY, beef is eaten almost daily, and on Sunday people really stuff themselves on it. Gout, once a disease of royalty and the wealthy, has trickled down to all levels of society!

In Puglia, there is still a tradition—albeit a waning tradition—of the man of the house doing the grocery and food shopping, as it was once considered unseemly for a woman to visit a butcher or market. And the sexist mentality that still has a strong influence on the culture says that only men have the qualities of discernment required to spend money wisely. Below, I have recreated for you a typical dialogue between a middle-class shopper from a small town and his butcher. This should help you understand the mentality regarding how much meat is needed on Sundays.

CUSTOMER: Peppì, give me a kilogram [2 1/4 pounds] of veal scaloppine for making meat rolls. Don't cut them too thin.

Then give me three-quarters of a kilogram of ground meat for meatballs; about a kilogram or a little more of small steaks, with the bones, that I'm going to roast.

Give me some pork trimmings for the sauce and throw in a few pieces of mutton and beef, maybe two or three small pieces of pork belly wouldn't be a bad idea either. That gives the sauce more flavor! Do you have any hand-chopped sausage?

Well, give me a kilo. I don't know whether I'll use it in the sauce or roast it with potatoes.

BUTCHER: *Anything else, signor Antonio?*

CUSTOMER: Well, as long as I'm here, give me a kilo of stew meat for broth on Monday. And you'd better throw in a piece of bone and a little veal fat. . . . You did not tell me you had calves' heads! My wife is crazy about those!
Give me a couple of those and I'll roast them tomorrow. Otherwise we never know what to eat on Sunday night.

Anyone thinking this sounds like a reasonable amount of meat for a large family to eat over the course of a week would be wrong. This is intended for a family of six, at the most, to eat on a single Sunday. They may have some leftovers for the next day, but not many.

It's almost as if people want to make up for the hunger their ancestors suffered for hundreds of years, and it is true that not long ago the parents of Puglia often had to send their children to bed hungry, or at least couldn't feed them heartily. With intelligence, hard work, and industrialization, though, we have been become one of the richest.regions in the center-south of Italy.

Now that the culture of meat has put down strong roots, there are many recipes for preparing it, but they aren't really traditional. I am providing only two recipes, each for a sauce meant to be served with boiled meat.

Red Sauce
Salsa rossa

Ingredients
- 1 clove garlic
- 4 tablespoons extra-virgin olive oil
- 3/4 cup tomato paste, diluted with a small amount of water
- 1 tablespoon capers
- 1 pinch salt
- 1 tablespoon sugar
- 3 tablespoons white wine vinegar
- 1/4 cup fresh flat-leaf parsley, chopped

In a medium pan or skillet, heat the garlic in the olive oil. When the garlic begins to color, remove and discard it, then add the tomato paste. Cook until the sauce thickens, then add the capers, salt, sugar, and wine vinegar. Cook for an additional 2 to 3 minutes, then stir in the parsley. Serve warm or cold.

Green Sauce
Salsa verde

Ingredients
- 1 hazelnut-size piece of crustless bread
- White wine vinegar
- 6 ounces fresh flat-leaf parsley leaves
- 1 hard-boiled egg, minced
- 2 tablespoons capers
- 1 anchovy in olive oil, boned
- 1/2 clove garlic, minced
- 3/4 cup extra-virgin olive oil
- Sea salt

Soak the bread in wine vinegar, then squeeze dry and mince. Combine in a bowl the bread, parsley, egg, capers, anchovy, and garlic. Add the olive oil and a pinch of salt and continue mincing until the ingredients are very fine and well-combined.

FISH IL PESCE

FISH is undeniably expensive. That's why most of the fish that's eaten in Puglia is oily, dark-fleshed fish, which costs less and has traditionally been eaten by the poor. Still, if this type of fish is fresh and prepared properly, it offers excellent nutrition and taste. More expensive fish remains something found mostly in restaurants and on the tables of the privileged few.

In Puglia, the counters of fish stores and markets are overflowing with anchovies, sardines, mackerel, mullet, needlefish, whiting, albacore tuna, skipjack, little tuna, sprats, and small mullet. Much rarer are white bream, sea bream, bass, and umbrine, all of which need to be ordered in advance.

When preparing oily fish, you can let your imagination run wild, and the resulting dishes have a lot more flavor than those made with more expensive types of fish. Cuttlefish, octopus, comber fish, and scorpion fish make excellent fish soups and stews that can also include black mussels, clams, and littleneck clams, and can be counted among the finest dishes ever.

Grouper, stone bass, and skate are excellent when cooked in tomato sauce, and that sauce can be served over *tubettini* and spaghetti.

In the spring and fall it's easy to find whitebait, tiny fish of various species that are fished using a very fine net. These are a real delicacy and are usually coated with a simple batter and fried, or topped with a mixture of olive oil, salt, pepper, garlic, parsley, bread crumbs, and grated pecorino and then cooked in the oven. Whiting and small mullet are also excellent fried and are often served as an appetizer.

In summer, fish markets are full of swordfish, which are a funny sight, because each sword has a piece of plastic stuck on it to keep shoppers from injuring themselves accidentally. Swordfish cut into steaks can be grilled or baked. Sea bream, mudfish, kingfish, and *marmora* should be roasted. Umbrine should be baked or cooked in salt; bass should be boiled; sole should be fried in butter. Mullet may be cooked in parchment or in tomato sauce and roasted, or fried, depending on its size.

Many fish markets also sell anchovies, an indispensable ingredient in orecchiette with broccoli rabe. These anchovies are salted, pressed, and preserved in ceramic *capase* containers. Many families still prepare them at home, and the homemade type are much better than those industrially produced, not to mention a good deal cheaper. When rinsed and boned, anchovies can also be preserved in olive oil. Tuna is also preserved in olive oil, although the preparation is different. Whole tuna can be preserved in olive oil, and tuna steaks can be roasted.

THE COAST of Puglia teems with cuttlefish and octopus. These are cooked as they are in other areas, but in the southern part of the Adriatic they are also eaten raw. They are simply cleaned and rinsed in seawater or dressed with a little lemon juice, salt, and pepper. I have watched tourists from the north stare in disgust and horror as a *pugliese* tears off the tentacles of an octopus with his or her hands and eats them with gusto. I must say, though, that after that first negative impression, they usually get curious and, feeling that "in Rome one must do as the Romans do," end up trying the raw octopus themselves—and are inevitably won over by the irresistible taste and scent of the sea.

The poor have long relied on *baccalà,* for it is very nutritious. Now *baccalà* has become a celebrated delicacy in refined culinary circles. In the Salento area, it is boiled, fried, or grilled.

VIEW OF TRANI'S PORT

Sea-Salted Anchovies

Alici salate

Ingredients

Fresh anchovies, heads removed, gutted
Sea salt, coarse ground

Rinse the anchovies in salted water and set aside to drain thoroughly. Arrange a layer of salt in a ceramic container, preferably a traditional *capasa,* and arrange a layer of anchovies on top of the salt in a sunburst pattern, with their tails in the center. Cover the anchovies with a generous amount of salt and repeat the layers until you have used up the anchovies. Finish with a layer of salt.

Put a wooden or stone disk that fits just inside the mouth of the *capasa* on top of the salt and weigh it down. The anchovies will begin to give off liquid, so drain off the liquid every day until the salt looks just slightly damp. At that point, remove the weights and leave just the wooden or stone disk on top. Cover the container with a sheet of thick paper and use a rubber band to hold the paper in place.

Occasionally check to be sure the salt hasn't dried up completely; if it does, add a very small amount of water.

After 1 month, the anchovies are ready to be eaten. When you want to use some anchovies, remove them from the container with a fork, wash them under running water, and bone them. They can be used immediately or can be preserved in a glass jar with olive oil to cover.

Tuna in Olive Oil

Tonno sott'olio

Ingredients

1 very fresh tuna, about 11 pounds, head and tail removed, gutted, and rinsed
1 1/2 pounds salt (for an 11 pound fish)
1 quart white wine vinegar (for an 11 pound fish)
Extra-virgin olive oil

Put the tuna in a large stockpot and add salt and wine vinegar (proportional to

its weight). Then add water to cover, bring to a boil, then simmer the tuna for at least 4 hours. Drain and cool the tuna. Clean the tuna carefully, removing and discarding all its skin and any black spots.

Divide the tuna among sanitized glass jars and add olive oil to cover to each jar. (Make the portion of tuna in each jar small, because once you open a jar you'll have to use up all the tuna.) Hermetically seal and cook in a bain marie for 5 to 6 minutes.

Once sealed, the jars may also be cooked at 250° in a wood-burning oven for about 30 minutes. Once cooled, the tuna can be stored in the unopened jars indefinitely.

Weigh the tuna before you start and adjust the amounts of salt and wine vinegar according to the weight of the tuna.

ANCHOVIES WITH ONION

Alici in salsetta

Serves 4

Ingredients

1 3/4 pounds fresh anchovies, heads removed
Flour for dredging
Extra-virgin olive oil
1 onion, thinly sliced
2 tablespoons white wine vinegar

Dredge the anchovies in flour. Coat the bottom of a large skillet with olive oil and fry the anchovies. Remove to a serving platter large enough to arrange them in a single layer and set aside.

When the frying oil has cooled, filter it and reheat it in another pan. Add the onion and when the onion has wilted, add the wine vinegar. Cook until the wine vinegar has evaporated. Pour this onion sauce over the cooked anchovies.

Left: tuna at market

MARINATED ANCHOVIES

Alici marinate

Serves 4

Ingredients

1 1/4 pounds fresh anchovies, heads removed, boned, rinsed
White wine vinegar
Lemon juice
Sea salt
Extra-virgin olive oil
Peperoncino, hot red chili pepper, sliced [or dried flakes] to taste

Arrange the anchovies in one layer on a large, deep platter and pour on wine vinegar to cover. Set the anchovies aside to rest until they turn white from "cooking" in the wine vinegar, about 2 hours. When the anchovies have turned white, remove them and arrange on a serving platter. Sprinkle with lemon juice and salt, then drizzle on oil. Sprinkle on the pepper. Allow to rest 1 additional hour before serving.

BAKED ANCHOVIES

Alici in tortiera

Serves 4

Ingredients

1 3/4 pounds fresh anchovies, heads removed, gutted, rinsed
4 to 5 cherry tomatoes, chopped
1 clove garlic, minced
Fresh flat-leaf parsley, chopped
Sea salt
Pepper
White wine vinegar
Bread crumbs
5 tablespoons extra-virgin olive oil

Place the anchovies in a single layer in a baking dish with low sides. Sprinkle on the chopped tomatoes, garlic, and parsley. Season with salt and pepper, then drizzle on wine vinegar and sprinkle with bread crumbs. Drizzle on the olive oil and bake in a preheated 350° oven for about 20 minutes.

WHITEBAIT FRITTERS

Frittelle di bianchetto

Serves 4

Ingredients

1 egg, lightly beaten
8 tablespoons flour
Fresh flat-leaf parsley, chopped
Sea salt
Pepper
10 ounces whitebait, rinsed and drained
Extra-virgin olive oil for frying

In a large bowl, make a batter by whisking together the egg, flour, and parsley. Season with salt and pepper. The batter should be of medium thickness—if necessary, thin it with a little milk or thicken it with a little more flour. Add the whitebait to the batter and toss to coat. In a heavy-bottomed pot, bring a generous amount of olive oil to a boil. Drop tablespoons of the whitebait into the olive oil and fry until golden. Remove cooked whitebait with a strainer and drain on paper towels before serving.

WHITEBAIT WITH BREAD CRUMBS

Bianchetto arracanato

Serves 4

Ingredients

Extra-virgin olive oil
1 pound whitebait, rinsed and drained
Bread crumbs
4 tablespoons grated pecorino
Sea salt
Pepper
1 clove garlic, minced
Fresh flat-leaf parsley, chopped

Oil a baking dish and put the whitebait in it. Smooth the top of the whitebait with a spoon so they are a level layer. Combine the bread crumbs and pecorino and sprinkle over the fish. Season with salt and pepper and sprinkle on garlic and parsley to taste. Drizzle on a small amount of additional olive oil and bake in a preheated 350° oven for about 15 minutes.

Breaded Sardines

Sarde impanate

Serves 4

Ingredients

1 1/4 pounds sardines, scaled, gutted, boned, heads removed, and butterflied
Sea salt
Flour for dredging
2 eggs, lightly beaten
Bread crumbs
Extra-virgin olive oil for frying

Set out a plate of flour for dredging. Season the sardines with salt. Dredge the sardines in flour, dip them in the eggs, then roll them in the bread crumbs. Fry in a generous amount of olive oil and serve hot.

Sardines with Herbs and Bread Crumbs

Sarde ammollicate

Serves 4

Ingredients

3/4 cup bread crumbs
Leaves of 1 sprig parsley, minced
Leaves of 1 sprig mint, minced
1 tablespoon fresh oregano
1 clove garlic, minced
4 tablespoons grated pecorino
Sea salt
Pepper
Extra-virgin olive oil
1 3/4 pounds sardines, scaled, gutted, and boned

In a bowl, combine the bread crumbs, parsley, mint, oregano, garlic, pecorino, and salt and pepper to taste. Oil a baking pan and arrange the sardines neatly in it. Sprinkle on the bread crumb mixture and drizzle with additional olive oil. Bake in a preheated 350° oven for about 20 minutes.

SARDINE CROSTINI

Crostini di sarde

Serves 4

Ingredients

4 tablespoons extra-virgin olive oil
1 tablespoon lard
3 cloves garlic, crushed
2 1/4 pounds sardines, scaled, gutted, boned, heads removed, chopped
Sea salt
Pepper
2 tablespoons capers
4 slices semolina/country bread

In a skillet, heat the olive oil and the lard. Add the crushed garlic and cook until the garlic begins to color, then add the sardines. Stir and season with salt and pepper. Add the capers and cook until the sardines begin to fall apart, about 30 minutes. Spread each slice of bread with the cooked sardine mixture, then arrange the slices on serving dishes. Pour any juices remaining in the skillet over them.

ROASTED GRAY MULLET

Cefalo al forno

Serves 4

Ingredients

3 to 4 lemons, sliced
1 gray mullet, about 2 1/2 pounds, scaled and gutted
or 2 gray mullets, about 1 1/4 pounds each, scaled and gutted
Fresh flat-leaf parsley, chopped
1 clove garlic, minced
1 cup water-cured black olives, chopped
Sea salt
Pepper
Extra-virgin olive oil
Lemon juice

Line the bottom of a large baking dish with lemon slices. Lay the fish over the lemon slices, and fill the belly with the parsley, garlic, and olives. Season with salt and pepper. Drizzle the fish generously with olive oil and roast in a preheated 350° oven for about 20 minutes or more if necessary, basting with lemon juice occasionally.

MARINATED EEL

Capitone marinato

Serves 4

Ingredients

1 large eel, about 2 3/4 pounds, cleaned, skinned, head attached
1/4 cup fresh flat-leaf parsley leaves
1 clove garlic, chopped
4 to 5 bay leaves
Sea salt
Pepper
1 cup extra-virgin olive oil
1 cup white wine vinegar

Coil the eel in a large pan with high sides just big enough to hold it. Toss the parsley, garlic, and bay leaves over it. Season with salt and pepper, then pour the olive oil and wine vinegar over the eel. The eel should be completely covered by the liquid. Cover the pan and cook over low heat until the wine vinegar has almost completely evaporated, about 1 hour. Cool and then refrigerate. The eel should be eaten within a few days.

FISH STEW

Zuppa di pesce

Serves 8

This also makes an excellent sauce to serve over spaghetti or linguine.

Ingredients

1 onion, thinly sliced
2 cloves garlic, minced
3/4 cup extra-virgin olive oil
1 1/2 pounds tomatoes, peeled, and puréed through a food mill
Sea salt
Pepper
4 1/2 pounds various types of fish, scaled and gutted: sliced cuttlefish, sliced calamari, peeled and deveined shrimp and scampi, scorpion fish cut into pieces, and whiting
Fresh flat-leaf parsley, chopped
8 slices semolina/country bread, toasted

In a very large stockpot, brown the onion and garlic in the olive oil. Add the puréed tomatoes. Season with salt and pepper and cook until thickened. Add the fish to the stockpot, starting with cuttlefish and calamari, then the shrimp and scampi, scorpion fish pieces, and ending with whiting. Cook uncovered over high heat for about 15 minutes. Add a generous amount of minced parsley. Serve the stew in bowls over toasted bread.

GRILLED SALT COD/BACCALÀ

Baccalà alla brace

Serves 4

Ingredients

1 3/4 pounds *baccalà*, salt cod, soaked in water until soft
5 tablespoons extra-virgin olive oil
2 tablespoons white wine vinegar
Pepper
Sea salt
Fresh flat-leaf parsley, chopped

Cut the salt cod into 8 pieces and remove the skin. In a deep dish large enough to hold the salt cod, combine the olive oil, wine vinegar, pepper and salt to taste, and the parsley. Add the salt cod and marinate for about 2 hours.

Remove the salt cod from the marinade. Reserve the marinade and place the cod pieces carefully on a grill [or in a non-stick grill basket]. Grill the cod over high heat, turning occasionally and brushing with the marinade.

To soften salt cod/*baccalà*, soak it in water for several days in the refrigerator, changing the water every 12 hours or so. It can be purchased presoaked.

Batter-Fried Salt Cod/Baccalà

Baccalà fritto in pastella

Serves 4

Ingredients

Flour
Sea salt
1 3/4 pounds *baccalà,* salt cod, soaked in water until soft
Extra-virgin olive oil

In a large bowl, make a batter by whisking together flour and water and a pinch of salt. The batter should have the consistency of a custard. Cut the salt cod into pieces and remove the skin. Toss the cod pieces in the batter to coat them lightly. Coat the bottom of a large skillet with a generous amount of olive oil, then fry the cod pieces. Turn them 2 or 3 times until they are browned and crisp. Serve piping hot.

To soften salt cod/*baccalà,* soak it in water for several days in the refrigerator, changing the water every 12 hours or so. It can be purchased presoaked.

Endive with Salt Cod/Baccalà

Indivia con baccalà

Serves 4

Ingredients

3/4 pound *baccalà,* salt cod, soaked in water until soft
8 small heads curly winter endive
4 tablespoons capers
8 salted anchovies, boned and rinsed
Water-cured black olives
Sea salt
Pepper
Extra-virgin olive oil

Wash the endive heads. Boil the salt cod in a pot of unsalted water. Remove and chop the cooked salt cod, removing any bones that you find. Gently spread out the endive leaves, taking care not to detach them. Stuff each head of endive with some salt cod, 1/2 tablespoon capers, 1 anchovy, and some of the black olives.

Season with salt and pepper. Tie each head of endive with kitchen twine. Arrange the stuffed endive in a large ovenproof pan with a lid. Drizzle with olive oil and season with salt. Add 1/2 cup water around the endive so the water sinks to the bottom of the pan and cook, covered, over medium heat for about 30 minutes. Transfer the pan to a preheated 400° oven and bake until the endive is thoroughly cooked, about 30 minutes. Serve warm.

SALT COD/BACCALÀ IN TOMATO SAUCE

Baccalà al sugo

Serves 4

This sauce can be served over spaghetti as well.

Ingredients

1 clove garlic
5 tablespoons extra-virgin olive oil
1 1/2 pounds *baccalà*, salt cod, soaked in water until soft, cut into large pieces
10 ounces (about 1 1/4 cups) tomato purée
Fresh flat-leaf parsley, chopped
Sea salt
Pepper
Water-cured black olives

In a skillet, heat the garlic in the oil, then remove and discard it. Add the salt cod pieces and brown on all sides. Add the tomato purée and parsley and season with salt and pepper. When the salt cod is almost cooked and the sauce has thickened, add the olives. Cook for an additional 10 minutes.

Fresh tomato purée: blanch and peel tomatoes, then purée them through a food mill.

UMBRINE IN A SALT CRUST

Ombrina al sale

Serves 4

Ingredients

2 1/4 pounds sea salt
2 umbrine about 1 pound each, or other fish suitable for roasting, gutted, but not scaled
Fresh black pepper (optional)

Rinse the fish. In an earthenware baking dish shaped specifically for baking fish, or, if not available, a regular baking dish, make a thick layer of salt. Top with the fish and then make a blanket of salt over the fish. Bake in a preheated 400° oven for about 30 minutes. Bring the fish to the table in the dish, then break the salt crust at the table and cut away pieces of fish to serve, leaving skin and bones behind. The only thing that should be added to this is a little bit of pepper, if desired.

GRILLED SWORDFISH

Pesce spada alla griglia

Serves 4

Ingredients

1/3 cup extra-virgin olive oil
1 clove garlic, minced
Fresh flat-leaf parsley, chopped
Fresh oregano
1 tablespoon white wine vinegar
Sea salt
Pepper
4 swordfish steaks, about 1 3/4 pounds total
Bread crumbs (optional)

In a bowl, combine the olive oil with the garlic, parsley, oregano, and wine vinegar. Season with salt and pepper. Marinate the swordfish in this mixture for about 1 hour.

Meanwhile, prepare a grill. When you are ready to cook the swordfish, remove it from the marinade, reserving marinade. If using the bread crumbs, dredge the swordfish steaks. Place all the steaks on the grill [or use a non-stick grill basket]. Cook, turning frequently, and brush from time to time with the reserved marinade.

SWORDFISH STEAKS

Cotolette di pesce spada

Serves 4

Ingredients

1 egg
Sea salt
Pepper
4 swordfish steaks, each about 1/2-inch thick
Flour for dredging
Bread crumbs
Extra-virgin olive oil

Set out a plate of flour for dredging. In a bowl, lightly beat the egg, season with salt and pepper, and set aside. Dredge the swordfish steaks in the flour, then in the beaten egg, and finally in the bread crumbs. Coat the bottom of a large skillet with a generous amount of olive oil, then fry the the steaks for 5 to 6 minutes, turning to brown both sides.

STUFFED CUTTLEFISH

Seppie ripiene

Serves 6

Ingredients

1/2 cup bread crumbs
2 ounces grated pecorino
1 egg, lightly beaten
1 clove garlic, minced
Fresh flat-leaf parsley, chopped
1 teaspoon capers
Pitted black olives
Sea salt
Pepper
2 1/4 pounds medium cuttlefish, ink sacs removed
Extra-virgin olive oil

In a bowl, combine the bread crumbs, pecorino, egg, garlic, parsley, capers, and olives and season with salt and pepper. Stuff this mixture into the cuttlefish and arrange the cuttlefish in a baking dish so that they are pressed up against one another. Drizzle with a generous amount of olive oil and bake in a preheated 350° oven for about 1 hour. Serve warm.

SHELLFISH I MITILI

THE SEA around Taranto is rich with varieties of mollusks, including sea dates, littleneck clams, larger clams, hairy mussels, and the murex [a rough-shelled mollusk] that we call *queccioli.* The secretions of the latter were used in ancient times to make purple dye.

The Mar Piccolo in Taranto is a deep bay closed off by two bridges, a stone bridge and a swing bridge. Its calm waters, made even less salty by freshwater springs due to Karstic phenomena in the area, provide an ideal environment for raising shellfish and oysters. Indeed, these shellfish have been a major part of the city's economy since ancient times.

Taranto mussels are well-known for their quality and their adaptability to all types of preparations. You'd be hard-pressed to find a Taranto resident who doesn't eat them every day, either raw (despite the risks) or cooked in one of the many creative preparations native to the area. Unfortunately, the area for cultivating shellfish is shrinking. At one time, oyster production flourished and there were as many oysters in the area as there were mussels, but today, plenty of people in Taranto are forced to do the unthinkable and eat oysters imported from France.

THE TRADITION lives on, though, as does the beauty of this body of water, enriched by the geometric arrangement of posts sunk into the sandy bottom and hung all around with long thick ropes that have bunches of black shiny shellfish hanging from them.

There is much demand in Puglia for murex. They are boiled in their shells in salted water acidulated with a slice of lemon and served as an appetizer. The meat is then extracted from the shells using a pin. (A real expert can crush a murex shell and grab the inside end of the murex as well; it has an even sweeter flavor.) Murex cooked this way are seasoned with extra-virgin olive oil, pepper, and lemon and served cold.

Another seafood that is eaten quite commonly in Puglia is sea urchin, at its peak flavor in late winter and in spring. Along the Adriatic and Ionic shorelines there are markets selling sea urchins that are opened very quickly with a pair of scissors and placed on tin trays, ready to be eaten by the many people strolling by.

In some areas there are tables with plastic tablecloths next to the stalls selling sea urchins where customers can sit and eat the sea urchin along with a little piece of bread that they use to scrape out the pink pulp. This snack is washed down with a glass of beer.

In short, the wide variety of seafood available has created a truly great culinary tradition.

Peppery Mussels

Impepata di cozze

Serves 4

Ingredients

4 1/2 pounds mussels, scrubbed and rinsed
Fresh black pepper
Toasted semolina/country bread

Put the mussels in a large pan over high heat. As they open, transfer the mussel meat to another pan, retaining their liquid, and peppering them generously as you do. When they are all open (discard any that resist opening), filter their cooking liquid into the second pan (where the mussel meat now sits) and add additional pepper. Serve piping hot with toasted bread.

Mussel Gratin

Cozze al gratin

Serves 4

Ingredients

4 1/2 pounds mussels, scrubbed and rinsed
5 tablespoons bread crumbs
3 tablespoons grated pecorino
Pepper
1 clove garlic, minced
Fresh flat-leaf parsley, chopped
Extra-virgin olive oil

Open the mussels by hand, leaving the meat in the bottom half of the shell but breaking off and discarding the empty top half. Open the mussels over a bowl and reserve any liquid. Arrange the mussels on the half-shell in a large baking dish, slightly overlapping. Filter any liquid that collected as you opened the mussels and pour it over them in the baking dish.

In a bowl, combine the bread crumbs and pecorino and season with pepper, then sift this mixture through a strainer with large holes over the mussels. Sprinkle on the garlic and parsley and drizzle on some olive oil, being sure to get some on each mussel. Bake in a preheated 400° hot oven until browned, about 15 minutes.

Fried Mussels

Cozze fritte

Serves 4

Ingredients

3 1/4 pounds mussels, scrubbed and rinsed
2 eggs
Sea salt
Flour for dredging
Bread crumbs for dredging
Extra-virgin olive oil for frying

Set out a plate of flour for dredging. Open the mussels by hand and discard shells. (If you are uncomfortable opening raw mussels, cook them briefly to open.) Lightly beat the eggs with a pinch of salt. Drain the mussels, dredge them in flour, then in the eggs, and then in bread crumbs. In a large skillet, fry them in a generous amount of very hot olive oil. When the mussels are golden, scoop them out with a strainer and place them briefly on paper towels to drain. Serve piping hot.

STUFFED MUSSELS

Cozze ripiene

Serves 4

Ingredients

2 3/4 pounds large mussels, scrubbed and rinsed
2 cloves garlic
5 tablespoons extra-virgin olive oil
1 pound ripe tomatoes, peeled and puréed through a food mill
Basil leaves
2 eggs, lightly beaten
2 tablespoons grated pecorino
Fresh flat-leaf parsley, chopped
Pepper
Bread crumbs

In a large skillet, cook the mussels over high heat to open them (discard any that resist opening). Set the mussels aside in their shells. Filter any resulting liquid and retain. In a large pan with high sides, fry 1 garlic clove in the olive oil. When the garlic browns, remove and discard it, and pour in the puréed tomatoes and basil. Cook for 20 minutes, thinning with the filtered liquid from the mussels.

Meanwhile, mince the remaining garlic and in a bowl combine it with the eggs, pecorino, and parsley. Season with pepper and add enough bread crumbs to make a fairly firm stuffing.

Keeping the shells intact, stuff a little of the bread crumb mixture into each one. Tie each mussel closed with kitchen twine. When all the mussels are stuffed, bring the tomato sauce back to a simmer if you've taken it off the heat, then add the mussels. Cook the stuffed mussels in the tomato sauce for 15 minutes.

MUSSELS IN SAUCE

Cozze in salsetta

Serves 4

These may be served as an appetizer.

Ingredients

3 1/4 pounds mussels, scrubbed and rinsed
5 tablespoons extra-virgin olive oil
2 tablespoons white wine vinegar
Juice of 1 lemon
Pepper

Open the mussels by cooking them in a large skillet over high heat (discard any that resist opening). Filter any resulting liquid and set aside. Remove the meat from the mussels and discard shells. Put the mussels in a bowl with a small amount of their liquid and season with the olive oil, wine vinegar, lemon juice to taste, and a generous amount of pepper. (Taste and add salt if necessary.) Stir well to combine and refrigerate for at least 3 hours.

STEWED MUSSELS

Zuppa di cozze

Serves 4

Ingredients

1/3 cup extra-virgin olive oil
1 clove garlic, minced
1 onion, minced
10 ounces ripe tomatoes, peeled and puréed through a food mill
Basil leaves
Sea salt
3 1/4 pounds mussels, scrubbed and rinsed
Pepper
Fresh flat-leaf parsley, chopped
Toasted semolina/country bread

In a large pot with a lid, heat the olive oil and add the garlic and the onion and fry until they begin to color. Add the puréed tomatoes, basil, and a pinch of salt. Cook until the sauce is very thick, then add the mussels. Cover the pot with a lid and cook for 10 minutes. Season with a generous amount of pepper and parsley. Serve hot with toasted bread.

STEWED SEAFOOD

Zuppa di frutti di mare

Serves 4

Ingredients

1/2 cup extra-virgin olive oil
1 clove garlic, minced
1 onion, minced
10 ounces ripe tomatoes, peeled and puréed through a food mill
Basil leaves
Sea salt
1 1/2 pounds mussels, scrubbed and rinsed
10 ounces littleneck clams, scrubbed and rinsed
10 ounces cockles, scrubbed and rinsed
10 ounces razor clams, scrubbed and rinsed
Pepper
Fresh flat-leaf parsley, chopped
Toasted semolina/country bread

In a stockpot, heat the olive oil and add the garlic and the onion and fry until they begin to color. Add the puréed tomatoes, basil, and a pinch of salt. Cook until the sauce is very thick, then add the seafood. Cover the pot with a lid and cook for 10 minutes. Season with a generous amount of pepper and parsley. Serve hot with toasted bread.

SEAFOOD SALAD

Insalata di mare

Serves 6

Ingredients

Lemon
3/4 pound baby octopus, cleaned
3/4 pound baby calamari, cleaned
Sea salt
3/4 pound shrimp, in shells
1 pound black mussels, scrubbed and rinsed
10 ounces clams, scrubbed and rinsed
1/2 cup extra-virgin olive oil
1 tablespoon white wine vinegar
1 clove garlic
Pepper
Fresh flat-leaf parsley, chopped

Cut 2 slices from the lemon. Juice the rest of the lemon and set the juice aside. In a stockpot, cook the octopus and calamari in boiling salted water with a slice of lemon added.

In another pot, cook the shrimp in boiling salted water with a slice of lemon. Put the black mussels and clams in a large pan and cook over high heat to open their shells, discarding any that resist opening. Shell the shellfish and transfer their meats to a large serving bowl. Transfer the octopus and calamari to a work surface and chop. Add to the large bowl. Shell the shrimp and add those to the bowl as well.

In a small bowl whisk together the olive oil, wine vinegar, reserved lemon juice, whole garlic, and a pinch of salt. Whisk vigorously with a fork, then remove and discard the garlic and pour the dressing over the seafood. Toss to combine thoroughly, then season with pepper and sprinkle on parsley. Set aside to rest for at least 20 minutes before serving.

SWEET AND SOUR SHELLFISH

Cognotti

This sweet and sour specialty has roots that reach far back in time, though it is almost completely unknown today.

Ingredients

- 2 1/4 pounds oysters or mussels, shelled
- Flour for dredging
- Extra-virgin olive oil
- 3 cups honey
- 5 cups white wine vinegar
- 7 tablespoons almonds, roasted and ground
- 4 tablespoons chestnuts, roasted and ground
- 4 tablespoons candied orange peel, minced

Set out a plate of flour for dredging. Drain the shellfish meats, then dredge them in flour. In a large skillet, fry them in a generous amount of olive oil. When they are golden, scoop them out with a strainer and drain on paper towels. Combine the honey and wine vinegar in a pot and bring to a boil. Stir in the fried shellfish and the almonds, chestnuts, and candied orange peel. Boil for a few minutes, then set aside to cool. When the mixture is completely cool, serve, or transfer to glass jars and seal hermetically.

Christmas Traditions

Tradizioni Natalizie 

In Puglia, Christmas starts early. In Taranto it begins on November 22, to be precise. That's the day dedicated to Saint Cecilia, and it's also the day that a very special home ritual is performed.

At the break of dawn, the woman of the house slips out of bed, heads into the kitchen, and prepares the dough for the fried treats known as *pettole* whose dough must rise for at least one hour. At the same time, a band begins marching up and down the streets, singing a song in the saint's honor. The music wakes children who, still rubbing the sleep from their eyes, are drawn to the delicious smell of the *pettole* that by then is filling their houses. Soon the whole family is gathered around the kitchen table for a truly unusual breakfast until they have to head off to school or work. That's the beginning of a period of joyous Christmas spirit that lasts through January 7.

Holiday eves that are celebrated most regularly are the Feast of the Immaculate Conception on December 7, Christmas Eve, and the Epiphany on January 5. In the past (and still today in some homes) people fasted on those days, so around six in the evening the entire family gathered around the table to eat dishes that were only prepared on those special occasions. *Pettole,* little balls of fried dough, were a must. These were eaten piping hot and were served with boiled broccoli rabe in place of bread.

There were no greenhouses, nor was there any artificial irrigation. Every vegetable had a very specific and limited season. Broccoli rabe began to sprout from the ground in the first ten days of December, so the first shoots were always part of the meal for the Immaculate Conception and on Christmas Eve.

As children, we would ask our grandmothers for permission to accompany the servants who were sent to gardens on the outskirts of town to gather those greens. The first course was *vermecidde,* small spaghetti broken in half-inch lengths that the women patiently cut off one at a time from a very thin sheet of pasta dough that they stretched by hand. This pasta was always served with either fish or tuna sauce. Meat and dairy were not allowed, so

Above: broccoli rabe

the second course, too, was always a fish dish. There were also prescribed desserts, such as *carteddate* [fried dough ribbons] and *purcidd* or *sannachiutili* [fried dough].

QUALITY and preparation varied with taste and traditions, but a large adult female eel always made an appearance. This eel was purchased by the head of the family, who knew exactly when the fish would arrive at the fish stall and passed that information on to the next generation. For those few days, the fishmonger was treated more respectfully than anyone else in town. Once a year, price was no object, and no one asked for a discount. Adults loved the eel, but children often balked at the idea of eating it, especially if they'd been present for its preparation. If the eel slipped from the hands of the person cooking it, it would wriggle to the floor like a big snake.

An impressive religious tradition was the ritual of the "nine lights." This began on December 16 and ended on December 24. Every morning at five a.m., women of all ages would wrap themselves in dark wool shawls decorated in paisley patterns and head to the closest church. On December 16 there would be nine lamps on the altar, and then each day there would be one fewer, in a kind of countdown to Christmas.

Every morning the atmosphere was more heated and impatient as the time left to prepare all the food for the holiday grew shorter. Christmas is a religious holiday, of course, but the celebration turned into a food-veneration rite. The kitchen became an altar amidst mystical experience of first waiting for the season to arrive, preparing all the food, and finally getting to enjoy it. All members of the family, from the youngest to the oldest, men and women, had their roles in loading the table with food. Families spontaneously gathered together. Grandparents, adult children, and even relatives who had emigrated far away all returned to contribute to an unforgettable Christmas reunion.

The holidays themselves have their own special menus. For the Feast of the Immaculate Conception, the menu wasn't strict, but Christmas and New Year's Day always featured broth made with a capon or turkey as a first course. There is a very good dish that is not well-known even in Puglia called *sagna stampata*. This lasagna dish uses turkey or pieces of leftover meat picked from the bones. The breast is set aside to be used as desired. The second course is boiled meat with

Left: broccoli rabe

various sauces, roast turkey with potatoes, and roasted rolls of offal. For some time now, there is a tradition throughout Italy of serving *cotechino* (sausage) and *zampone* (pig's feet) with lentils on New Year's Day. There are also traditional sweets that must be served.

It was up to the mother and any small children to decorate the tree and assemble the crèche. For once, small children had a say in something. Only after endless discussion and after various arrangements had been tried out were the two most important Christmas symbols ready to be admired by relatives and friends, who were always plied with questions about whether the current year's decorations were better than those of the previous year. Proud and happy, family members went back to preparing the meal, and they lit a fire in the fireplace, itself a symbol of family unity. They made desserts, prepared sauces, exchanged gifts, gave each other items from their gardens, and paid visits to each other.

THE EVENING before the Epiphany had a culinary character all its own. Tradition called for nine different courses to be eaten, one after the other, but it wasn't necessary to eat a real meal. Lupini beans or dried figs could serve as a course, for example. However, herring was always served. After dinner the real celebration started, but first adults had to call on all their organizational skills. First came the near impossible task of convincing the children to go to bed. This was done by explaining that if they were still awake, the Befana (the kind witch who delivers gifts on the Epiphany) would refuse to come down the chimney and bring them their gifts. Eventually, the children would give in. They'd hang their stockings with their wish lists, and then they'd set out a very frugal meal on a table for the Befana, who was sure to arrive tired and cold from her rounds to all the houses where good little children lived. The menu for the Befana was always the same: ricotta, bread, cheese, a little fruit, and a small cup full of cherries in alcohol, which were supposed to reinvigorate the poor old lady. Even the donkey that the Befana rode on got something—a little bit of hay was always left on the floor next to the offering for the Befana. The next morning, delighted children woke to find a few leftovers and some fruit peels on the table, and a few stray bits of hay on the floor and their belief extended another year. But the night the Befana was expected to arrive,

TRADITIONAL HOLIDAY FOODS

CHRISTMAS AND NEW YEAR'S DAY
Turkey lasagna; *sciusciello* with ricotta; greens in broth. Roast turkey; roast capon; boiled meats with various sauces; offal; lamb roasted in various ways. Fritters with cooked wine must; fried dough; fried dough ribbons; sweet ravioli; almond milk; Christmas cake; brittle.

EASTER AND EASTER MONDAY
Maccheroni timballo; chicory *timballo*; savory pie; offal rolls; roasted lamb and potatoes; lamb stew; grilled salt cod; Easter breads; black pepper *taralli*; sweet turnovers; sweet *taralli*; horse-shaped sweet *tarallo*; sponge cake; nougat; almond tart.

CARNEVALE
Fried offal bits; wheat berries; blood pudding; sugared almonds.

excited by all the activity, children always managed to stay up a little later than usual, even though they knew the legend that at midnight "the walls become ricotta and the animals talk."

If they did stay awake, the warning continued, they would get to see these strange phenomena, but the Befana would never come back again. Even as children got a little older and began to get suspicious, there was a last-ditch strategy for goading them into remaining believers a little longer. A family member who had been absent until that moment would dress up in old women's clothing, cover his or her head with a shawl, and sling a large burlap sack over his or her bent shoulders. This person wandered around in the yard until someone inside claimed to have seen something through the steamed up windows. The curious children would approach a window and exclaim with wonder, swearing that they had spotted the Befana. At this point they ran to go to bed, fearing the old woman would get impatient with them for still being awake and pass them by without leaving any gifts.

Once the children were all tucked in, adults sprang into action. They opened bags and unwrapped packages that had been carefully hidden. They wrote the name of the recipient on each gift, and in the middle of the table set for the Befana they left a letter addressed to all the children, thanking them for the dinner and giving each of them a special suggestion: try to be neater, or study harder, or listen more attentively to your parents. The letter always ended with a warning that they needed to be good in order to receive more gifts and less coal the following year. The sight of a fireplace surrounded with gifts still brings me back to my childhood. Even now, if I close my eyes I can see the bright colors and the excitement of children racing to the fireplace to find out if their wishes had been fulfilled. There were a few toys and always a lot of candies and chocolates. The mantelpiece always sported a row of neatly arranged tangerines as big as oranges that were bought only for special occasions, as well as dried fruit and other sweets. The adults were all smiles, too, because they were glad to see their hard work appreciated.

ALL THIS enthusiasm was due to the fact that in earlier times, until the 1960s or so, there weren't as many gifts as there are now. Children got one gift a year for the Epiphany. Adults and children alike awaited the holidays, the former because they got joy from giving, and the latter because they got joy from receiving. Even the poorest families could not have denied their children gifts, although sometimes the one gift was a tin sword for boys or a rag doll—sewn lovingly in secret by their mother—for girls.

Jams, Jellies, and Preserves

Le Marmellate

The large amount of fruit harvested in Puglia has led to another tradition—the making of jams, jellies, and preserves.

One rule of farming culture is that nothing is ever thrown away, so any extra fruit is made into preserves. The most common fruit in Puglia is the pear. Wild pear trees grow spontaneously everywhere in Puglia, even in areas with rocky, inhospitable soil. Since a farmer never passes up any opportunity, in February, almost for fun, he begins to graft all these small trees that like magic grow new branches and begin to bear fruit the following year. Once the farmer's family has eaten as many fresh pears as they like, the remaining pears are made into preserves. Grapes, too, are made into preserves. During the grape harvest, a few bunches are always left on the vines. A few days later, the farmer walks among the vines and collects any fruit the grape pickers missed. The farmer's wife selects the best fruit and cooks it in a large pot without any added sugar. These preserves have come to be known as *mostarda.*

Peaches, apricots, and plums are also cooked into compote. Quinces are best made into jam. The fruit is cut into slices and peeled and then boiled in water and, finally, passed through a sieve. With the right amount of sugar added, the fruit produces an excellent jam with a slightly acidic (pleasantly so) taste. The water used to cook the quince is filtered and then combined with sugar to make a very soft, delicate, and transparent natural gelatin. This gelatin decorates pastries and cakes, especially those made with fresh fruit, lends these desserts an excellent flavor, and keeps fruit juices from leaking out of the pastries.

Traditionally, quince was considered a fruit with great medicinal powers. Families that lived on farms guarded their fruit jealously during the winter, as it was believed to cure many ills. For example, a piece of quince boiled with dried figs, carob, almond shells, barley, mallow leaves, bay leaves, and other aromatic herbs made a concoction that was believed to cure coughs. Quince seeds were boiled and then made into a poultice that was an excellent remedy for the dry nipples of some nursing mothers. It was rare to go to a doctor and drugs were expensive. People without means used these home cures for many illnesses.

FIG TREES are numerous in Puglia. They grow easily and often are planted close to homes so that their large wide leaf growth provides refreshing shade. In addition to being planted for esthetic reasons, fig trees are also planted in the region because their fruit is a favorite. In late spring and early summer, early figs are picked and eaten or served with prosciutto as an appetizer and they are called *fioroni.* Figs picked later in the summer are mostly dried or used in preserves and are called *fichi.*

Every day ripe figs are picked from the trees, cut in half, left on their stalks, and spread out on mats known as *cannizze.* They are left out in the sun for an entire day, then taken inside in the evening to avoid becoming damp. This is repeated for four or five days until the figs are completely dry. At this point they can be handled in various ways. They may be baked and then stored in earthenware or glass containers. Before they are baked, they may have almonds, pieces of bitter chocolate, or pieces of lemon peel tucked into them.

Below: figs

These figs are called *mmaritati* (dialect for "married"). Dried figs, along with almonds and walnuts, were a fixture on every table, especially on winter evenings. Farming families appreciated their high calorie content; wealthier families considered them an excellent dessert. Fig jam is not very common in Puglia, although some people do make it. It is used to make tarts and small stuffed pastries.

Sour cherries, on the other hand, are used only in preserves or syrups or soaked in alcohol. While these cherries are occasionally used in baking, they're relatively rare in Puglia.

One of the most common sweets in Puglia is the *zeppola,* which is associated with Saint Joseph's Day on March 19. Fried or baked *zeppole* are always topped with whipped cream with a little bit of sour cherry preserves, or made with sun-dried sour cherries. Homemade sour cherry syrup tastes completely different than store-bought industrial syrup. Cherry preserves are fairly common.

Wonderful cherry groves have been planted in Puglia, especially in the modern era. The cherries of Turi, Conversano, Gioia del Colle, and Putignano are particularly well-known and are exported as well as being sold within the region. Every field in the Salento area has a cherry tree, especially in those areas that are slightly cooler.

Before turning to the recipes, I'd like to make a general observation. The exact point at which preserves are cooked properly can be judged by dipping a wooden spoon into the mixture and then lifting it out quickly. The preserves are properly cooked when they fall slowly from the spoon in large drops.

*Preserving note

Follow safe preserving procedures when making these recipes. Always put ingredients in sanitized, dry glass jars (boiled or put through a dishwasher). Cover jars using airtight, hermetically sealed lids. After opening the jars, always refrigerate them.

Cherry Preserves

Marmellata di ciliegie

Ingredients

2 1/4 pounds pitted cherries, stems removed
2 3/4 cups sugar
Alcohol [pure, distilled]

Combine the cherries and the sugar in a bowl and set aside, stirring occasionally, until the sugar has dissolved, about 3 to 4 hours. Transfer the fruit mixture to a heavy-bottomed pot and cook over high heat for 30 minutes. Lower the heat and cook, stirring constantly with a wooden spoon, until the fruit has reached the proper consistency. Transfer the preserves to heated glass jars that have been cleaned and dried.* Allow to cool. Then cover, inserting a disk of wax paper moistened with alcohol between the preserves and the lid before sealing.

*See Preserving note

Sour Cherry Preserves

Marmellata di amarene

Ingredients

2 1/4 pounds pitted sour cherries, stems removed
5 1/2 cups sugar
Alcohol [pure, distilled]

Combine the cherries and the sugar in a bowl and set aside, stirring occasionally, until the sugar has dissolved, about 3 to 4 hours. Transfer the fruit mixture to a heavy-bottomed pot and cook over high heat for 30 minutes. Lower the heat and cook, stirring constantly with a wooden spoon, until all the liquid has evaporated. Transfer the preserves to heated sterile glass jars.* Allow to cool, then cover, inserting a disk of wax paper that has been moistened with alcohol between the preserves and the lid before sealing. *See Preserving note

Sour Cherries Syrup

Sciroppo di amarene

Diluted with four parts cold water to one part syrup, this makes an excellent beverage.

Ingredients

2 1/4 pounds pitted sour cherries, stems removed
5 1/2 cups sugar

Follow the Sour Cherry Preserves (*Marmellata di Amarene*) recipe. About 10 minutes after the cherries and sugar come to a boil, use a ladle to remove most of their juices and a few tablespoons of the fruit. Pour into a wide-mouthed glass jar and allow to cool.* Continue cooking the rest of the contents of the pot to make preserves.

*See Preserving note

Sun-Dried Sour Cherries Syrup

Sciroppo di amarene cotte al sole

This syrup makes a delicious drink when diluted with water. The cherries are a lovely decoration for pastries, too.

Ingredients

2 1/4 pounds pitted ripe sour cherries, stems removed
2 cups sugar

Fill a wide-mouthed glass jar* to the top with the cherries, adding the sugar in small amounts as you do so that all the empty space between the fruit is filled with sugar. Hermetically seal the jar, inserting a disk of wax paper between the fruit and the lid. Set outside on a windowsill and allow to rest for 15 days. (Be sure to bring the jar in the house at night so it doesn't acquire moisture overnight.) When the natural heat of the sun has melted the sugar, bring the jar back inside. Wait at least 1 month before eating the syrup. *See Preserving note

Peach Preserves

Marmellata di pesche

Ingredients

2 1/4 pounds peaches, pitted, peeled, and sliced
3 cups sugar
Alcohol or rum

Mix the peach slices with the sugar in a bowl and set aside to rest 6 to 7 hours. Transfer the fruit to a heavy-bottomed pot and cook, stirring constantly, until the fruit has reached the proper consistency, about 1 hour. Allow to cool, then transfer to clean, dry glass jars.* Cover the mouth of each jar with a disk of wax paper moistened with alcohol or rum, then a lid, and then hermetically seal.

*See Preserving note

Apricot Preserves

Marmellata di albicocche

Ingredients

2 1/4 pounds ripe apricots, pitted and sliced
3 cups sugar
Alcohol or cognac

Mix the apricots with the sugar in a bowl and set aside to rest 2 to 3 hours. Transfer the fruit to a heavy-bottomed pot and cook over medium heat until the fruit has reached the proper consistency, about 1 hour. Allow to cool, then transfer to clean, dry glass jars.* Cover the opening of each jar with a disk of wax paper moistened with alcohol or cognac, then a lid, and then hermetically seal. *See Preserving note

Fig Preserves

Marmellata di fichi

Ingredients

2 1/4 pounds ripe figs, peeled and halved
2 cups sugar
Rum

Put the figs and sugar in a pot and add about 3/4 cup water. Cook over medium heat, stirring constantly. After about 1 hour, check the consistency and if it's right, remove from heat. Once the fig mixture has cooled, transfer it to clean, dry glass jars.* Insert disks of wax paper soaked in rum between the preserves and the lids before sealing tightly.

*See Preserving note

Strawberry Preserves

Marmellata di fragole

Ingredients

2 1/4 pounds strawberries, washed and hulled
3 cups sugar
Juice of 1 lemon
Cognac

Macerate the berries with the sugar and lemon juice and set aside to rest for 2 hours. Transfer the mixture to a heavy-bottomed pot and cook over high heat for 30 minutes, stirring constantly. Remove from heat and allow to cool. Transfer to clean, dry glass jars.* Insert disks of wax paper moistened with cognac between the preserves and the lids and seal tightly.

*See Preserving note

Blackberry Jelly

Marmellata di more

Ingredients

Blackberries
Sugar
Alcohol

Gather together all the adults and children you can and go into the countryside and collect a lot of blackberries. In an earthenware pot, combine the berries with about 1/2 cup of water and bring to a boil. When the berries are cooked properly, pass them through a sieve. Weigh the amount of juice that results and mix it with an equal amount (by weight) of sugar. Put the juice and sugar over the heat and cook, stirring constantly. The jelly is ready when, once cool, you drip it onto a plate and it thickens there.

Transfer to clean, dry glass jars* and insert a disk of wax paper soaked in alcohol between the preserves and the lids and seal tightly.

*See Preserving note

Chestnut Preserves

Marmellata di castagne

Ingredients

2 1/4 pounds chestnuts
Sea salt
1 tablespoon fennel seeds
1 cup Marsala
2 1/2 cups sugar
1 cup milk
1/2 cup cognac
Alcohol [pure distilled]

In a heavy-bottomed pot combine the chestnuts, salt, and fennel seeds and add water to cover. Cook over medium heat. When the chestnuts are halfway cooked, remove them from the pot, peel them, and then put them in a pot with the Marsala, 1 cup of sugar, and water to cover and finish cooking.

When the chestnuts are cooked, reserve their cooking liquid and purée them through a sieve. Then combine the puréed chestnuts with the milk.

In a small bowl, dissolve the remaining sugar in 3 to 4 tablespoons of the cooking liquid from the chestnuts. Cook this sugar mixture into caramel and combine it with the puréed chestnuts, stirring vigorously with a wooden spoon until thoroughly combined. Stir in the cognac. Allow the mixture to cool, then transfer it to clean, dry glass jars.* Insert disks of waxed paper soaked in alcohol between the preserves and the lids. Seal hermetically.

*See Preserving note

Pear Preserves

Marmellata di pere

Ingredients

2 1/4 pounds pears, peeled, cored, and diced
1 1/4 cups sugar
Alcohol

In a bowl combine the pears and sugar and set aside to rest for 2 to 3 hours. If you prefer preserves with a smooth consistency, force the pears and sugar through a sieve after they have rested, then transfer to a heavy-bottomed pot. If you prefer chunkier preserves (they are excellent this way), simply transfer the mixture to a heavy-bottomed pot.

Use summer pears for this recipe. The pears in Salento are small and juicy—but any kind will work well in these preserves.

Cook over high heat until this begins to break down. Turn the flame down to low and continue cooking, stirring continuously, until the preserves reach the proper consistency and are a golden brown color. Allow to cool. Transfer the preserves to clean, dry glass jars* and insert a disk of wax paper soaked in alcohol between the preserves and the lid before sealing hermetically.

*See Preserving note

Grape Preserves

Marmellata di uva

No sugar is added to the grapes because they are sweet enough on their own. These preserves are good for pastries and tarts.

Ingredients

- 2 1/4 pounds grapes (any variety), seeded
- Alcohol [pure, distilled]

Put the grapes in a heavy-bottomed pot and cook until they give up their liquid and the liquid evaporates completely. Allow to cool. Transfer the preserves to clean, dry glass jars* and insert disks of wax paper soaked in alcohol between the preserves and the lids. Seal hermetically.

*See Preserving note

Orange Marmalade

Marmellata di arance

Ingredients

- 2 1/4 pounds thin-skinned freshly picked oranges
- 5 cups sugar
- Juice of 1 lemon
- Alcohol [pure, distilled]

Peel half the oranges and slice thinly. Slice the remaining oranges, with peels. Put the orange slices in a ceramic bowl, sprinkling the sugar in between the layers of fruit. Leave for 8 to 10 hours. Add the lemon juice and stir to combine, then transfer to a heavy-bottomed pot and cook over medium heat, skimming off the foam occasionally. Stir frequently and cook until the fruit has reached the proper consistency, meaning it should no longer slide off of an inserted wooden spoon.

Transfer the warm marmalade to clean, dry glass jars* and place disks of wax paper soaked in alcohol between the preserves and lids.

*See Preserving note

Quince Preserves

Marmellata di mele cotogne

Ingredients

- 2 1/4 pounds quince, cored and diced
- Sugar
- Rum

Put the quince in a pot and add enough water to cover. Bring to a boil and cook until soft, then purée through a food mill and weigh the resulting cooked fruit purée. For every 2 1/4 pounds of purée, add 2 3/4 cups sugar. Stir to combine in a large heavy-bottomed pot and cook until the preserves reach the proper consistency.

Cool and transfer to clean, dry glass jars.* Insert disks of wax paper soaked in rum between the lids and preserves and seal hermetically.

*See Preserving note

Quince Gelatin

Gelatina di mele cotogne

Ingredients

1 quart quince cooking water
3 cups sugar
Extra-virgin olive oil (if making individual portions of quince gelatin)

Follow the recipe for Quince Preserves (*Marmellata di Mele Cotogne*). After cooking the quince, remove the cooked fruit with a slotted spoon and reserve 1 quart of the quince cooking water. Combine the water and sugar and boil in a heavy-bottomed pot until the liquid looks gelatinous and has a ruby red color. If the gelatin is going to be used to decorate cakes, remove it from the heat when it is still fairly liquid and transfer to glass jars.*

If you wish to make individual portions of quince gelatin (which is served as a dessert), wait for the mixture to thicken further and then transfer to small oiled aluminum or tinfoil cups. If making individual portions of quince gelatin, set the cups aside for 2 to 3 days to harden and then carefully run a knife around the inside of each cup to loosen the individual portions of gelatin, then unmold them.

*See Preserving note

Quince Jellies

Cotognata

Ingredients

2 1/4 pounds quince, cored and diced
Sugar
Superfine sugar

Cook the quince in a small amount of water in a heavy-bottomed pot until they are extremely soft and falling apart. Purée them through a food mill. Make a mixture of about 1 cup water and an amount of sugar equal (by weight) to the quince purée. Boil the sugared water for a long time, then add the quince purée before the sugar begins to caramelize.

Cook, stirring constantly until the mixture turns a deep pink color. Lightly oil a large, flat surface (such as a cutting board, marble slab, a porcelain plate, or a sheet of tin foil) and pour the cooked mixture onto the surface. Smooth the surface of the mixture with a spatula. It should be about 1 inch thick.

Set aside to dry in a well-ventilated place for 2 to 3 days, or more if the weather is humid. Cut the hardened quince mixture into small cubes or other shapes, toss each piece in superfine sugar, and arrange in fluted papers. Store in a tightly sealed wooden or tin box with wax paper between the layers of jellies.

*See Preserving note

Plum Preserves

Marmellata di prugne

Ingredients

2 1/4 pounds pitted plums
3 3/4 cups sugar
Juice of 1 lemon
Alcohol [pure, distilled]

Combine the plums, sugar, and lemon in a heavy-bottomed pot and place over high heat. When the mixture reaches a boil, skim off any foam. Cook, stirring constantly, until the preserves reach the proper consistency. Allow to cool somewhat, then transfer to clean, dry glass jars.* Insert disks of wax paper soaked in alcohol between the preserves and the lids.

*See Preserving note

Green Tomato Preserves

Marmellata di pomodori verdi

Ingredients

2 1/4 pounds green tomatoes, chopped
4 cups sugar
1 lemon, sliced
Cognac

Arrange the green tomato pieces in layers in a bowl, sprinkling the sugar between the layers. Set aside to macerate for 24 hours. Put the tomatoes in a pot (preferably earthenware) and add the lemon slices. Cook over medium heat until the tomatoes turn an amber color. Transfer the cooled preserves into clean, dry glass jars,* inserting a disk of wax paper soaked in cognac between the preserves and the lids. *See Preserving note

Pitted Sour Cherries in Alcohol

Amarene sotto spirito snocciolate

Ingredients

Sour cherries, pitted
Sugar
Alcohol [pure, distilled]

Combine equal amounts (by weight) sour cherries and sugar. Mix together in a large, wide-mouthed glazed ceramic dish with low sides such as a large soup bowl. Put the fruit in the sun for about 15 days, stirring occasionally. (Be sure to bring the bowl in the house at night so it doesn't acquire moisture overnight.) When the sour cherries have shriveled but are not completely dried, transfer them to glass jars* and add alcohol to cover. *See Preserving note

Cherries in Alcohol

Ciliegie sotto spirito

Use sweet [Bing] cherries and follow the instructions for *Grapes in Alcohol.*

Sour Cherries in Alcohol

Amarene sotto spirito snocciolate

Ingredients

2 1/4 pounds sour cherries or black cherries, stems removed
2 cups sugar
1 cinnamon stick
10 cloves
1 cup alcohol [pure, distilled]

In glass jars combine the cherries, sugar, cinnamon stick, and cloves. Cover the jars and set the fruit in the sun for about 25 days, bringing it indoors at night so it doesn't acquire moisture. Add the alcohol and set in the sun for 1 additional day.* Wait at least 2 months before serving.
*See Preserving note

Grapes in Alcohol

Uva sotto spirito

Ingredients

2 1/4 pounds table grapes
10 cloves
1 cinnamon stick
1 1/4 cups sugar
2 cups alcohol [pure, distilled]

Rinse the grapes, let them drip dry, then with shears cut the stem of each grape, leaving the longest stems possible. Arrange the bunches in glass jars* and add the cloves and cinnamon. In a small heavy-bottomed pot, combine the sugar with 3/4 cup water and stir over low heat until dissolved. Set aside to cool, then add the alcohol to the sugar syrup and pour the liquid into the jars to cover the grapes. Seal hermetically and set aside to age for at least 2 months before serving.
*See Preserving note

Liqueurs I rosoli

In southern Italy, there is a long tradition of preparing liqueurs. Due to their innate sense of hospitality, Puglia's hosts never allow their visitors to leave without offering something to eat or drink.

Having liqueurs around meant the host could always offer "a little glass" of something to drink. In fact, the word *bicchierino*, which literally means "little glass," is synonymous with liqueurs. The woman of the house usually asks, "Would you like coffee, or a little glass?"

In earlier times, the middle class and farmers didn't drink liqueurs with high alcohol content. They tended to reach for vermouth, *Strega* (an herbal liqueur), anisette, and especially homemade liqueurs.

Weddings years ago were not the luxurious and expensive affairs that they are now in southern Italy. They were events celebrated in the home, as were baptisms and confirmations. The largest room in the house or apartment, sometimes the only room, was emptied completely. Rows of chairs were arranged along the walls, and once the guests were seated they stayed seated for the rest of the reception. Usually, the number of chairs needed was so large that hosts had to borrow them from neighbors who were happy to help out on these special occasions.

If there were a great number of guests, the church's chairs also would be borrowed for the occasion. The sexton would load up a cart with chairs and bring them to the home of the newlyweds, who paid a rental fee to the church or made an offering for the poor in return.

The luxuriousness of the reception could be judged by the number of times the hosts made a complete round of the room, serving their guests pastries or liqueurs. To make it clear that the refreshments were abundant and varied, a different color liqueur was offered to the guests on each round.

THE WOMEN of the house, assisted by neighbors and friends, began preparing desserts and liqueurs at least ten days in advance. The liqueurs were made first, as they needed to rest for at least a week. The most common were: ruby red cherries; mint, a bright green liquid resulting from adding peppermint leaves to water and alcohol; and a bright yellow lemon liqueur made by soaking lemon peel from freshly picked fruit in alcohol. Dark brown coffee liqueur, a must as well, was made with sugared coffee mixed with a certain amount of alcohol.

After an impressive number of bottles of liqueur had been prepared, the desserts were tackled. The first were usually made of almond paste, which would stay firm for a fairly long time, followed by cookies filled with preserves, and so on until the small pastries were made at most a day in advance. If the family's economic situation allowed, the hosts served cream-filled pastries made by a baker as the last round to impress their guests.

HOME RECEPTIONS preceding funerals had similarities. Those were moments when human solidarity was expressed to its fullest, and relatives and friends were involved in a moving kind of competition to see who could be the kindest. The relatives of the deceased could not be left alone for a single moment during the two days preceding the funeral. The house would be transformed radically so that, in addition to the viewing room, two other rooms were emptied of their usual furnishings, then filled with chairs supplied by the church in exchange for a modest donation or a tip for the sexton.

One room was for men and one for women. Visitors went immediately to their rooms and stayed seated in absolute silence for at least one hour—or longer, in proportion to their relationships and friendships with the deceased and family.

It was assumed that the people closest would spend the night holding a wake over the body. As the hours wore on and those keeping watch grew tired and hungry, someone had to take care of them. (It was also assumed that they were in too much pain to take care of things like this themselves, or even to think about them.) Pots of coffee and cappuccino, trays of pastries, and pots of broth, sent by friends or more distant relatives, began to trickle into the kitchen.

Intermittently, the family's closest friends would approach and whisper a few words in the ears of the relatives of the deceased and, after much denial, they would convince them to get up and go into the kitchen, where they were quickly given refreshment.

Close friends, servants, and anyone who had come from far away received the same treatment. Tact and discretion were required, even though everyone knew why they were getting up. But in even earlier times, this ritual resembled a true reception even more closely. During the wake, trays were circulated by hand among all the attendees, who could take coffee and sweets. It would have been rude to refuse, so they all served themselves.

In the hot summers in the south, it wasn't unusual for a tray to appear bearing dishes of ice cream. Broth was always served for lunch—it was considered light and nourishing—sometimes with meatballs or "sponge cake" pasta.

THIS TRADITION, referred to in dialect as *u cunz,* dates back to very ancient times, and the expression seems to be an etymological descendent of the Latin *consolatio.* It seems the Romans had a similar way of observing funerals. Among the wealthy, *u cunz* went on as long as eight days and was funded by the closest friends of the deceased, who not only prepared lunch which they shared as well, but also provided utensils, dishes and glasses, and table linens so as not to burden the family members. This is another tradition that is fading with the passage of time and the introduction of new social mores. *U cunz* still occurs today in many towns, but only among the lower-middle classes. Mostly it occurs in the form of an offering of liqueurs, coffee, and sugar on the part of relatives and friends. After the funeral, these are divided up among the relatives.

Following are recipes for liqueurs and desserts that were normally served at these in-home receptions that families still prepare today.

Left: lemon trees

LEMON LIQUEUR

Rosolio di limone

Ingredients

Zest of 6 large freshly picked lemons
1 quart alcohol [pure, distilled]
5 cups sugar
4 1/2 cups water

In a tightly sealed bottle, soak the zest in alcohol for 48 hours. Occasionally shake up the contents of the bottle. In a heavy-bottomed pot, combine the sugar and water. Boil for about 2 minutes then remove from heat. Allow the syrup to cool and then add the lemon-steeped alcohol. Stir to combine, then filter the liquid and pour back into a clean, dry bottle. Hermetically seal the liquid in the bottle and set aside for at least 1 week before serving.

ORANGE LIQUEUR

Rosolio di arance

Ingredients

Zest of 7 freshly picked oranges
1 quart alcohol [pure, distilled]
5 cups sugar
4 1/2 cups water

Follow the instructions for making Lemon Liqueur *(Rosolio di Limone)* above.

TANGERINE LIQUEUR

Rosolio di mandarini

Ingredients

Zest of 8 freshly picked but not extremely ripe tangerines
1 quart alcohol [pure, distilled]
5 cups sugar
4 1/2 cups water

Follow the instructions for making Lemon Liqueur *(Rosolio di Limone)* above.

SPANISH LIME LIQUEUR

Rosolio di lima di Spagna

"Spanish limes" are citrus fruits that are very similar to lemons but are smaller and sweeter—so sweet that I'd almost call them flavorless. They have a lovely aroma, but they can be hard to find in stores.

Ingredients

Zest of 8 Spanish limes, minced
1 quart alcohol [pure, distilled]
5 cups sugar

Follow the instructions for making Lemon Liqueur *(Rosolio di Limone)* above.

Citrus liqueurs may be varied as follows—Caramelize 1/4 cup sugar, add the liquid caramel to the prepared liqueur and wait for it to dissolve completely. Then filter the liquid. The liqueur will have an amber color and a sweeter flavor. The resulting liqueur is less tart, but also loses its characteristic bright color.

ESPRESSO LIQUEUR

Rosolio al caffè

Ingredients

Espresso
Sugar
Alcohol [pure, distilled]
Coffee essence [available in specialty stores]

Prepare a full espresso maker with coffee 4 times and pour into a pot. While the espresso is still hot, add 1 teaspoon of sugar for each serving of espresso (enough to fill a small espresso cup). Stir to combine. Transfer the sweetened coffee to a pitcher, let cool, then add an equal amount of alcohol and the coffee essence. Stir well to combine and then filter. Transfer to tightly sealed bottles, and allow to rest 10 days before serving.

Coffee Liqueur

Liquore moka

Ingredients

- 1/2 pound roasted, freshly ground coffee of excellent quality
- 1 quart alcohol [pure, distilled]
- 3 cups sugar
- 3 cups water

Combine the coffee and the alcohol in a pot and set aside to steep for 15 days. In a pot, dissolve the sugar in the water and boil for 2 minutes, then remove from heat immediately. Set aside to cool, then add the cooled syrup to the coffee mixture. Allow to rest an additional 8 days, then filter and transfer to clean, dry bottles. Hermetically seal the bottles. Allow to rest at least 10 days before serving.

Old Lady's Milk Liqueur

Liquore latte di vecchia

Ingredients

- 1/2 lemon, diced
- 5 cups sugar
- 1 quart milk
- 1 quart alcohol [pure, distilled]

Drop the lemon pieces into a wide-necked bottle. Add the sugar, the milk, and the alcohol. Seal hermetically and set aside to rest for 15 days, shaking the contents of the bottle every morning and evening. Filter the liqueur, transfer to clean, dry bottles. Hermetically seal the bottles.

Mulberry Liqueur

Rosolio di mora di gelso

Use the Morus Nigra *variety for this recipe. These are black mulberries with a tart taste.*

Ingredients

- 10 ounces black mulberries
- 2 cups alcohol [pure, distilled]
- 2 cups sugar
- 2 cups water

Combine the mulberries and the alcohol in a large jar, seal tightly, and set aside for 15 days, shaking the contents of the jar occasionally. Put the sugar in a pot with the water and bring to a boil for about 2 minutes. Set aside to cool, then pour into the jar with the mulberries and the alcohol. Transfer to wide-necked clean, dry bottles. Keep the fruit in the liquid. Add additional mulberries when serving if you like.

Sour Cherry Liqueur

Rosolio di amarene

Ingredients

- Sour cherry pits
- 2 cups alcohol [pure, distilled]
- 2 1/2 cups sugar
- 2 cups water

Sour cherry liqueur, which tastes like cherry brandy, is made usually when making sour cherry preserves, because the pits of the sour cherries are used to make the liqueur.

After pitting the sour cherries, put their pits (which usually have a little fruit clinging to them) in a wide-necked 1-quart bottle. Fill the bottle halfway with the sour cherry pits, then add 2 cups alcohol to cover the pits. Seal and infuse for 30 days, shaking up the contents of the bottle occasionally. In a pot, make a syrup by bringing the sugar and water to a boil, then boiling for about 2 minutes. Cool, and add to the alcohol. Stir to combine and filter. You may want to filter the liquid twice, because the sour cherry pulp can make the resulting liqueur fairly cloudy. Seal hermetically.

WALNUT LIQUEUR

Nocino

A digestive.

Ingredients

- 25 green, not yet ripe, walnuts, picked between June 20 to June 25, quartered (not shelled)
- 1 quart alcohol [pure, distilled]
- 5 cloves
- 1/2 cinnamon stick
- Peel of 1 lemon
- 2 1/2 cups sugar
- 3/4 cup water

(Wear gloves, as these young walnuts are coated with a strong natural dye.) Wash the walnuts and dry them.Put the walnut pieces in a jar with the alcohol, cloves, cinnamon stick, and lemon peel. Seal hermetically and allow to steep for 40 days, shaking up the contents occasionally.

After 40 days, make a syrup in a pot with the sugar and water and boil for a few minutes. Filter the alcohol, discarding the walnuts or set aside for *Ratafia* (following) and other items, and combine with the cooled syrup. Filter again and transfer to bottles. Seal hermetically. Wait at least 3 months before serving.

WALNUT RATAFIA

Ratafià di noci

This light liqueur tastes something like Port.

Ingredients

- Walnuts from making Walnut Liqueur
- 1 quart dry white wine
- 2 cups sugar

Ratafia is made when making the Walnut Liqueur (*Nocino*) above. After removing the walnuts from the alcohol, combine them with the wine and sugar in a jar. Macerate for 30 days and then filter. Transfer to a clean, dry bottle and seal hermetically.

EGGNOG

*Vov**

Ingredients

- 2 egg yolks
- 2 cups sugar
- 1 cup Marsala
- 3/4 cup alcohol [pure, distilled]
- 1 packet powdered vanilla [or 1 teaspoon extract]
- 2 cups milk

In a large bowl, beat the egg yolks and sugar until foamy, then add in the Marsala, alcohol, and vanilla. Add the milk last. Stir until well combined, then filter. Transfer to a clean, dry bottle and seal hermetically. Store in the refrigerator, as it won't keep for long.

*Brand name of an Italian liqueur.

MINT LIQUEUR

Rosolio di menta

A digestive.

Ingredients

Peel of 1 lemon
50 fresh mint leaves, peppermint is best
2 cups alcohol [pure, distilled]
2 1/2 cups sugar
1 1/2 cups water

In a bowl, macerate the lemon peel and the mint leaves in the alcohol for at least 24 hours. Combine the sugar with water in a pot and boil for about 2 minutes to make a syrup. Cool the syrup and combine it with the alcohol. Filter the liquid and transfer to bottles. Seal tightly and allow to rest for at least 1 week before serving.

BASIL LIQUEUR

Rosolio di basilico

Ingredients

30 fresh basil leaves
2 cups alcohol [pure, distilled]
2 1/2 cups sugar
1 1/2 cups water

Soak the basil leaves in the alcohol in a tightly sealed bottle for at least 24 hours, shaking up the contents of the bottle occasionally. Combine the sugar with water in a pot and boil for about 2 minutes to make a syrup. Cool the syrup and combine it with the alcohol. Filter the liquid and transfer to bottles. Seal tightly and allow to rest for at least 1 week before serving.

BAY LIQUEUR

Rosolio di alloro

A digestive.

Ingredients

60 fresh bayberries *or* 20 fresh bay leaves, halved
2 cups alcohol [pure, distilled]
2 1/2 cups sugar
1 1/2 cups water

Soak the berries or the halved bay leaves in the alcohol for at least 24 hours. Combine the sugar with water in a pot and boil for about 2 minutes to make a syrup. Cool the syrup and combine it with the alcohol. Filter the liquid and transfer to bottles. Seal hermetically and allow to rest for at least 2 days before serving.

This is best used within 2 months, or it starts to lose some of its flavor.

STRAWBERRY LIQUEUR

Rosolio di fragole

Ingredients

Strawberries, rinsed, hulled, and drained
2 1/2 cups alcohol [pure, distilled]
2 1/2 cups sugar
1 2/3 cups water

Fill a 1-quart bottle with a wide mouth halfway with strawberries. Add the alcohol and set aside to steep for 1 week. Combine the sugar with water in a pot and boil for a few minutes to make a syrup. Let the syrup cool and combine it with the strawberry infusion. You can serve the liqueur with the fruit in it. Seal hermetically and allow to rest a few days before serving.

FRIED DOUGH

Purcidd o sannacchitili

Ingredients

- 1/2 cake yeast [or 1/2 package active dry yeast]
- About 1 1/4 cups white wine, lukewarm
- 5 3/4 cups flour
- 3/4 cup extra-virgin olive oil
- 1 tablespoon salt
- 4 cups honey
- 1 cup water
- Peel of 1 lemon
- Candy-coated anise sprinkles

Dissolve the yeast in the wine. Then make a dough out of the flour, olive oil, salt, and the dissolved yeast. If the dough seems dry, add a little wine; if it is too sticky, add a little flour. The resulting dough should be fairly firm. Break off pieces of the dough and shape them into rolls. Cut these rolls of dough into pieces about 1 inch long and make grooves on them by pressing them against the tines of a fork or the teeth of a grater. In a heavy-bottomed casserole, bring a generous amount of olive oil to a boil and deep-fry them until they turn golden. Scoop them out with a strainer and arrange them on a dish towel.

In a large skillet or pan, make a mixture of the honey and water. Add the lemon peel and bring to a boil. Add the fried dough pieces to the pan a few at a time (about 1 cup of them at a time) and toss vigorously in the honey mixture. Remove the coated pieces of dough with a skimmer and arrange them in a ring on a serving platter. When all the pieces of dough have been coated with the honey, scatter the sprinkles over them. This dessert keeps for a long time, but must be stored in a dry place as humidity ruins it.

Fried Dough Ribbons

Carteddet o carteddate

Ingredients

1/2 cake yeast [or 1/2 package active dry yeast]
About 1 1/4 cups white wine, lukewarm
5 3/4 cups flour
3/4 cup extra-virgin olive oil
1 tablespoon salt
4 cups honey
1 cup water
Peel of 1 lemon
Ground cinnamon or candy-coated anise sprinkles

Prepare the same dough as the *Purcidd* recipe. Dissolve the yeast in the wine. Make a dough out of the flour, olive oil, salt, and the yeast dissolved in the wine. If the dough seems dry, add a little wine; if it is too sticky, add a little flour. The resulting dough should be fairly firm.

Use a pasta machine to roll the dough into very thin sheets. With a serrated pastry wheel, cut the dough sheets into strips about 2 inches wide. These can be shaped in many ways. The most common way is to cut the strips into 4 inch lengths and pinch each strip in the center so that it looks like a bow. Another common form is to roll an 8-inch long strip into a spiral so that it looks like a rose. In a heavy-bottomed casserole, bring a generous amount of olive oil to a boil and deep-fry these until they turn golden. Scoop them out with a strainer and arrange them on a dish towel.

In a large skillet or pan, make a mixture of the honey and water. Add the lemon peel and bring to a boil. Add 3 to 4 fried dough pieces at a time and coat with the honey mixture, working carefully as they break easily. Remove the coated pieces of dough to a serving platter. Sprinkle with cinnamon or scatter anise sprinkles over them. This dessert, too, keeps for a long time, but must be stored in a dry place as humidity ruins it.

Fritters in Cooked Wine Must

Pettole al cotto

Ingredients

1 batch fritters *(pettole)*
1 quart cooked wine must *(cotto di vino)**
Honey (optional)

The fritters *(pettole)* recipe may be made into a dessert by boiling them in cooked wine must. Make the *pettole* following the recipe on page 55 and drain them well.

In a heavy-bottomed pot, dilute the cooked wine must with some lukewarm water and bring to a boil. Drop in the pieces of fried dough and boil 2 to 3 minutes, then transfer to a bowl. Serve cold. These may also be served in the wine must or with honey.

*Wine must is the first juice pressed from wine grapes. Before the fermentation process begins, some of this juice is removed, cooked slowly until thickened, and then bottled as *cotto di vino*. (See page 253.)

SWEET RAVIOLI

Ntreme di vicchie

Ingredients

- 5 3/4 cups "00" flour
- 1 1/4 cups (10 ounces) walnuts, chopped
- 7 tablespoons golden raisins
- Zest of 2 lemons
- Sea salt
- 1 quart cooked wine must

Make a firm dough with the flour and some water. On a smooth work surface, use a rolling pin to roll the dough out into very thin sheets. Cut irregular 3 inch squares using a serrated pastry wheel.

In a bowl, combine the walnuts, golden raisins, and lemon zest. Place a teaspoon or so of this filling on each square. Close the squares like little bundles, bringing together the 4 tips to close.

Cut tagliatelle noodles out of any leftover dough. The tagliatelle, too, should be irregularly shaped.

In a heavy-bottomed pot, bring a large amount of salted water to a boil, drop in and and cook both shapes of dough for 6 to 7 minutes. Meanwhile, pour the cooked wine must into another large pot and bring to a boil.

Remove the cooked pieces from the boiling water with a strainer and transfer them to the boiling wine must. Boil an additional 10 to 15 minutes until the must has thickened.

Transfer the pieces to a bowl and serve cold.

ALMOND MILK PASTA

Latte de l'amenue (latte di mandorle)

This is a specialty of the Salento area, where it is always served at the end of Christmas lunch. It's very unique and not well-known elsewhere.

Ingredients

- 1 cup flour
- 2 1/4 pounds blanched almonds
- 3 tablespoons cornstarch
- 5 1/2 cups sugar
- Ground cinnamon
- 3 quarts water

On a smooth work surface, make a dough with the flour and a little water. Working with 1 small piece of dough at a time, roll it between your hands to make spaghetti about 1/2 inch long.

Meanwhile, grind the almonds until they form a fine paste. In a mixing bowl, dissolve the ground almonds in 6 cups water, mixing them together with your hands. Pour this mixture through a piece of cheesecloth over a bowl and squeeze to extract as much liquid as possible. Then pour the liquid into a large heavy-bottomed pot.

Mix the ground almonds (now squeezed dry) with another 6 cups water and repeat the process, again collecting the liquid extracted, then pouring it into the pot with the first batch. Pour about 1/2 cup of the liquid into a small bowl and dissolve the cornstarch in it. Then strain this mixture into the large pot with the almond liquid.

Stir the sugar into the mixture, then bring to a boil over medium heat. Add the spaghetti to the boiling liquid and cook until the pasta is cooked through.

Transfer to a serving bowl or distribute among individual serving dishes and sprinkle cinnamon. Allow to rest for a few hours in the refrigerator and serve cold.

HERE ARE TWO OLD RECIPES FROM THE NOTEBOOK OF A LOCAL WOMAN.

CHRISTMAS CAKE

Pizza Natalizia

Serves 6 to 10

Ingredients

- 14 tablespoons butter (1 stick plus 6 tablespoons), softened
- 12 eggs, separated
- 1 1/4 cups sugar
- 2 slices day-old rye bread, ground into bread crumbs
- 6 tablespoons grated chocolate
- 7 tablespoons blanched almonds, ground
- 1/2 teaspoon ground cinnamon
- 1 pinch ground cloves
- Zest of 1 lemon
- 1 cup flour
- Confectioners' sugar

Put all the butter in a large bowl and beat until it is soft and creamy. Add the egg yolks 1 at a time. (Set aside the whites.) When the butter mixture is lightened and soft, whip the egg whites to soft peaks and then fold them into the mixture. One at a time add: sugar, bread crumbs, chocolate, almonds, cinnamon, cloves, lemon zest, and flour, beating to incorporate between additions. Butter and flour a cake pan with low sides, or a rectangular baking pan, and pour the batter in. Bake in a preheated 350° oven until golden. Sprinkle with confectioners' sugar before serving. This cake should be made one day before it is to be served.

ALMOND BRITTLE

Croccante

Ingredients

- 5 1/2 cups sugar
- 1/2 cup water
- 2 1/4 pounds blanched almonds, toasted and chopped with a mezzaluna
- Olive oil
- 1 lemon, cut in half
- Sugar coated almonds or sprinkles (optional)

In a heavy-bottomed pot, pour the sugar in the water and heat until the sugar has dissolved. Stir in the chopped almonds. Oil a copper pan and pour the mixture into it. Use a lemon slice as a tool to shape the mixture however you prefer. If using sugar-coated almonds or sprinkles, scatter them on while the mixture is still hot. Set aside to cool. When cool, unmold to a serving dish.

Sweet Turnovers

Ficarelli o ficazzedde

Ingredients

Filling

1 1/4 cups cooked wine must
Semolina flour
Zest of 1 lemon
1 1/4 cups (10 ounces) walnuts, chopped
1/3 cup water

Dough

3 cups "00" flour
1 1/2 teaspoons salt
1/3 cup extra-virgin olive oil
1/4 cake yeast [or 1/4 package active dry yeast] dissolved in warm water
White wine, brought to room temperature

Glaze (optional)

To make the filling, dilute the wine must with some lukewarm water in a large heavy-bottomed pot and bring to a boil. When it begins to boil, slowly add semolina flour, sifting as if raining. Stir constantly until the mixture is as thick as fruit preserves. Remove from heat and add the lemon zest and walnuts. Stir to combine and set aside.

Meanwhile, make a fairly firm dough of the flour, salt, olive oil, dissolved yeast, and wine. Use a pasta machine to make fairly thin sheets of dough. Using a drinking glass or cutter, cut circles out of the dough. Place about 1 teaspoon of the filling on each circle of dough and fold these into semicircles. Seal the semicircles with a pastry wheel. Bake in a preheated 350° oven until golden. Brush with glaze if desired.

Rosata

Ingredients

1 1/4 cups sugar
1 cup (8 ounces) blanched almonds, finely ground
Zest of 1 lemon
1 packet vanillin [1 teaspoon vanilla extract]
7 eggs, separated
Communion or other round thin wafers (optional)

In a heavy-bottomed pot, combine the sugar with a small amount of water and bring to a boil to dissolve. Add the ground almonds, lemon zest, and vanilla extract. Cook, stirring constantly, until all the water has evaporated. Set aside to cool.

When the mixture has cooled, add the egg yolks one at a time, stirring to combine between additions. Put the egg whites in a clean, dry bowl and whip them to soft peaks, then fold the whipped whites into the yolk mixture. Line a baking pan with thin wafers or ungreased wax paper. Pour in the mixture and bake in a preheated 350° oven until golden. Let cool and remove from pan, turning over onto a serving dish.

SPONGE CAKE

Pan di Spagna

Ingredients

6 eggs, separated
1 1/4 cups sugar
1 pinch salt
1 cup flour
1 cake yeast [or 1 package active dry yeast]

Whip the 6 egg yolks with the sugar until they are light in color and frothy. Separately, beat the egg whites to soft peaks with the salt, then fold them into the egg yolks. Very slowly add in the flour and yeast, sifting as if raining, while whisking constantly. Pour the batter into a buttered and floured baking pan. Bake in a preheated 350° oven for about 30 minutes. Let cool and remove to a serving dish.

SWEET TARALLI

Pucciatidd o taralli cull'ova

These are traditionally an Easter treat.

Ingredients

Dough

5 3/4 cups flour
12 eggs, lightly beaten
3/4 cup extra-virgin olive oil
1 1/2 teaspoons salt

Glaze

1 very fresh egg white
(no yolk whatsoever)
Water at room temperature
2 cups confectioners' sugar
1 packet vanillin
[1 teaspoon vanilla extract]

Make a dough out of the flour, eggs, olive oil, and salt. On a smooth work surface, roll the dough into 1-inch thick cylinders. Form traditional circular-shaped *taralli*, 1-inch thick and 3 inches in diameter, with ends crossing over each other. Set aside to rest on the work surface for at least 1 hour.

Bring a large pot of water to a boil and submerge a few *taralli* at a time. As soon as they bob to the surface, scoop them out with a strainer and arrange them on a dish towel, and continue until they've all been boiled. With a sharp knife, make a small cut the long way around the edge of each one, place on a baking sheet, and bake, preferably in a wood-burning oven, for about 20 minutes. Set aside to cool.

While the *taralli* are cooling, prepare the glaze. Whip the egg white to a firm peak. Add 3 tablespoons of water and very slowly stir in the sugar and vanilla extract. When it is all well combined and thick (if necessary add an additional tablespoon or 2 of water), brush the glaze on the *taralli* and let them dry completely. Store in a dry place.

PEPPER TARALLI

Taralli col pepe

Ingredients

5 3/4 cups flour
3/4 cup extra-virgin olive oil
1 tablespoon salt
Freshly ground black pepper
1 cake yeast, dissolved in lukewarm
white wine

Mix and knead the flour, olive oil, salt, a generous amount of black pepper, and the yeast and wine mixture. Roll the dough into cylinders that are about 1/2 inch thick. Shape those into small *taralli* that are about 1 1/2 inches in diameter. Set aside to rest for 1 hour.

You can vary these by incorporating 2 tablespoons of fennel seed into the dough.

Bring a large pot of water to a boil. Add a few of the *taralli* at a time and when they bob to the surface scoop them out with a strainer. Arrange them on a dish towel, covered. Continue until they've all been boiled. Transfer these to a baking sheet and bake in a preheated 350° oven, preferably a wood-burning oven, for about 20 minutes.

Horse-Shaped Sweet Tarallo

Cavaddistr

A *cavaddistr* is made with the same ingredients as the *Sweet Taralli* recipe. The difference is the shape and the symbolic significance. A *cavaddistr* was exchanged by an engaged couple.

On Palm Sunday, the fiancé went to the house of his fiancée to give her a gift of an olive branch (the palm) painted gold, a symbol of peace. He also gave her a piece of gold jewelry as a gift. In return, the fiancée gave him a palm and, funds permitting, a small gold object.

On Easter Sunday, the fiancé again went to his fiancée's house. This time he brought a *cavaddistr*, a horse-shaped dessert. The fiancée broke off the head and then gave it back to him as a symbol of her future submission to the head of the family. Later she went to the fiancé's house and brought her future mother-in-law a sweet that she had made.

This tradition is the source of the saying, "Golden palm, sugared Easter"!

Here's how to prepare a *cavaddistr.*

On a smooth work surface, make the dough for sweet *taralli*. Roll the dough into a sheet about 1 inch thick and cut out a shape in the form of a large horse. Make a harness as well. Let the dough rest on the cutting board for 1 hour.

Bring a wide pot of water to a boil and immerse the horse into the water. After 2 to 3 minutes, remove it carefully with a strainer and arrange it on a dish towel for a few minutes. Then bake it until golden, and when it has cooled, brush on the glaze. Before the glaze hardens, sprinkle on candy-coated fennel seeds.

EASTER BREADS

Palomme o scarcelle

Traditionally these aren't sweet, although many people make them out of a dough that's similar to a cookie dough. These are another traditional Easter specialty. Palomma *is dialect for dove.*

Ingredients

5 3/4 cups flour
3/4 cup extra-virgin olive oil
1 tablespoon salt
1 cake yeast [or 1 package active dry yeast], dissolved in lukewarm water
Freshly ground black pepper
1 egg (in the shell)
2 peppercorns

Mix and knead the flour, olive oil, salt, dissolved yeast, a generous amount of pepper, and enough water to make a fairly firm dough. Form the dough into a ball and put in a lightly oiled bowl. Turn the dough to coat all sides, then cover the bowl and set aside to rise for about 1 hour.

Traditionally the dough is made into various shapes—a dove, snake, purse, rose, a man known by the name Marcantonio (who knows why), and other objects that spring from the creator's fantasy and imagination.

Here's how to prepare one.

As an example, we'll use a snake. Take a piece of dough and make a roll about 8 inches long and 1 inch thick. Wet the egg, dry it slightly, and then shape the roll of dough into a spiral with the egg in the center. Squash the end of the roll of dough slightly to form the snake's head, then stick in 2 peppercorns to serve as the eyes.

Bake in a preheated 400° oven until the dough is browned and the egg is hard-cooked. Eat the egg with salt and accompany it with the bread.

These breads are eaten at picnics on the day after Easter.

ALMOND PASTE COOKIES

Paste di mandorle

Ingredients

2 1/4 pounds blanched almonds, skins removed
4 cups sugar
5 eggs, lightly beaten
1 pinch vanillin [scant vanilla extract]
Zest of 1 lemon
Whole almonds or candied cherries, halved, or candied orange peel, chopped

Grind the almonds with the sugar, then mix in the eggs, vanilla, and lemon zest to make a paste. Fill a pastry bag fitted with a serrated tip with the almond paste and use it to make small, round cookies, not touching, on floured baking sheets. Top each cookie with a whole almond or half a candied cherry or a piece of candied orange peel. Bake in a preheated 350° oven until golden for about 20 minutes.

ALMOND TART

Barchiglia

This is a traditional dessert from Puglia most frequently served on Easter.

Ingredients

Crust
- 1 1/2 cups flour
- 8 tablespoons (1 stick) butter, cut into pieces
- 1/2 cup sugar
- 1 pinch salt
- 3 egg yolks

Glaze
- 2/3 cup sugar
- 1 ounce dark chocolate

Filling
- 3 eggs, separated
- 2/3 cup sugar
- 3/4 cups blanched almonds, skins removed, ground
- 1 pinch salt
- 1 pinch ground cinnamon
- Zest of 1 lemon
- Pear preserves, a few tablespoons

To make the pastry crust, mound the flour on a smooth work surface, make a well, then put the butter pieces in it. With a pastry cutter or your hands, cut the butter into the flour until it resembles coarse crumbs. Reshape the mixture into a well and place the sugar, salt, and egg yolks in the center. Hand mix vigorously until combined. Flatten the dough on the work surface using the palms of your hands, then fold it over and flatten it again with your hands. Shape the dough into a ball, wrap it in aluminum foil, and refrigerate for 1 hour.

To make the filling, beat the egg yolks with the sugar and stir in the ground almonds, salt, cinnamon, and lemon zest. Beat the egg whites to stiff peaks and fold them gently into the egg yolk mixture.

Butter a round baking [tart] pan. Roll out the cooled dough into a disk about 1/8-inch thick and transfer to the buttered pan. [Press dough up along edges of the pan.] Spread a few spoonfuls of pear preserves on the dough, and then pour in the egg and almond mixture and smooth. Bake in a preheated 350° oven until a skewer inserted into the center of the tart comes out clean and dry, about 30 minutes. Set aside to cool.

While the tart is cooling, prepare the chocolate glaze. In a small pan, dissolve the sugar in a small amount of water and cook into a syrup. In a double boiler, melt the chocolate, then stir in the syrup. Stir to combine, then pour over the tart while still hot. Set tart aside until glaze is cool.

Ricotta Crêpes

Dita di apostoli (Apostles' Fingers)

Serves 6

Everybody loves this dessert, which is frequently served on Easter.

Ingredients

Crêpes

1 3/4 cups flour
2 cups milk
1 pinch salt
3 eggs

Filling

10 ounces ricotta
Sugar to taste, about 2/3 cup
Zest of 1 lemon
7 tablespoons dark chocolate, finely chopped
1/2 cinnamon stick, finely chopped
Minced candied citron (optional)

Topping

3/4 cup honey
Ground cinnamon

To make the crêpes, whisk together in a bowl the flour, milk, and salt. Add the eggs one at a time, whisking until smooth between additions. Whisk until the batter is perfectly smooth, with no lumps whatsoever.

Butter or oil a small non-stick 5 inch pan. Put the pan over low heat and when it is heated, pour in enough batter to cover the bottom. Move the pan occasionally to be sure the crêpe isn't sticking. As soon as the crêpe is golden, flip it to cook the other side. Transfer to a plate, and continue making crêpes with the remaining batter.

When all the crêpes are ready, make the filling. Beat the ricotta and sugar in a bowl, until they are smooth and have no lumps. Stir in the grated lemon zest, chocolate, cinnamon stick, and candied citron, if using. Stir to combine and then top each crêpe with about 1 tablespoon of this mixture. Roll up the crêpes as if they were cigars and arrange them on a serving dish.

In a small pot, combine the honey with 3 tablespoons of water and bring to a boil. As soon as the honey starts to boil, drizzle it over the crêpes. Sprinkle a little ground cinnamon on top and refrigerate for at least 1 hour before serving.

Saint Joseph's Doughnuts

Zeppole di San Giuseppe

A superstition from the Salento area calls for 13 diners to eat 13 courses on Saint Joseph's Day. The meal should start with Ciceri e Trie, *or Chickpeas with Tagliatelle and end with these* zeppole.

Ingredients

Dough

8 ounces lard, or 2 1/2 cups margarine
1 pinch salt
2 cups water
2 3/4 cups flour, sifted
10 to 12 eggs

Cream
3 egg yolks
3 tablespoons sugar
4 tablespoons flour
2 cups milk
Several peels of lemon
Sour cherries in syrup, or sour cherry preserves, or chopped cinnamon stick
8 cups lard or margarine for frying

To make the dough, put the lard or margarine in a pot and add the salt and water. Bring to a boil, then slowly sprinkle in the flour. Stir until the dough starts to pull away from the sides of the pot and form a ball. Pour the dough onto a cutting board and set aside to cool.

Knead in 1 egg at a time and continue to knead until the dough is somewhat stiff and yellow, like a very thick custard cream. (The number of eggs you use will depend on their size. Stop when the dough is the proper consistency.)

Transfer the dough to a pastry bag fitted with a serrated tip. Cut out 3 inch circles of thick wax paper and pipe a circle of dough about 2 1/2 inches in diameter on each circle. To fry the dough, divide the lard or margarine for frying between two heavy-bottomed casseroles, and place them over the heat.

Add 4 to 5 *zeppole* at a time to the first pot. To add them to the pot, slip in the waxed paper, then immediately pull out the paper. The *zeppole* should slip right off into the pot. Keep the first pot at a low simmer and cook the *zeppole* in it until they are puffy and soft. Use a strainer to transfer the puffy soft *zeppole* to the second pot, which should be boiling over higher heat. The hotter second pot will give them a golden crust. As the *zeppole* turn golden in the second pot, transfer them with a strainer to paper towels to drain and cool.

When all the *zeppole* are cooked, prepare the cream. In a non-stick pot, whisk the egg yolks with the sugar. Whisk in the flour and then the milk, whisking smooth between additions. Add the lemon peels and place over low heat. Cook, stirring constantly, until the cream thickens. Remove the lemon peels. Set the cream aside to cool. When it is cool, transfer it to a pastry bag fitted with a serrated tube and pipe two dots onto each of the pastries. Put a cherry or about 1/2 teaspoon sour cherry preserves or a bit of chopped cinnamon stick on each dot of cream.

Pudding
Budino

Ingredients

- 1 1/2 cups sugar
- 1 quart cold milk
- A few peels of 1 lemon
- 4 eggs
- 4 egg yolks

Make the caramel. In a 1-quart pan with a tube in the center [a heat-resistant bundt pan], dissolve 1/2 cup of the sugar in 4 to 5 tablespoons of water. Cook until this caramel turns brown. As soon as the sugar starts to smoke, wearing oven mitts, quickly pick up the pan and move it in a circular motion to coat the bottom evenly. When the sugar is no longer liquid, set the pan aside to cool.

Meanwhile, in a large bowl combine the milk, 1 cup sugar, and lemon peel. Stir to dissolve the sugar. In a clean bowl, beat the 4 eggs plus 4 egg yolks as if making a frittata. Add the beaten eggs to the milk mixture and whisk to combine, then pour the mixture through a strainer into the pan with the caramel.

Bake in a bain marie in a preheated 475° oven for 1 hour. If the surface of the pudding begins to burn, place a lid or a piece of aluminum foil on top. When you remove the pan from the oven, immerse the pan in a bowl of cold water and let it rest for 30 minutes, then refrigerate for at least 3 hours. Serve cold.

Carmelized Almonds
Mandorle atturrete (alla maniera del torrone)

Ingredients

- 1 pound whole almonds
- 2 3/4 cups sugar
- 1 cup water

Put the almonds in a wide non-stick pan and stir in the sugar and water. Bring the mixture to a boil, stirring occasionally. When the water has evaporated completely, start stirring constantly until the sugar begins to caramelize. When the almonds and sugar look reddish in color, remove from the heat and immediately spread out on a wooden or marble surface to cool.

Keep a close watch on the almonds when they are cooking. If you cook them too long, the almonds won't come apart from each other and will turn into nougat.

WINE IL VINO

UNTIL just a few decades ago, taverns were still a large part of the social fabric of Puglia. They had small groups of regular customers and served thick, dark, and highly alcoholic wine, which was often mixed with lighter white wine.

In Puglia, custom calls for drinking wine only with food. The people who patronized these taverns were usually unemployed or worked at the humblest of jobs.

That same dense, dark wine is still made today on the plains of the Salento area and is used as a "cutting wine." Some excellent white grapes are grown in the Murgia hills, which only the patient work of farmers has rendered hospitable to growing crops. *Verdeca* and the white grape from Alessano are used to make white wines with a low alcohol content that are dry and light green in color and that have appeared on tables in Puglia forever.

Before the birth of industrial winemaking, wine was produced on site by farmers. Vineyards were small, and each farmhouse had a winepress next to it, and next to that a small shed with enormous *capasuni,* large ceramic jugs with holes for taps, that were full of wine. One local and strictly seasonal product was *pero,* an extremely light wine with little flavor that was made by adding water to marc [grape residue] and pressing it. This had a low alcohol content, which meant it had to be consumed quickly or it would turn to wine vinegar. Some of the must [juice and residue] from pressing grapes would be used to make *cotto di vino,* or cooked wine must. The must was poured into a large pot and boiled for hours over a coal fire. It was removed from the heat once it had been reduced to one quarter of its initial volume. Once it cooled, it was stored in large glass bottles, tightly sealed. Later it would be used as an ingredient in *pettole natalizie* or mixed with snow.

The latter treat was prepared on the rare occasions when it snowed. Must and snow were vigorously beaten together with a wooden spoon until the mixture resembled ice cream. Adults and children alike ate it with great enthusiasm.

The grape harvest was a community ritual. It was announced far in advance so that friends and relatives could be recruited to lend a hand; even children joined in picking the grapes.

Grape picking began at six o'clock in the morning. Activity came to a halt briefly at about ten for a substantial breakfast, *sferra,* of bread and *pilacca* (a sauce made with peppers), eggplant, and fried peppers. A fancier breakfast would have included mortadella and provolone, all washed down with the previous year's wine.

Work started up again an hour later and kept going until all the grapes had been brought to the wine press. Meanwhile, in homes, the woman of the house boiled water and heated up the sauce and meatballs prepared the night before. The rustic meal was served to all in a large bowl full of orecchiette with sauce, topped with meatballs.

SOME OF THE WINE produced in these small vineyards was used by the the landowners, while the rest was sold to wholesale dealers and taverns. The taverns were located in ground floor spaces. Outside, they normally sported a grapevine and a small bottle full of wine to indicate the business that went on inside.

Customers at these taverns usually played cards or a game called *padrone e sotto* [master and servant] in which wins and losses were paid in wine that was then drunk according to a complex ceremony. The taverns served food, usually a meal of horse *braciole* or meatballs, accompanied by semolina or country bread. Regular customers could also run a tab.

Often, as a tavern's wine began to turn into vinegar, it was used to pickle large amounts of peppers, cucumbers, and eggplant, so these pickled vegetables were on the menu as well. The cucumbers, peppers, and eggplant were left whole and unpeeled and placed in large ceramic jars, then covered with wine vinegar and salt. After thirty days they were ready to be eaten. The peppers were peeled and seeded, then cut into strips and drizzled with olive oil. Eggplants were cut in half with a spoon and the pulp was removed. This, too, was drizzled with olive oil and then served as a side dish for boiled meat or fava bean purée.

[Commercial wine-making activity in Puglia has grown enormously in the last decades, both in quantity and quality and many table wines are considered top wines in Italy. Puglia's wine producers have become major exporters of table wines.]

Since these few words on wine are the close of my work, I'd like to end with a very original recipe—one that I don't believe has ever been published before—that has nothing to do with wine, but is related to grapevines. Perhaps some of my readers will know that grapevines sprout not only leaves and grapes, but wiry little bits of growth that end in a spiral. These tendrils can be eaten raw when they're young. They taste a little sour. I suggest that anyone who has the patience to collect a substantial number of these tendrils in late spring should make use of this one last recipe and prepare a dish that is a true gastronomic curiosity.

TENDRIL SALAD

Insalata di viticci

Ingredients

Grapevine tendrils
White wine vinegar
Extra-virgin olive oil
Mint
Sea salt
1 clove garlic, minced

Boil the tendrils in a mixture of water and wine vinegar. In a small bowl, make a dressing by whisking together olive oil, mint, salt, and garlic, to taste. Drain the cooked tendrils and transfer them to a bowl. Toss with the olive oil dressing to coat and serve cold.

View of Lecce's arch with Saint Oronzo

Index of Recipes

Resources 

Authentic ingredients as well as fresh, seasonal produce are essential for Italian cookery. Here are selected companies providing Italian regional products. Check for their store locations and mail order information.

A. G. Ferrari Foods	agferrari.com	877-878-2783
Balducci's	balduccis.com	800-225-3822
BuonItalia	buonitalia.com	212-633-9090
Citarella	citarella.com	212-874-0383
Corti Brothers	cortibros.biz	800-509-3663
Dean & DeLuca	deandeluca.com	800-221-7714
De Medici Importers	demedici.com	914-651-4400
Di Palo Fine Foods		212-226-1033
	gustiamo.com	718-860-2949
Manicaretti	manicaretti.com	888-952-4005
Todaro Brothers	todarobros.com	877-472-2764
Vivande Porta Via	vivande.com	415-346-4430
Zabar's	zabars.com	212-496-1234
Zingerman's	zingermans.com	888-636-8162

Of course, look to your local organic food shops and farmers markets for fresh, seasonal produce.

or grow your own!

Seeds from Italy	growitalian.com	781-721-5904

Photo Credits

Cover: Jörg Jahn; Joanna Wnuk, pages 2/3, 4; Claudio Colombo, pages 7, 13/14, 62, 68/69, 193; condor35, pages 8/9; iofoto, page 11; rj lerich, page 18; "8781118005", page 19; "649386629", page 31; Lori Sparkia, pages 35, 148; Claudio Baldini, page 48; David Smith, page 53; Charlotte Moss, pages 60, 109; Matka Wariatka, page 70; Antonio Esperraga, page 73; Silvio Verrecchia, page 78; Wally Stemberger, page 84; Sarah McHattie, page 86; Jim Mills, page 93; Lezh, page 98; Elena Schweitzer, pages 103, 162; "ale 1969", page 111; Pawel Strykowski, pages 115, 119; Vladimir Popoviv, pages 120, 266; Ronald Summers, page 126; Christina Ferrari, pages 129, 164/165; Kerry Muzzy, page 130; Blanche Branton, page 133; luri, pages 134/135; Goruppa Mihaylovich, page 136; Nathalie Dulex, pages 144, 221, 222; Sebastian Duda, page 151; Giovanni Mattinata, page 152; Montero Verdu, page 154; Ollirg, page 156; Thomas Perkins, page 158; Yanta, page 161; Maria Vera, pages 162/163; Mario Savoia, page 169; Joy Neish, page 173; Sasha Radosavjevich, page 179; Elisa Locci, page 185; Blazej Maksym, page 194; Artykov Andrey, page 196; Pedro Nogueira, page 199; Michelle Marotta, page 201; Michael Damklev, pages 202/203; Joriah Mosin, page 214; S. Duffett, page 225; Jamey Ekins, page 226; Albo, page 234; David Lee, page 236; Gianluca Fantini, page 241; Mark Grenier, page 251; Vladimir Koskins, page 253; Mariano Heluani, page 256